CURRENT ENGLISH USAGE

CURRENT ENGLISH USAGE

USAGE

A Concise Dictionary

FREDERICK T. WOOD

First published 1962
Reprinted 1962 (twice), 1963, 1964, 1965,
1969, 1970 (twice), 1974, 1975, 1978

Published by
THE MACMILLAN PRESS LTD
London and Basingstoke
Companies and representatives throughout the world

ISBN 0 333 07359 2 (hard cover)
0 333 01078 7 (paper cover)
0 333 04797 4 (ELBS edition)

Printed in Hong Kong

PREFACE

THE aim of this book is a practical one: to provide an easy work of reference for those who wish to write good English. To some extent, therefore, it is necessarily prescriptive. It deals with points of syntax, punctuation, style, idiom, spelling and modern usage generally. With grammar as such it is not concerned; though specific grammatical points or constructions which may present difficulty have, of course, been included; but it has been assumed that anyone who uses the book will have a knowledge of the basic grammatical terms. Where differences of opinion exist, or where usage is changing, I have tried to avoid being too dogmatic, though I have usually counselled conservatism. In general I have sought not to encroach on the province of the ordinary dictionary, but I have felt it justifiable to draw attention to words which are often mis-spelt, misused or mispronounced. A number of examples of incorrect English are taken from newspapers, magazines and other periodicals, as well as from published reports of business houses and official bodies. Occasionally the name of the publication concerned has been given, but more often I have indicated merely the kind of publication, as 'a daily newspaper', 'a Free Church weekly', 'a women's magazine', 'a church magazine', and so on. This anonymity has been dictated by three considerations: first, because even Homer may nod; secondly, because the author of a book such as this must necessarily collect his examples mainly from the limited number of periodicals which he reads fairly regularly, and it would be unfair to give the impression that these journals were culpable beyond the rest, or that the examples quoted were typical of the general standard of English to be found in their pages; and thirdly because many come from signed articles or from the correspondence columns. Anyone using the book, however, may rest assured that all such examples are genuine.

Certain words and constructions have been described as Americanisms. This does not necessarily mean that they are bad

English. Many Americanisms (though not all) are good English — in America. But where British and American usage differ, British writers and speakers should follow the British idiom, not the American. The foreign student is at liberty to decide for himself which he will adopt, or to let his teacher decide for him.

A note should perhaps be added on pronunciation. The only really satisfactory way to indicate the pronunciation of a word is by one of the recognised systems of phonetic symbols. But as most of those who will use this book are not likely to have a knowledge of phonetics, to use such symbols would merely mystify rather than help them. Other methods have therefore had to be used, though it is recognised that they are not so accurate as phonetic symbols would be.

Finally I wish to express my indebtedness to Mr Thomas Mark, who read the whole of the book when it was at the manuscript stage, and made many valuable suggestions. Without his advice it would have contained many more imperfections than it does.

FREDERICK T. WOOD

Sheffield

PUBLISHER'S NOTE (1976)

The text has been revised to replace old-currency references in examples by decimal-currency usage.

ABBREVIATIONS USED

C.O.D.   *The Concise Oxford Dictionary of Current English.*

M.E.U.   H. W. Fowler, *A Dictionary of Modern English Usage.*

O.E.D.   *The Oxford English Dictionary.*

R.C.R.   Horace Hart, *Rules for Compositors and Readers at the University Press, Oxford.*

A

A, AN (Indefinite Article). (i) The general rule is, use *a* before consonants and *an* before vowels, diphthongs or the unsounded *h*. Into this last class fall *heir, honest, honorary, honorarium, honour, hour* and their derivatives. *An hotel*, though not incorrect, is now old-fashioned; we usually sound the *h* and write *a hotel*. When used in an English context, French words beginning with *h* take *an*, since in French an initial *h* is unsounded: e.g. *an habitué, an hors-d'œuvre*.

(ii) The terms 'vowel' and 'consonant' are phonetic terms; that is, they refer to sounds, not to letters. Words which have the initial letters *u* or *eu* pronounced like an initial *y* do not, therefore, begin with a vowel but with a consonant, and take *a*: *a university, a united effort, a Unitarian, a European country*.

(ii) A few words in which an initial *h* is normally sounded may nevertheless take *an* when, owing to their position in the sentence, the distribution of stress makes it difficult to give the aspirate its full value: *an habitual action, an heretical opinion* and (occasionally) *an historical survey*.

(iv) Which we use before initials depends on whether, in reading aloud, we pronounce the names of the individual letters, or the words for which they stand: thus *an L.C.C. school, an M.A.*, because we say *ell-see-see* and *emm-aye*; but *a N.C.B. circular*, because we read it as *National Coal Board*.

Note : Always *an H.M.I.* (we could not possibly say 'a Her Majesty's Inspector') and *a MS.* (pronounce *manuscript*, not *emm-ess*).

(v) Beware of the intrusive article, exemplified in such expression as *no bigger a salary, no better a scholar*. The *a* should be omitted. It is idiomatic English with the positive degree (*as big a salary, as good a scholar*), but not with the comparative.

(vi) On the question of *kind* (*sort*) *of a thing* as against *kind* (*sort*) *of thing*, see under KIND and SORT.

(vii) Note the omission of the article in sentences of the type 'He is more fool than knave', where the noun is used in a descriptive capacity and has thus something of the force of an adjective (*foolish, knavish*), though it is stronger than the actual adjective would be.

ABBREVIATIONS

I. **The full stop.** Fowler (*M.E.U.*) recommended that no stop should be used if the last letter of an abbreviated word was written, and this recommendation may be followed if one so desires; but it has not been universally accepted. Even the Oxford University Press, which publishes Fowler's work, does not recognise it. Moreover, it gives rise to a number of difficulties; for instance, most plural abbreviations have the final *s*; are we, then, to use the stop for *log.* (*logarithm*), *prefab.* and *mac.*, but not for their plurals *logs*, *prefabs* and *macs*?

All things considered, we advise the use of the stop for abbreviated words whether the last letter is written or not, subject to the following exceptions:

 (i) No stop for *Mr* and *Mrs*, as these have come to be accepted as the full spelling.

 (ii) No stop for words like *pub*, *pram*, *cab*, *taxi*, *zoo*, which, though actually abbreviations, have come to be accepted as colloquial words in their own right. (*Exam.*, *maths.* and *prom.* have not quite attained this status yet, so the stop should be used.)

 (iii) No stop for familiar names like *Fred*, *Will*, *Tom*, *Doll*; but *Geo.*, *Chas.*, *Wm.*, *Thos.*, *Eliz.*, etc., where the full name is pronounced though the shortened form is written, must have the stop.

 (iv) Though the names of most of the English and Welsh counties, when written in abbreviated form, take the stop, none should be used with *Hants*, *Northants*, *Salop* and *Devon*. (Though one may, of course, be needed if they come at the end of an address.)

 (v) No stop after the ordinal numbers when written as 1st, 2nd, 3rd, 4th, 5th, etc.

 (vi) No stop in those rare cases where a genitive of an abbreviated word has to be written. Thus *Messrs. T. J. Jones & Co.* will have the stop after *Co.*, but it will be omitted in *Jones & Co's sausages*. The apostrophe serves to denote both the genitive and the omission.

N.B.—A fairly detailed list of abbreviations which the writer of ordinary prose will have less occasion to use, with their recommended pointing, is given in *R.C.R.* Many of them refer to scientific, technical and mathematical treatises.

II. **Initials.** Generally a full stop should be placed after each letter that stands for a full word, as *P.T.O.*, *R.S.V.P.* With combinations like MS. (manuscript), TV. (television) a stop is required after the last letter only, since the first does not represent a separate word. For points of the compass, NW., SW., SE. (only one stop), but for London postal districts, N.W., S.W., S.E. (two stops).

A practice has recently grown up of omitting the stops in the case of well-known organisations which are normally known (in spoken English at least) by the initials rather than by the full name (e.g. the BBC, the WEA, the GPO, BOAC, the NUT, the TUC). This is allowable, but it is better to insert the stops, especially in matter of a formal or official character. Where it has become the common practice to pronounce the initials as a word, no stops should be used: e.g. UNESCO, NALGO, NATO, UNICEF.

For the plural of initials the addition of a small *s* is advised (M.P.s, J.P.s, H.M.I.s), leaving the apostrophe for the genitive ('an M.P.'s duties, J.P.s' qualifications'). Note, however, that the plurals of *p.* (page) and *l.* (line) are *pp.* and *ll.* respectively.

III. **Abbreviation of Latin Words.** The non-Latinist, or anyone else who is not quite sure, had better make certain which of the Latin words or phrases that are commonly used in English are abbreviations and which are not. In the case of phrases, sometimes neither word is abbreviated (*pro rata, sine die*), sometimes only one (*ad lib., infra dig.*), sometimes both (*nem. con., verb. sap.*). Most English dictionaries have an appendix giving such expressions, correctly pointed.

IV. **The Apostrophe.** Use the apostrophe, not the full stop, to indicate the omission of letters from the end or the beginning of a word to indicate slovenly or affected pronunciation (*at 'ome, huntin', shootin' and fishin'*), as well as for contractions by the omission of letters internally (*can't, isn't*). The following points, however, should be noted.

(i) See that the apostrophe is correctly placed. (It is surprising how many examination candidates write *is'nt* and *could'nt*.)

(ii) If there are two omissions in a word, only the second is normally indicated (*shan't, can't*).

(iii) If both the beginning and the end of a word are omitted, only the first omission is indicated. Thus *'flu*, not *'flu.*, as the abbreviation of *influenza*. (Though see point iv, below.)

(iv) Use no apostrophe for *bus*. It may also be omitted from *phone* (especially when used as a verb) and *flu*, but must be inserted in *'plane* (for aeroplane).

V. The Use of Abbreviations. (i) In a colloquial or informal style the contractions *didn't*, *haven't*, *shouldn't*, etc. are allowable, but in more formal writing the full forms should be used.

(ii) Even in an address at the head of a letter or on an envelope it is better not to use the abbreviated forms *Cromwell Rd.*, *Church St.*, *Gordon Sq.*, etc., and the words should certainly be spelt in full when they occur in a sentence. Do not write 'Theophilus Lindsey established a church in Essex St., just off the Strand'.

(iii) Do not use the abbreviations *Dr.* and *Prof.* unless they stand before a personal name. Even then it is better to write *Professor Thompson* than *Prof. Thompson*, though *Dr. Jackson* is to be preferred to *Doctor Jackson*.

VI. Abbreviations to Avoid. (i) The following are permissible in conversational English but should not be used in writing except of the most informal kind (e.g. in letters between friends, where a conversational style is adopted): *chrysanth.* (chrysanthemum), *'flu*, *fridge*, *lab.*, *lino.*, *maths.*, *meth.* (methylated spirit), *prep. school*, *turps.*, *vet.* (veterinary surgeon), *on spec.* (speculation).

(ii) The following 'dainty' words may be suitable for women's magazines or for the women's page of a popular newspaper, but they should not appear in serious writing: *hanky* (handkerchief), *pinny* (pinafore), *nightie* (night-dress), *tummy* (stomach). (See also CHILDISH WORDS.)

(iii) Do not write *boro'*, *tho'*, *altho'*, *thro'*. There are no places named *Scarboro'*, *Gainsboro'*, *Wellingboro'* or *Hillsboro'*.

(iv) The following abbreviations are vulgarisms, and should not be used in either speech or writing: *advert.* (advertisement), *on appro.* (on approval), *gent.* (gentleman), *Jap.* (Japanese), *an invite* (an invitation), *a recommend* (a recommendation). Unlike *'plane* for *aeroplane*, the abbreviated form *'copter* for *helicopter* is not yet recognised.

ABIDE BY. When used with its usual sense of 'stay', the verb *abide* has the past tense and the past participle *abode*, but *abide by* (a decision, a promise, etc.) has *abided*. 'He abided faithfully by his promise.' 'He has always abided by his word.'

ABORIGIN.S. The singular is *aboriginal* not *aborigine* or (worse still) *aboriginee*.

ABSTRACT LANGUAGE. It was over forty years ago that Fowler gave the advice, in *The King's English*, 'prefer the concrete term to the abstract', and more recently this has been reinforced by Sir Ernest Gowers (*Plain Words*). It would be unfortunate, however, if this were to lead to a rather conscious avoidance of all abstract terms. They cannot be dispensed with altogether; one must use discretion. 'The Chairman expressed his appreciation of the loyalty of the staff and the workpeople' is much to be preferred to '. . . said he appreciated the way that the staff and the workpeople had been loyal', and 'There is no denying the seriousness of the situation' is no more objectionable than 'There is no denying that the situation is serious'. If the abstract style is concise, clear and euphonious there seems no objection to it; a change to the concrete may be a change for the worse. But of recent years there has grown up, especially in official documents and in journalism, a woolly kind of style which uses circumlocutory, periphrastic abstractions which are clumsy in construction and which say rather ineffectively what could have been said much more clearly in far fewer words. This should certainly be avoided by anyone who wishes to write good English. Below are a few examples. A simplified version is given after each one.

What is the position with regard to the availability of a house? (Is a house available?)

There is no likelihood of an early finalisation of the plans. (It is unlikely that the plans will be put into a final form for some time.)

The implementation of the scheme would involve the expenditure of a large sum of money. (It would be very costly to carry out the scheme.)

The situation with regard to the export of cars has shown a slight improvement. (Rather more cars have been exported.)

In the eventuality of this being the case. (If this is so.) In view of the fact that. (As.)

If the weather situation permits. (If the weather permits, or 'weather permitting'.)

Under active consideration. (Being considered.)

This last example is particularly stupid, though in official circles it now seems to have become an accepted cliché. No one has yet been honest enough to say that a matter is under passive consideration.

ACADEMIC: ACADEMICAL. Generally speaking, *academic* has to do with learning or scholarship, *academical* with an academy or place of learning: thus 'an academical institution', but 'academic distinction', 'an academic education', 'a point of purely academic interest'. We speak of *academic dress*, but *full academicals*.

ACCENT. 'In this year's dress shows the accent is on green.' Does this mean any more than 'Green is the most popular colour'? Avoid this use of the word; it has become something of a vogue word of recent years.

ACCENTUATE. 'The steel shortage has been accentuated, and will particularly hit the motor industry.'—*The Financial Times*.
'In America cotton, hessian and paper share the important bagging market. With the first two in short supply, the trend towards paper sacks is accentuated.'—*Ibid*.
These two sentences exemplify a misuse which has become very common in the last few years. 'To accentuate' means to throw into relief or into prominence (e.g. 'The microphone accentuates certain defects of intonation'). It does not mean to increase, to aggravate, to make more acute, and the several related meanings which modern usage (or abusage) gives it.

ACCEPTANCE: ACCEPTATION. We beg a person's acceptance of a gift, a government signifies its acceptance of the findings of a Royal Commission, and the newspapers announce Mr Blank's acceptance of an honour or a position. *Acceptation* is an academic word meaning an agreed interpretation to be placed upon a word, or upon a clause in a document.

ACCORD. The idiom is '*of* one's own accord', not '*on* one's own accord'.

ACCORD: ACCORDANCE. 'In accord with your instructions' or 'In accordance with your instructions'? It depends on the meaning to be expressed. When the sense is 'following out' or 'obeying' *accordance* is required ('In accordance with your instructions we have suspended work on the heating apparatus'); when it is that of 'agreement', then *accord* is used ('What he has done is not in accord with your instructions').

ACCORDING. This cannot be used as an adverb. 'We will ascertain their wishes, and act accordingly'— not *according*.

ACCUSTOMED. When *accustomed* is intended to express the notion that something is customary, or is generally done, it is followed by the infinitive ('She was accustomed to sleep for an hour after her lunch'); when it is followed by *to* plus the gerund, it means 'is/was used to, or inured to' ('I am not accustomed to walking long distances'). As a verb, *accustom* is followed by a gerund, not an infinitive: 'You must accustom yourself to getting up early', not 'You must accustom yourself to get up early'.

ACOUSTICS. 'The acoustics of the hall *are* not all that could be desired', but 'Acoustics *is* an important subject in the training of an architect'.

ACQUAINT. We acquaint a person *with* (not *of*) a fact. The expression, however, is best avoided, since it is usually no more than a piece of pretentious English for the simpler *inform*, *tell* or *let know*.

ACQUIESCE. Followed by the preposition *in*.

ADD UP TO. 'What it adds up to is . . .' A piece of modern jargon for *amounts to*, *comes to* or sometimes simply *means*. Allowable perhaps colloquially, but should not be used in serious writing.

ADDICTED. The sentence 'He is addicted to drink' has perhaps given rise to the unidiomatic use of an infinitive after *addicted*. 'To drink' is here not an infinitive, but a noun preceded by a preposition. *Addicted* is always followed by *to* plus a noun or a gerund: *addicted to drugs*, *addicted to gambling*, but not *addicted to gamble*.

ADEQUATE. (i) *Adequate* is always followed by the preposition *to*, not *for*: 'adequate to one's needs', etc.
   (ii) Since *adequate* means 'just suffiicent', *adequate enough* is a solecism, and *more adequate* an absurdity. Logically, there is no objection to *more than adequate* ('The time you were allowed for the work should have been more than adequate'), but *more than enough* or *more than sufficient* is to be preferred.

ADHERENCE : ADHESION. *Adhesion* means 'sticking to' in the literal sense (the adhesion of a stamp to an envelope, or of flies to a fly-paper); *adherence* is 'sticking to' in the figurative sense, as adherence to a plan, to one's principles, etc.

The verbal counterpart of both is *adhere*: wallpaper adheres to the wall, and a person adheres to his plans.

Adherence gives the adjective *adherent*, and *adhesion* the adjective *adhesive* (as 'adhesive tape', 'an adhesive plaster'). Both adjectives may be converted to nouns: *adhesives* (paste, gum, etc.), a person's *adherents*.

ADJECTIVE OR ADVERB? (See under Adverb.)

ADMISSION: ADMITTANCE. When *admit* means 'confess', the noun is always *admission* (the admission of one's guilt, the admission that one was to blame); when it means 'allow in' *admission* is also the more usual word ('Admission fifty pence'. 'Admission by ticket only'). *Admittance* is more formal or official, and means 'leave or right to enter': e.g. 'No admittance except on business'.

ADMIT: ADMIT OF. (i) *Admit* may take a personal subject, and indeed usually does, but *admit of* (= allow of, leave room for) cannot: e.g. 'I admit breaking the window', 'She admitted having read the letter', but 'The position admits of no delay', 'The regulations admit of no variation'. 'I cannot admit of your doing that' is incorrect (amend to 'I cannot allow you to do that'), but 'The regulations do not admit of your doing that' is perfectly good English.

(ii) 'In spite of all the evidence against him, he refused to admit to the allegation.' *Admit to* something that is charged against one (perhaps on the analogy of 'confess to a crime') is occasionally to be found in modern writing, but it is not yet established as idiomatic, and is best avoided.

ADOPTED PARENTS (FATHER, MOTHER). Sometimes heard in speech, and occasionally seen in print (e.g. 'The Reverend Joseph Evans, the adopted father of Joseph Hunter'), but, strictly speaking, incorrect. It is the child who is adopted by the 'parents', not vice versa. Substitute *adoptive parents* (*father*, *mother*). *Adopted child*, *son*, *daughter* is, of course, correct.

ADULT. The modern tendency is to put the stress on the second syllable, though it is permissible to stress the first.

ADVANCE (Noun): ADVANCEMENT. *Advance* = 'progress' or 'going forward' (or sometimes 'coming on'): the advance of an army, the advance of science, the advance of medical know-

ledge, the advance of old age. *Advancement* = 'promotion' or
'helping forward': to seek advancement, to work for the advancement of a cause, the Royal Society for the Advancement of
Science. We say that with the advance (not the *advancement*)
of winter the days grow shorter.

ADVERB OR ADJECTIVE? (i) There are some pedantic people
who, under the impression that they are being 'correct', insist
on changing 'new-mown hay' to 'newly mown hay', and 'fresh-
ground coffee' to 'freshly ground coffee'; but the change is
not necessary. These adjective-participle combinations (other
examples are *new-laid eggs, new-won freedom, a new-born baby*)
are quite idiomatic, and as a matter of fact express a slightly
different idea from the participle preceded by the adverb.
Fresh-ground coffee is coffee which is fresh because it has just
been ground, whereas *freshly* ground coffee is coffee which has
been ground afresh (as though it might have been ground
before). But 'a newly painted house' is correct, for here the
sense is 'painted recently'. 'New-won freedom' is freedom
which is new because it has only just been won ; 'newly won freedom' is freedom which has been enjoyed before, lost temporarily, and then won anew. There is an obvious difference
between an egg which is hard-boiled and one which is hardly
boiled.
    Note that the adjective-participle combination must have the
hyphen. There is normally no hyphen when the adverb is used.
    (ii) 'Don't speak so loud' (or *loudly* ?). *Loudly* is to be pre-
ferred, but *loud* is often used, and can be defended on the
ground that it is descriptive of the sound rather than of the
manner of speaking. Similarly we might justify 'Speak a little
slower', 'No-one can walk quicker than that', 'The bus will
get you there as quick as the train'. (See also under QUICKER,
HARD, HIGH, TIGHT.)

ADVERTISEMENT. In British English the stress is on the
second syllable (*advértisement*). The Americans, however, say
advertísement, with the stress on the third syllable. A pronunciation with stress on the first syllable (the same as in *advertise*) is
common in certain parts of northern England, but it is not
accepted as correct by speakers of Standard English.

AFFECT : EFFECT. The verb corresponding to the noun
effect is *affect* (to produce an effect upon) : 'The climate affected
his health', 'The increased tariffs recently announced by the
Australian government are bound to affect our exports to that

country'. *Affect* also means 'to assume, as a form of affectation', as in the phrase 'to affect a superior air'.

Effect, when used as a verb, means 'to bring about' or 'to achieve', e.g. to effect an escape, to effect a change.

The plural noun *effects* may mean 'results' ('The full effects of the measures have yet to be felt') or it may mean 'personal property or belongings', as in the expression 'one's household effects'.

AFFINITY. There is an affinity *between* two things, or one has an affinity *with* (not *to*) the other. Fowler (*M.E.U.*) condemns 'an affinity *for*', but it is recognised in scientific language. One substance is said to have an affinity *for* another when it has a tendency to unite with it. Outside this rather specialised use, however, 'an affinity for' is incorrect.

AFORESAID. Except in the language of legal documents, an archaic word, which has a slightly absurd or humorous effect (e.g. 'the aforesaid Mr Smith'). Do not use it in ordinary English.

AGENDA. Though strictly a Latin plural (meaning 'things to be done'), in English this word is treated as a singular. Say 'The agenda *has* not yet been drawn up'. Plural: *agenda* or *agendas*, preferably the former.

AGGRAVATE. Commonly misused in the sense of 'to annoy, to irritate': 'Don't aggravate your aunt in that way', 'It is very aggravating to be constantly interrupted when you are engaged on an important piece of work'. The mistake is a very old one. Jerry Cruncher, in *A Tale of Two Cities*, it may be recalled, referred to his wife as 'an aggrawater'. The only legitimate meaning is 'to make worse something that is already bad'. 'The measures designed to remedy the situation only aggravated it.'

AGO. 'It is ten years ago since his father died.' This sentence illustrates a very common mistake. *Ago* normally takes the past tense; it refers to a point of time in the past, and reckons backwards from the present. It cannot, therefore, be combined with *since*, which reckons *from* a point of time in the past *up to* the present (e.g. 'I have not seen him since last Christmas'). The alternative constructions are: (i) It was ten years ago that his father died, (ii) It is ten years since his father died, (iii) His father died ten years ago.

'Is it only ten years? It seems longer ago than that.' Here the present tense *seems* is justified, since the sentence is an ellipsis of 'It seems *that it was* longer ago'.

AGREE. (i) To agree *with* a suggestion or a course of action is to regard it with approval; to agree *to* it is to give consent to it. Thus we may agree *to* something without agreeing *with* it: e.g. 'He was forced to agree to the proposals, though he did not like them'.

(ii) 'The Inspector of Taxes has now agreed your claim for expenses.' This transitive use of *agree* has now become firmly established in accountancy, and it ill becomes a layman to criticise it there. The accountants are entitled to use the idiom of their profession. Unfortunately, however, it is beginning to creep into the newspapers and into official announcements, where it is not recognised: e.g. 'The committee have agreed wage increases for nurses and hospital staffs'. If they have accepted increases that were already proposed, then they have agreed *to* them; if they have discussed them with representatives of the nurses and the hospital staffs, and have finally reached agreement, then they have agreed *on* them. In the active voice at least the transitive use should be kept within the strict bounds of accountancy; outside these bounds it sounds unnatural and is unidiomatic, though the passive 'wage increases have been agreed' or 'the terms have now been agreed' is less objectionable — perhaps because the preposition would come at the end, and since it is an insignificant word its absence is not noticeable.

AGREEMENT OF VERB AND SUBJECT. The rule is that a verb must agree with its subject in number and person. The following points should be noticed:

(i) When a subject consists of two singular words co-ordinated by *and* it normally becomes a plural subject and must take a plural verb: 'Your aunt and uncle *have* arrived'. But combinations like *bread and butter*, *fish and chips*, *whisky and soda* are singular.

(ii) Alternative subjects to the same verb each apply to it separately; if each of the alternatives is singular, therefore, the verb is singular ('Either John or James *is* the culprit') but if the alternatives are each plural the verb is plural ('Neither the boys nor the girls *have* done well in the examination').

(iii) When there are alternative subjects which each demand a different verb form, the form used is that which is appropriate to the subject which comes immediately before it: 'Either you or I *am* to go', 'Neither Sheila nor her parents *were* there'.

(iv) Care is necessary when a singular subject is separated from its verb by a plural enlargement (e.g. *a bunch of grapes*), or when the verb is followed by a plural complement. The verb must still be singular, though there is a tendency for it to get attracted into the plural. The following example comes from the *Birmingham Post*: 'The price of easier-flowing and safer traffic are the sights of the old Bull Ring—the hawkers, the orators, the flower-bedecked stalls and the fascinating crowds'.

(See also under SINGULAR OR PLURAL? and THERE (*Formal Subject*).)

AGRICULTUR(AL)IST.   *Agriculturist* is to be preferred. Similarly *horticulturist*.

AIM. The idiomatic construction is 'aim at doing something'. *Aim to do* is gaining ground, but it is not yet recognised as Standard usage. Say 'This book aims at giving a general out line of the subject', not 'This book aims to give a general outline of the subject'.

AIRPLANE. Some English newspapers seem to have adopted this spelling, but though it is normal in America it is not generally accepted in British English. Use *aeroplane*.

ALARM: ALARUM. The second word is the one regularly used in the expression 'alarums and excursions', and some people may prefer to speak of an 'alarum clock' rather than an 'alarm clock'. For all other purposes use *alarm*.

ALIAS. In Latin *alias* means 'at another time'. In English it is used to indicate an assumed name by which a person is known for a certain part of his life or in certain circles (William Arthur Jenkins *alias* Samuel Henderson). It may also be used as a noun, with the plural *aliases*: 'He had had several aliases'. It must, however, be confined to names: it cannot be used of a disguise or an assumed character, an incorrect use which is exemplified in the sentence 'He gained admission to the premises under the alias of a police officer'. Amend to 'under the guise of' or 'by posing as'.

ALIBI. *Alibi* is a Latin adverb meaning 'elsewhere'. In legal language an accused person proves an alibi when he is able to show that at the time when the crime with which he is charged was committed he was elsewhere. The word does not mean an excuse, a justification, extenuating circumstances and the various related ideas that popular misuse has given it in the past few years. The following are examples of this misuse:

'The Government is entering on a new phase. Up to now ministers have been carrying on where Labour left off, and have been able to plead various alibis as a result.' — *The Observer* (1952).

'It is unfortunately true . . . that directors couch their dividend forecasts in terms which provide them with a complete alibi if profits go sour, and they cannot fulfil their forecasts. I am getting a trifle fed up with these alibis, which must confuse unsophisticated shareholders.' — *The Stock Exchange Gazette* (1961).

The legal sense is the only legitimate one, but that is certainly not the sense that the writers of the above sentences intended.

ALL. (i) *All: all of*.
(a) Though *of* is used when a simple pronoun follows (*all of .it, all of us, all of them*), it should be omitted if the pronoun is itself followed by a noun in apposition: *all you boys*.

(b) Before a noun, or a noun qualified by an adjective, *all* is more usual, though *all of*, in contrast to *some of, few of*, etc., is allowable if the reference is to number ('All his children are now grown up', or 'All of his children are now grown up'); but it should not be used for amount, quantity, distance, length of time, etc. (*all the milk, all the morning, all the way* — not *all of*).

(ii) *All day*, etc. *All day, all night*, and sometimes *all morning* and *all afternoon*, are the only expressions of this kind where the definite article is omitted. In certain parts of the country, *all week* is frequently heard, but Standard usage insists on 'all *the* week'.

(iii) *All together: altogether, all ready: already*. See under the latter term in each group.

ALLERGIC. In the literal sense a medical term, meaning 'highly sensitive, so that the slightest amount of a certain substance produces a violent reaction'. It does not mean a strong dislike, and the recent use of it metaphorically in this sense ('I am allergic to people who are always thrusting their politics or religion upon others') is to be deprecated. In the medical sense a person may be allergic to something of which he is very fond, e.g. strawberries.

ALLOW: ALLOW OF. *Allow* means 'permit', *allow of* means 'give scope for' or 'leave room for'. ('The regulations do not allow of any variation'. *Allow of* cannot take a personal subject; we cannot say 'He would not allow of my going'. (See also ADMIT.)

ALLUSION: ILLUSION. *Allusion* = a passing or a veiled reference: *illusion* = a deceptive appearance. The adjectives are *allusive* and *illusory*.

ALMOST: NEARLY. (i) In many contexts *almost* and *nearly* are, for all practical purposes, interchangeable: e.g. 'It is almost ten o'clock', 'It is nearly ten o'clock'. Which we use depends on our attitude of mind towards the fact concerned. *Almost* is what we might call a 'minus' word; it subtracts from the idea of the word it modifies. *Nearly*, on the other hand, represents an approach towards it, and therefore gives it more emphasis. *Almost* is a genuine adverb of degree; *nearly* is not. The tendency seems to be to use *nearly* rather than *almost* when some special significance is implied. If someone asks us the time we might reply that it is either *almost* or *nearly* ten o'clock; but we should probably use *nearly* to the exclusion of *almost* if we wished to express surprise at the fact, or if someone had asked us to tell him when it was ten. 'It is almost five miles to the next village' is a simple statement of distance. If we wish to suggest that it is too far to walk, or that it is farther than one would think, then we are more likely to say that it is *nearly* five miles. Similarly, 'It cost me almost twenty pounds' is a mere statement of price, but 'It cost me nearly twenty pounds' suggests that it was more than might have been supposed, or more than I wished to pay.

(ii) When we wish to say that we come near to doing something, but then refrain from doing it, or avoid it, *nearly* is used in preference to *almost*: 'I nearly ran over that dog'. 'We nearly called to see you last Saturday'. 'I nearly offered to give them a lift'.

(iii) Verbs and adjectives denoting feeling or state of mind take *almost*, not *nearly*: 'I almost wish I had taken his advice'. 'You could almost imagine you were in Switzerland.' 'I almost dread going.' 'I am almost glad that the project has failed.'

ALREADY: ALL READY. When *ready* has the meaning of *prepared*, two words are required: 'We are all ready to start'. 'They came all ready for a day in the country.' Note the difference between 'The meal is already on the table' and 'The meal is all ready on the table'.

ALRIGHT. A very common misspelling. The only correct form is *all right*. On *all right by me*, see BY.

ALSO. *Also* is an adverb, not a conjunction; it should therefore not be used:
(a) at the beginning of a sentence or of a clause, (b) after a comma, to co-ordinate two nouns, unless it is preceded by *and* or *but*. *Examples*:

He had spent a good deal of his life on the Continent. Also he had lived for a year or so in India. (Correct to 'He had also lived', etc.)

She sold her diamond ring, also a pearl necklace. (Correct to 'and also a pearl necklace'.)

The following sentence, from a published report, is a particularly glaring example of careless style:

'Preparation of the book was deferred so that an account of the opening proceedings could be included, also photographs of the new building.'

Correct to '. . . so that an account of the opening proceedings and photographs of the new building could be included'.

Some defence of the initial *also* is possible, however, in sentences like the following:

'Also on the platform were the Mayor, the Town Clerk, and the Borough Librarian'.

By bringing forward the phrase that would otherwise stand at the end, we give greater prominence to the names of the persons in question by leading the reader up to them as a kind of climax. But the notion expressed by the opening phrase must have an obvious connexion with that of the previous sentence.

ALTERNATE: ALTERNATIVE. *Alternative* implies a choice between (strictly) two things (either one or the other); *alternate* means 'first one, then the other, in turn', as 'We play football and hockey on alternate Saturdays', i.e. football one Saturday, hockey the next.

Note also:—(i) Though, as stated above, *alternative*, strictly speaking, implies only *two* things or courses, it is no longer limited to that number. Only the pedant will object to our speaking of 'several alternatives'.

(ii) The term 'alternative accommodation' (as applied to housing) is now so strongly rooted in the vocabulary of officialese that it is probably useless to object to it, though usually the accommodation offered is not an alternative, since the unfortunate householder is not free to choose whether he accepts it or remains where he is.

(iii) The construction *no alternative but* (e.g. 'I had no alternative but to do it'), used, as it generally is, to mean that only one course was open, is what Fowler calls 'a sturdy indefensible'. It is illogical, but usage has established it as accepted idiom. The use of *but* implies that the course in question *is* an alternative, though the only one. But an alternative must be an alternative to something else; if there is no other which one might have chosen instead, then the course that one is obliged to take is not an alternative at all. Logically we should say 'I had no alternative to doing it', but one rarely does.

ALTHOUGH. (See THOUGH.)

ALTOGETHER: ALL TOGETHER. The first spelling should be used only when the sense is 'completely'. When *all* has a separate meaning, denoting number or quantity, it must be written as a separate word.

He took several pieces of string and tied them all together.

Now we will say the poem all together (i.e. in chorus).

I found the missing papers all together in a drawer of my desk, but the letter that I thought was with them seems to have vanished altogether.

ALWAYS: ALL WAYS. *Always* means 'at all times', *all ways* 'in every possible way'.

We have tried all ways to get the information, but without success.

AMBIGUOUS: AMBIVALENT. An ambiguous term or statement is one where only one meaning was intended, but a second is possible (e.g. Was the motorist driving on the *right* side of the road?). An ambivalent term is one which is intended to have a double meaning. Thus when Chaucer, in the Prologue to the *Canterbury Tales*, says of the Friar that he knew 'all the worthy women of the town' we can take *worthy* at its face value, as meaning 'well-off' or 'highly respected', or we may take it as a euphemism for 'disreputable' or 'loose-living'.

AMENABLE. Followed by the preposition *to* plus a noun (*amenable to discipline, amenable to reason,* etc.). An infinitive, whether active or passive (*amenable to learn, amenable to be taught*), is incorrect.

AMEND: EMEND. *Amend* = alter (usually for the better); *emend* = correct an error. Nouns: *amendment, emendation.*

AMOK: AMUCK. The latter spelling is to be preferred.

AMONG: AMONGST. (i) There is no difference of meaning, and no rule as to which should be used in particular circumstances, though *M.E.U.* suggests that *amongst* is more usual before a vowel. The deciding factors are really euphony and the rhythm of the sentence.

(ii) Both must be followed by a plural noun or pronoun, or by one which, though singular in form, has a plural sense (such as *clergy, staff, family*). *Amongst a pile of rubbish* is incorrect.

(iii) At one time grammarians insisted that a thing is shared *between* two people, but *among* (or *amongst*) more than two; but this distinction is no longer observed. Modern usage permits *between* where the purist would insist on *among*, but not vice versa. (See BETWEEN.)

AN (Indefinite Article). See A.

ANARCHY: ANARCHISM. *Anarchy* = a state of political disorder. *Anarchism* = a political philosophy which would reduce laws to a minimum and allow the individual the maximum of liberty to follow his own reason and conscience.

AND. (i) *And* is a co-ordinating conjunction, and must therefore join two syntactic units *of the same kind*, whether the units are single words, phrases or clauses. The following sentences are therefore incorrect.

It was decided that all books must be returned promptly, and a fine of one penny per day to be imposed on defaulters. (Noun clause + infinitive.)

He had with him a friend from somewhere in the Midlands, and whom I had never seen before. (Adj. phrase + adj. clause.)

(ii) Care is necessary with the subjects of clauses co-ordinated by *and*. Normally each will have its own subject. The subject may be omitted from the second, only if it is the same as that of the first, so that the one can serve for both. There is thus no objection to the sentence 'There are some people who rest during the day and work at night', since *who*, the subject of the first subordinate clause, is understood in the second. The construction 'Children whose parents are badly off and are unable to provide them with sufficient clothing' is also quite idiomatic, since *whose parents* is the subject of both verbs. But the following, from *A Guide to Bath Abbey*, is clearly incorrect:

'For visitors whose time is limited and are unable to learn

the history and examine the building in detail on the spot, it is suggested that the following itinerary be followed.'

Who is required before *are unable*. As the sentence stands we must understand *whose time*, from the previous clause, and this would make nonsense. *Whose* and *who* always need watching. Sometimes, as in the above sentence, *who* is required after *whose*, but sometimes it would be wrong to insert it. There is, for instance, a great temptation to write 'Children whose parents are badly off and who are unable to provide them with sufficient clothing'; but it would be incorrect, for the antecedent of *who* would be *children*, not *parents*. It would mean that the children were unable to provide the parents with sufficient clothing.

(iii) Contrary to a very widespread belief, there is no rule against beginning a sentence with *and*; in the Bible hundreds of sentences begin with it. Often it is the most appropriate word to begin with, as it links what is to follow to what has gone before; but this does not mean that it can be used arbitrarily. Two principles at least must be observed:

(a) The second sentence must introduce a new idea; it must not be just an extension or continuation of the first. The following should clearly have been written as one sentence, not as two.

After we had finished tea my wife settled down to sew. And I read the newspaper.

(b) The second sentence must have its own subject. If one subject has to do service for two verbs, then both verbs must go in the same sentence. The following (from *The Observer*) is an example of a violation of this rule.

'Johnny lives alone in two rented rooms. He's been in the district all his life. And is prepared to live it out there.'

The last two sentences should have been written as one.

(iv) Should a comma be used before *and*? If *and* joins two words or two short phrases the comma is best omitted, but if it joins two clauses, or two phrases of some length, then it should be used. It should never be omitted if its absence might lead to misunderstanding, or cause the reader to follow a false scent: e.g. 'He shot the landlord, and the barman only escaped by ducking behind the counter'. (See under COMMA.)

ANOTHER. (i) For alternatives, where only two things are concerned the correct idiom is *one or the other*, where more than two *one or other*, though *one or another* is also found.

(ii) *Some way or another* is incorrect. The alternatives are *one way or another* and *some way or other*. Similarly the compounds with *some-* as their first element (*someone, somehow, somewhere,* etc.) must be followed by *other,* not *another.* ('We shall have to do it somehow or other'—not *another.*)

(iii) Strictly speaking, *one another* should be used of three or more, and *each other* of two only, but the distinction is no longer rigidly observed.

ANTICIPATE. This verb has been so long misused, as though it meant *expect,* that it is perhaps useless to protest, especially when the error appears in a publication of a university examining board ('We do not anticipate that many candidates will enter for the paper'). Its only accepted meaning is 'forestall' or 'foresee, and take action against'. ('The enemy had anticipated our move.')

ANY. (i) *Than any.* 'London is more densely populated than any city in the world.' This is an example of a very frequent mistake. 'Any city in the world' includes London. Correct to 'any *other* city in the world.'

(ii) *Of any.* 'Dickens was the most widely read of any of the nineteenth-century novelists.' Incorrect. The alternatives are 'more widely read than any other' and 'the most widely read of all'.

(iii) *Any* used adverbially in interrogative and negative sentences ('I didn't like it any', 'Does the radio disturb you any?') is American. It is not recognised in British English. Use *at all.*

ANYONE : ANY ONE. (i) *Anyone* is singular and should therefore be referred to by a singular pronoun or possessive adjective. ('Has anyone a dictionary he can lend me?'—not *they.* 'Anyone who does that is risking his life'—not *their.*) But in contexts where *anyone* is used in a general, and not an individual or specific sense, so that it has the force of 'all, without exception', a plural is allowable, since the singular would sound incongruous: e.g. 'Anyone can enter for the competition, can't they?'

N.B.—The above observations also apply to *anybody.*

(ii) The compound *anyone* can be used only of persons : when the reference is to things two separate words must be used: 'Which screwdriver do you want?' — 'Any one will do.'

(iii) Even for persons, if *one* has a numerical sense two separate words are necessary : 'It took two of them to do the work that any one of us could do'.

APOSTROPHE. There are three uses :

(i) To indicate the omission of one or more letters from the spelling of a word. (See ABBREVIATIONS.)

(ii) For the plural of words which, not being nouns or pronouns, do not normally have a plural form (*if*'s, *and*'s and *but*'s. He gets mixed up with his *will*'s and *shall*'s); for the plural of letters of the alphabet ('Mind your p's and q's.' 'How many *l*'s are there in *travelling*?'); and for the plurals of numbers when written as figures ('He makes his 8's like 3's. The 1930's'). But if a number is written as a word, no apostrophe is used: 'A woman in her fifties. Things are at sixes and sevens.'

(iii) To indicate the genitive case of a noun. The following points should be noted:

(a) The general rule is that the apostrophe is placed before the *s* for the genitive singular (*my father*'s *car*) and after the *s* for the genitive plural (*a girls*' *school*, *a dogs*' *home*). But those nouns which do not make their plural in *s* add an '*s* to both the singular and the plural forms (*a child*'s *toys*, *children*'s *toys*, *a woman*'s *hat*, *a women*'s *college*, *a man*'s *overcoat*, *men*'s *clothing*). If there is any doubt, a safe guide is to substitute a preposition. *A woman*'s *hat* = a hat for a woman (hence the apostrophe follows *woman* and precedes the *s*); *a women*'s *college* = a college for women (hence the apostrophe follows *women* and precedes the *s*); *a dogs*' *home* = a home for dogs (hence the apostrophe follows *dogs*).

(b) Close compounds like *lady*'s *maid*, *mariner*'s *compass*, *bird*'s *egg*, may make the plural *lady*'s *maids*, *bird*'s *eggs* or *ladies*' *maids*, *birds*' *eggs*, etc., but where the genitive word must obviously be a plural if the whole compound is plural (as in *birds*' *nests*) the apostrophe must follow the *s*. Where such compounds are used in a transferred, figurative sense, however, the '*s* is used for the plural: *crows*' *nests* (literally), *crow*'s-*nests* (on ships), *bulls*' *eyes* (literally), *bull*'s-*eyes* (sweets). 'He scored several bull's-eyes' (hit the centre of the target several times).

(c) For personal names ending in *s*, add an '*s* if an additional syllable is pronounced for the genitive (*Jones*'s, *James*'s, *Charles*'s) but if no extra syllable is pronounced, then place the apostrophe after the existing *s*: *Mr Humphreys*' *house*. (It would be very difficult to say *Humphreys-iz.*) For euphonic reasons names which sound like the plural of a common noun (*Masters*, *Stones*, *Fields*, *Knights*, *Vickers*) do not add an extra syllable, so the genitive should be written *Masters*', etc.

French names ending in *s* or *x*, when used in an English context, take '*s* for the genitive (*Dumas*'s *novels*, *Fourneaux*'s *letters*). Latin names ending in *s* which have not been adopted as English names also, place the apostrophe after the existing *s* whether an additional syllable is pronounced or not: *Brutus*' *wife*, *Horatius*' *heroism*, *Ceres*' *blessing*. (This is the recommendation of *R.C.R.*)

(d) When two names are to be taken together as a 'joint' genitive, the genitive inflexion is added only to the last: *Gilbert and Sullivan's operas* (joint authorship), *William and Mary's reign* (they were joint sovereigns), but *Trollope's and Thackeray's novels*.

(e) Note the 'free' or independent genitive in *St. Paul's, She was staying at her aunt's, I am going to the butcher's/baker's/barber's*. It is helpful to think of these as short for . . .'s cathedral, church, house, shop, etc. (Incidentally *barber shop*, instead of *barber's shop*, is to be deprecated. It is commoner in America than in Britain, but many Americans do not like it.)

Many houses with names that are genitive by origin omit the apostrophe (e.g. Mascalls); so do some place names (St. Ives, St. Helens) but others do not. If in doubt, consult an atlas or a gazetteer.

(f) The names of companies, commercial firms and business houses which actually are singular are often given an *s* ('This book is published by Macmillans/Harraps/Heinemanns'). This is a specialised use of the ordinary plural and requires no apostrophe; but it does raise the question, do we buy a thing from *Woolworths* or *Woolworth's*? The best principle to go on is, if the firm is intended, then use no apostrophe ('Woolworths will probably have it'); if the shop, then insert the apostrophe ('I bought it at Woolworth's', 'Meet me outside Woolworth's'). The verb may sometimes be a guide: if the verb is singular its subject must also be singular, so the *s* sound must represent the genitive ending (What time *does* Woolworth's open?), but if the verb is plural it implies a plural subject (What time *do Woolworths open?*).

There are several Woolworths, Woolworth's or Woolworths' in this town (?). The form without the apostrophe is advised as the most satisfactory. The logical form, of course, would be *Woolworth'ses*, but we never say it.

(g) Use the apostrophe (after the *s*) in *two hours' time, a three days' journey, two weeks' wages, three months' notice, three weeks' holiday*, etc. These are often written without the apostrophe, but the analogy of the singular, where the *s* sound that is heard in pronunciation can only be a genitive (*an hour's time, a day's journey*) suggests that the plural is genitive also.

(h) Note the 'post-genitive' in such expressions as *a friend of my father's, a poem of Shelley's, a relative of her husband's*. This usually occurs only in the singular, but a plural is possible, and care must be taken to recognise it and to place the apostrophe correctly: *that car of Smith's* (belonging to Mr Smith), *that car of the Smiths'* (belonging to Mr and Mrs Smith or to the Smith family).

(On the difference between *my friend* and *a friend of mine*, see under GENITIVE.)

(i) Should we write *One of my friend's parents*, or *One of my friends' parents*, if we mean the parents of one of my friends (not one of the parents of my friends)? Neither is really satisfactory, and the construction is best avoided, but if it is really necessary to write it, the apostrophe *after* the *s* is to be preferred. The difficulty is, of course, that the genitive idea really belongs to *one*, not to *friends*.

(j) Finally, note that there is no apostrophe in the possessive adjective *its*. *It's* is short for *it is* or *it has*. Similarly there is no apostrophe in the possessive pronouns *hers*, *ours*, *yours*, *theirs*, or in such combinations as *Accounts Department*, *Parks Committee*, *Lotteries Act*, where we have a plural noun used attributively to convey the meaning 'concerned with'.

The indefinite pronoun *one* has the genitive *one's* (*to do one's duty*), but there is no apostrophe in *oneself*.

APPENDIX.   *Plural*: appendices (to books, documents, etc.), appendixes (anatomical).

APPOSITION.   In apposition *to* (not *with*).

APPROPRIATE.   Appropriate *to* (not *for*) the occasion, etc.

APPROVE: APPROVE OF.   *Approve* = 'give consent to' (*approve a scheme*): *approve of* = 'think well of, regard with favour'. ('He did not approve of his daughter's marriage'). *Approve* is often used in the passive ('The plans have been approved by the local authority'), *approve of* is usually found in the active voice, though a passive is not impossible.

APPROXIMATELY.   *Very approximately*, in the sense of *roughly*, intended to suggest a greater margin of possible error than *approximately* alone would suggest, is absurd (e.g. *The area is very approximately* 100 *square yards*). Since *approximately* means 'approaching near to', *very approximately* should mean 'approaching very near to', and suggest a greater degree of accuracy. But in any case, it should not be used ; *approximately* alone is sufficient.

ARAB (Adj.): ARABIAN: ARABIC.   *Arab* refers to race (*Arab tribesmen*, *Arab warriors*), *Arabian* more specifically to Arabia (*the Arabian desert*, *Arabian perfumes*), *Arabic* to the language, either as spoken or as written (*an Arabic dialect*, *Arabic characters*, *Arabic numerals*). Note, however, *gum arabic*.

ARCHAISMS. Archaisms are words and expressions, like *eft-soons, verily, peradventure, anent, vouchsafe*, which were at one time current English but are no longer part of the living language. They may still have their place in verse, or in prose written for devotional purposes (e.g. prayers and collects), where they have an evocative value, and a few of them may not be altogether incongruous in other kinds of prose of a serious or elevated character, but generally speaking they should be avoided.

More strongly to be condemned than genuine archaisms, however, are what we may call 'spurious archaisms', where quaint spellings are supposed to represent 'old English'. It is nothing but snobbish affectation that prompts a café to call itself *Ye Olde English Tea-Shoppe*. And why must churches and chapels hold a *Christmas Fayre* (or, even worse, a *Xmas Fayre*), instead of a *Christmas Fair*? There is something cheap and vulgar about it — rather like imitation antique furniture.

AREN'T I? The recognised interrogative form (colloquially) of *I am*. Strictly speaking the spelling should be *an't* (as *cannot* becomes *can't*, so *am not* becomes *an't*), and in late eighteenth and early nineteenth century novels this is sometimes found, but it is now obsolete. The modern spelling has arisen, of course, by analogy with *aren't you?* and *aren't they?*

ARISE. (See Rise.)

AROUND. 'He spent the whole afternoon sitting around doing nothing', 'The papers were left lying around', 'I shall be home around five o'clock'. This use of *around* is an Americanism and is to be deprecated in British English. Use *about*.

AROUSE. (See Rouse.)

ARRIÈRE-PENSÉE. Not an afterthought, but an unspoken thought at the back of one's mind, or a mental reservation.

ARTIST: ARTISTE. The latter term means 'performer', and is used of either sex.

AS. (i) *Case of Pronouns.* 'You seem to dislike him as much as . . .' *I* or *me*? It depends on the meaning. If it means 'as I do', then *I* is the correct word; if it means 'as you dislike me', then *me* must be used. The same principle applies to *he/him*, *she/her*, *we/us*, *they/them*. The test is to complete the ellipsis.

(ii) *The Mis-related Phrase*. 'As a heating engineer, your readers may be interested in my experience of central heating of large premises' (Letter to the *Financial Times*). But were the readers of the *Financial Times* a heating engineer? Recast to read 'As a heating engineer I think your readers, etc.', or better still, 'As a heating engineer I have had considerable experience of central heating, etc.'.

'As a solicitor in a county market town, Unitarianism was probably a serious disadvantage.'—*The Inquirer*. But was Unitarianism a solicitor? Recast to read 'As a solicitor in a county market town, he probably found Unitarianism a serious disadvantage.'

'As Chairman of the T.U.C., may I ask you . . .?'—from a B.B.C. interview. But the person who put the question was not Chairman of the T.U.C., as the sentence suggests he was. The question was put *to* the Chairman of the T.U.C.

Descriptive phrases of this kind, introduced by *as*, must be followed by the noun or pronoun to which they are intended to refer. But when *as* carries a meaning something akin to *for*, the same rule does not apply; the phrase may legitimately be brought forward for the sake of emphasis: e.g. As an example of a prose satire we may take *Gulliver's Travels*.

(iii) *As . . . as: so . . . as*. *As* is used with positive statements, *so* is more usual with negative ones. 'That story is *as* old as the hills.' 'He is not *so* old as he looks.' *As*, however, may be used with a negative, especially when the sentence is intended to deny an assumed or suggested positive: 'I shouldn't dream of doing it; I'm not as foolish as all that'. 'He is not as ill as he makes out.'

(iv) *Equally as*. In *equally as good*, *equally as cheap*, etc., *as* is redundant. The alternatives are *just as good* and *equally good*. One thing is *as good as* another, or the two are *equally good*.

(v) Care is needed with comparative clauses introduced by *as* or *than* where the normal subject-verb order is inverted. The verb must agree with the subject which follows it, irrespective of whether a singular or a plural noun precedes: *as was the case*, *as was our intention*, *as were our intentions*, *than were the effects*.

(vi) When the comparative clause is elliptical, the number of the verb can be determined only by supplying the ellipsis:

'There were not so many tickets available as *were* asked for'—an ellipsis of 'as tickets were asked for'.

'There were not so many tickets available as *was* expected'—an ellipsis of 'as it was expected there would be'.

Similarly, 'There were not so many casualties as *was* feared' —not *as were feared*, since it is short for 'as it was feared there would be'.

(vii) When *as* is a kind of conjunctive pronoun (= *and this*, or *but this*) functioning as the subject of a verb and referring back to the whole of a previous statement, the verb must be singular : 'Objections were raised by a number of Opposition members, as *was* to be expected'.

(viii) Akin to the redundant *as* noticed under (iv) above, is the intrusive *as* exemplified in such sentences as the following :—

'As much as I admire him, I cannot excuse his faults.'

'As poor as they are, they never refuse to give to charity.'

The first *as* should be omitted ('Much as I admire him', 'Poor as they are'). The introductory clause is not comparative, but concessive, meaning 'Though I admire him much', 'Though they are poor'.

(ix) On *as* and *like*, see under LIKE.

AS FOLLOWS. Invariable in form, whether accompanied by a singular or a plural. 'The chief points are as follows' (not *as follow*).

AS FROM. In most cases when this expression is used it is used wrongly : e.g. 'As from Sunday next the bus will leave the City terminus at 9.45 a.m.' Here *from* alone is sufficient. *As from* should be used only retrospectively : e.g. 'The new scale of salaries will be paid as from April 1st last'.

AS IF : AS THOUGH. (i) Despite the attempts of purists to insist on a distinction, in actual usage there is none. *As if* is the more logical, but *as though* is used almost as frequently.

(ii) Many grammarians (again mostly purists) insist that both *as if* and *as though* must be followed by a subjunctive, not by an indicative verb, since they put an imaginary case (*as he would if he were*, etc.). But do they? There is surely a distinction between 'He walks as if he were drunk' (implying 'but he is not') and 'He walks as if he is drunk', meaning 'He is drunk, judging from the way he walks'. Similarly we have 'It looks as if it is going to rain' (= It is going to rain, by the look of it), 'It looks as though we shall have to do the work ourselves'. For these the indicative seems justifiable.

AS TO. (i) There are legitimate uses of *as to*. It is, for instance, used legitimately when it introduces an infinitive construction denoting result : e.g. 'I am not such a fool as to believe that'.

Again it is used legitimately at the beginning of a sentence to draw attention to the subject with which the sentence is to be concerned: 'As to the allegation that he deliberately concealed the information, it has been investigated, but no evidence can be found to support it'.

(ii) It is used illegitimately when it merely replaces a simple preposition, as in the sentences 'We have no information as to his present employment'. 'They could tell us nothing as to the probable cost of such a scheme.' Substitute *about, concerning,* or some other suitable preposition, according to the context.

(iii) In the following sentences *as to* is wholly superfluous, and should therefore be omitted. 'You had better inquire as to whether they will need lunch.' 'There is some doubt as to whether he will come.' 'I have often wondered as to where it [some money] had vanished' (W. H. Davies, *The Autobiography of a Super-Tramp*).

(iv) *As to* (when used in its legitimate sense) 'picks up' something which has already been mentioned or which is presumed to be already in the mind of the speaker and of the person to whom the remark is addressed. When we wish to introduce something new, or an issue that has not already been raised, *as for* is used: 'Much pasture land is under water; and as for the grain, most of that has been ruined'. 'The substance of his lecture was quite good, but as for the delivery . . .!'

AS WELL AS. (i) 'The mother, as well as her three children, were taken to hospital.' 'The mother, as well as her children, all perished.' Both these sentences are incorrect. *As well as* does not co-ordinate the two nouns; it introduces a parenthesis. In the first sentence, therefore, a singular verb is required (the subject is *the mother*), and in the second *all* should be omitted.

(ii) Care is necessary when *as well as* is followed by a verb. If an adverb clause of comparison is involved ('You know that as well as I do', 'She does not play tennis as well as she used to'), a finite verb must, of course, be used. But when *as well as* has the force of a compound conjunction, meaning 'in addition to', and joins two verbal forms, it *cannot* be followed by a finite verb. The following is therefore incorrect: 'He spent all his money, as well as wasted his time'. If the first verb is a simple tense form, as it is here, then *as well as* must be followed by a gerund (*as well as wasting his time*), as can be seen if we imagine it transferred to the beginning of the sentence. If the first verb is a compound tense, or is made up of *can, may, must,* etc. followed by an infinitive, then *can, may, must* or the auxiliary of the compound is understood after *as well as*, and the appropriate non-finite part must be used: 'She can cook as well as sew'. 'We are repairing the roof as well as pointing the walls.' If the first verb of the pair is an infinitive, then the second must also be an infinitive, but without the *to*: 'You cannot expect her to do the housework as well as look after the children'. A frequent mistake with this last type is to use the gerund ('as well as looking after the children').

(iii) There is often a temptation to use an accusative pronoun after *as well as* when a nominative is required. The case depends on whether the pronoun is a subject or an object. 'They have invited you, as well as me' (accusative because it is the object of *have invited*). 'You agreed to his suggestion, as well as I' (nominative, because it is the subject of *agreed*). 'You helped him, as well as I'='You and I both helped him'. 'You helped him as well as me'='You helped both him and me'.

ASIAN. Over the past twenty years *Asian* (an older word revived) has been gradually displacing *Asiatic*, and the latter word may, before long, fall out of use. Perhaps the change started during the war of 1939–45, when an adjective was needed for the compound noun *South-East Asia*. *South-East Asiatic* would have sounded awkward, and *South-East Asian* solved the problem. Some people may still prefer *Asiatic* as the adjective, but *Asian(s)* is to be preferred as the noun, denoting the peoples of Asia. *Asiatics* has something of a disparaging suggestion about it.

ASIDE: A SIDE. *Aside* is an adverb (*turn aside, put aside, set aside, stand aside*, etc.). When the sense is 'on each side' two words (*a side*) are necessary: 'The passengers sat four a side'. 'They played seven a side.' When the expression is used as a compound adjective, two hyphens are needed: 'a seven-a-side competition'. (*Seven-a-sides* is a solecism.)

ASPHALT. Note the spelling and the pronunciation of the first syllable (*as*-, not *ash*-). The latter pronunciation is very common in some parts of the country, but it is incorrect.

ASSURE: INSURE. In commercial usage there is a technical difference; one *assures* against something that is bound to happen (e.g. death), and *insures* against something that may or may not happen (e.g. fire, burglary, etc.). In ordinary English, however, we need not trouble ourselves about this distinction. We may speak of insuring our life, our house, our car or our luggage, irrespective of what the insurance (or assurance) companies call it. Of course, in writing to a company we must use the word by which it describes itself. Most call themselves *assurance* companies, but some have the word *insurance* as part of their name.

The verb meaning to make sure, or make certain, is *ensure*, not *insure*, e.g. to register a letter, to *ensure* that it reaches its destination.

ATE. Pronounced *et*. The pronunciation rhyming with *hate* is dialectal.

ATTENDANT: ATTENDER. 'For over thirty years he was a regular attendant at morning service' (From an obituary notice in a church magazine). The objection might be considered hair-splitting, but it would have been better if the writer had used *attender*. An attendant is one who attends on others: one who attends a service, a meeting, a lecture, etc., is an *attender*.

AUTHORESS. A needless feminine form. A woman who writes a book should be referred to as an author, not an authoress, a word which, like *poetess*, has come to acquire a slightly disparaging connotation.

AUTUMN (Adjective): AUTUMNAL. 'The autumnal social will be held on October 3rd.' Amend to 'the autumn social'. When the sense is merely that of 'occurring or falling in the autumn' the adjective is *autumn*, e.g. 'an autumn day', 'the autumn term' (in a school). *Autumnal* means 'having the qualities or characteristics that one associates with autumn'. We may say that the countryside looks 'quite autumnal' even though it is not yet autumn, while we may have autumnal weather in late summer. *Autumnal* is to *autumn* what *wintry* is to *winter*.

AVAIL. (i) Notice the idioms, 'All his efforts were *of no avail*' (adjectival), and 'He made repeated attempts, but *to no avail*' (adverbial).

(ii) As a verb, *avail* is used either intransitively ('All his efforts did not avail'), transitively, with a personal object ('All his efforts availed him nothing'), or with a reflexive object followed by *of* ('You should avail yourself of this opportunity', 'I shall avail myself of your offer'). It cannot, however, be used in the passive voice. 'The opportunity was not availed of', 'I am sorry that your kind offer cannot be availed of' are incorrect.

AVERSE. Followed by the preposition *to*; to insist on *from*, on purely etymological grounds, is pedantic. The only part of the verb that can follow *averse* is the gerund ('I am averse to gambling', not 'averse to gamble').

AWAIT. (See WAIT.)

AWAKE (Verb.). (See WAKE.)

AWFUL: AWFULLY. *Awful* is a word that should be used rarely, since the occasions or situations when it is really applicable will be rare. An awful scene is a scene that fills one with awe. When the hymn-writer spoke of God's 'awful purity' he was using the term correctly, to signify purity before which a mere mortal stands in awe; but popular usage has emptied the word of its real meaning, so that it has come to take its place with *nice*, *terrible* and *frightful* as an example of debased currency. It should never be used merely as an intensive ('an awful headache', 'an awful cold') or in a derogatory sense ('an awful bore', 'awful weather', 'an awful journey').

A similar warning is necessary about the adverbs *awfully*, *terribly* and *frightfully*. To describe a lecture as 'awfully boring', the weather as 'terribly cold' or a person as 'frightfully clever' is to degrade words to the point where they really express nothing at all. The late Aneurin Bevan once told a rally of Labour Party supporters that the Socialist experiment in the nationalisation of basic industries was 'of frightful importance to the whole world'. If he really meant what he said, it was an example of unusual candour on the part of a politician.

AWHILE: A WHILE. The compound *awhile* is perhaps best avoided, but if it is used it should be only in a strictly adverbial sense, when the meaning is 'for a short time': e.g. 'Wait here awhile', 'Let us rest awhile'. But even this can be expressed by two words. Two separate words must always be written when (a) a preposition precedes, as 'for a while', 'after a while', (b) when the expression is modified by an adverb, as in 'quite a while'.

B

BACK OF. *Back of*, in the sense of *behind* ('Back of the house was a small garden') is an Americanism, and not a very elegant one at that. It is not accepted as British English. Even in America, according to Margaret Nicholson (*A Dictionary of American-English Usage*), it is deplored by scholars and avoided by careful speakers. Say *at the back of* or *behind*, whichever is the more suitable to the context.

BACTERIA. A plural noun. Do not speak of *a bacteria*.

BADE (past tense of *bid*). Pronounced *bad*, not *baid*.

BALE OUT (from aircraft, etc.). Strictly speaking, the spelling should be *bail out*, but *bale out* has become accepted and is now the more usual.

BALEFUL : BANEFUL. *Baleful* = evil, *baneful* = harmful, destructive.

BALMY : BARMY. *Balmy* = fragrant, sweet-smelling, as 'the balmy air', 'the balmy breezes'. The slang word meaning *crazy* is spelt *barmy*.

BAR. 'Everything bar the clock was silent.' Apart from a few traditional expressions like 'It's all over bar the shouting', use *except*, or *but*.

BARBARISM : BARBARITY. *Barbarism* = an uncivilised mode of life, *barbarity* = savageness, cruelty.

BE. The use of *be* for an imaginary or assumed condition ('If it be alleged . . .', 'If the question be asked whether . . .', though not incorrect, is rather old-fashioned and savours of pedantry. Use the indicative *is*.

BECAUSE. (i) 'The reason he is absent from work is because he is ill.' Incorrect. The alternatives are 'He is absent from work because he is ill', and 'The reason he is absent from work is *that* he is ill'. 'The reason is because' is a mixture of the two.
(ii) 'Because another person cheats is no reason why you

30

should.' 'Because you don't like a person is no excuse for being
rude to him.' Again incorrect: an adverb clause is made the
subject of the verb *is*. Amend to 'The fact that . . .'

(iii) *Because* or *for*? In the following sentence *because* is used
where *for* would be more appropriate. 'The evenings were
getting chilly, because it was late September.' *Because* is a
subordinating conjunction, *for* is a co-ordinating one; *because*
therefore shows a more definite relationship between the two
facts than does *for*. With *because* the emphasis is on the reason,
which is presented as the really important fact, it being assumed
that we already know the fact given in the main clause. With
for it is the first fact that is important and which we are really
concerned to state; the second is added by way of explanation,
but almost as an afterthought.

This should be distinguished from sentences of the type:
'We shall have to hurry, because the shop closes at five o'clock'.
Here *because* is correct, despite the fact that the really important
clause is the first one. The second clause does not give the
reason for the fact stated in the first clause, but the reason why
the statement is made.

BEG. 'I beg to inform you . . .', 'I beg to state . . .' A meaningless cliché adopted by some letter-writers under the impression that it is a mark of courtesy. Occasionally it may
have a point, but it usually smacks of servility. Avoid it. It is
particularly stupid when the information is something for which
the writer has been asked, or which he is required to give in
an official capacity, and even more stupid when attached to verbs
like *acknowledge, thank*, etc. — as though one needed to apologise
for thanking a person, or for acknowledging a letter or a cheque.

BEG THE QUESTION. Not 'evade the question', or 'skilfully
avoid answering the question', but 'base an argument upon the
assumption of the truth of the very thing that has to be proved'.
E.g. 'We must believe that God exists, since it says so in the
Bible, and the Bible is God's infallible word.' Here our 'proof'
of the existence of God is based upon an assumption of his
existence; hence it amounts to no proof at all.

BEGIN: COMMENCE. (i) Wherever possible, use *begin*.
Commence is the formal word, used for the announcement of
meetings, concerts, etc. Wyld (*Universal English Dictionary*)
says that apart from such contexts 'the word has now fallen to
vulgar use'.

(ii) There are, nevertheless, certain traditional expressions, like *commence author*, *commence playwright*, where only *commence* can be used. They are perhaps now a little old-fashioned.

(iii) *Begin* may be followed by either the gerund or the infinitive (*begin doing something* or *begin to do something*), the infinitive being more usual when we are concerned only with the inception of an activity, without any reference to its possible continuance ('It began to rain', 'He begins to look old'), the gerund when the inception is thought of as initiating a process that continued or is to continue ('Don't begin writing until I tell you', 'They have begun building the house'). *Commence* takes only the gerund.

BEHALF. The idiom is *on behalf of*, not 'on *the* behalf of' or '*in* behalf of'.

On behalf of means 'acting for'; it must therefore be followed by a noun or pronoun denoting the person or persons for whom the deputy is acting, and only with a verb in the active voice can the subject of the verb denote the deputy (e.g. 'I am writing to you on behalf of my mother'). This does not mean that *on behalf of* cannot be used in passive sentences: it can (e.g. 'A telegram of congratulation was sent to him on behalf of the Queen', 'Greetings were conveyed by the Archdeacon on behalf of the Bishop'), but the subject of a passive verb cannot be represented as the deputy for those specified afterwards. 'The captain accepted the cup on behalf of the team' is correct: 'The captain was presented with the cup on behalf of the team' is not — unless (which is unlikely) it means that the cup was a presentation to him *from* the team. There is, however, nothing wrong with 'The Chairman was asked to make the presentation on behalf of the committee'. It is true, the subject of the passive verb (*The Chairman*) is represented as the deputy for the committee; but then the subject of the passive verb is here also the subject of the active infinitive *to make*, and it is this infinitive, not the finite verb, that *on behalf of* modifies.

The following sentences exemplify errors which, though perhaps not common, do sometimes occur.

'I am writing to you on behalf of your family to express my sympathy in your bereavement.' (If the writer was acting on behalf of anyone's family it was his own, not that of the bereaved person.)

'At the end of the lecture the Chairman moved a vote of thanks on behalf of the speaker.' (He moved a vote of thanks *to* the speaker, on behalf of the audience.)

'Much of the delay is due to inefficiency and bad organisation on behalf of the railways.' (Here *on behalf of* is wrongly used for *on the part of*.)

BEHOLDEN TO (someone). Not 'beholding to'.

BEING. '*Being as* we were strangers, we had to ask our way.'
A solecism and a vulgarism. The idiomatic alternatives are (i)
Being strangers, (ii) As we were strangers.

BEREAVED : BEREFT. *Bereaved* by death : *Bereft* (i.e. deprived) of speech, one's senses, etc.

BESIDE : BESIDES. Use *besides* only when the meaning is 'in
addition' ; for all other senses *beside* is the word : 'He sat beside
the driver', 'She was beside herself with joy'.

BETTER. (i) 'I have not been well, but I am better now.' 'He
got better very quickly.' This use of *better* in the sense of *well*
may be accepted as sanctioned by usage (strictly speaking, of
course, a person may be better, but still far from well), but
quite better is not permissible.
    (ii) The negative of *you had better* is *you had better not*. In
Cumberland *you better hadn't* is heard.

BETWEEN. (i) *Between* is a preposition, and any pronoun that
follows it must therefore be in the accusative case : *between you
and me*, not *you and I*.
    (ii) 'A space of three feet must be left between each of the
desks'. 'There will be an interval of ten minutes between each
act.' Incorrect. *Each* is singular, and we cannot have 'between'
one. Amend to 'between each desk and the next', and 'between
the acts'.
    (iii) We have to choose between one thing *and* another, not
or another.
    (iv) The rule, at one time insisted upon, that *between* is used
of only two things or persons, and *among* of more than two, is
no longer strictly observed. 'We shall do the work more quickly
if we share it between us' may refer to more than two people,
and so may the expression 'between ourselves', meaning 'in
confidence'. 'There does not seem much difference between the
three of them' is quite acceptable English. Even if *among* is
used when the sense is distributive, *between* is always required
when aggregation or co-operation is expressed : 'The three
children saved over a hundred pounds between them.' 'Between them the passengers managed to push the bus to the side
of the road.'

BEVERAGE. There is rarely any justification for this word, which is usually a piece of official jargon (e.g. 'Hot beverages are provided with the midday meal for those who require them'). Use *drink*, unless the word would be ambiguous or misleading (which is seldom).

BEWARE (OF). (i) Despite Shakespeare's 'Beware the Ides of March' and Lewis Carroll's 'Beware the Jabberwock, my son', the modern tendency is to use *of* before a noun or a gerund: 'Beware of the dog', 'Beware of flatterers', 'Beware of falling into bad ways'. Before a clause *of* is never used: 'Beware that he does not deceive you'. As an alternative to *that . . . not* we may have *lest*: 'Beware lest you take a false step'.

(ii) Since it is made up of the verb *be* and an old adjective *ware* (=careful, cautious), *beware* can be used only where the simple *be* would be possible, i.e. as an imperative, as an infinitive, and after *shall, will, should, would, must, may, can, ought*. There are no participles, no past tense, and no perfect or continuous forms. We cannot say 'They bewared of the dog'. Nor is a passive voice possible; we may say 'You should beware of flatterers', but not 'Flatterers should be bewared of'.

BI-ANNUAL: BIENNIAL. *Bi-annual*=twice a year. *Biennial* =once every two years.

BIBLE. (i) No inverted commas should be used, and in print the word should not be italicised. The same applies to the individual books of the Bible.

(ii) The adjective *biblical* always has a small letter: *a biblical reference, a biblical scholar*; so do the derived nouns *bibliolatry* and *bibliolater*.

BIG-HEADED. Not an accepted English word. Use *swelled-headed, swollen-headed* or *conceited*. *A big-head* (a conceited person), like *a big-mouth* (a talkative, boastful person), is slang.

BLAME. 'He blamed it on to me.' Acceptable colloquially, but in writing (except when reproducing dialogue) and in more formal speech say, 'He blamed me for it' or 'He put the blame on me'.

BLOND(E). The masculine form (without the *e*) does not occur in English; *blonde* is used for both sexes, though the word is very rarely applied to men. Though it is not impossible to describe a man, or his hair, as blonde (adj.), *a blonde* (noun) always means a woman.

BLUEPRINT. A very much over-worked piece of official jargon, which is best avoided. Use instead *plan, scheme, project, diagram, design, sketch,* or whatever the appropriate word is.

There is, of course, a correct literal use for *blueprint* in drawing offices and in engineering and constructional work.

BONA FIDE: BONA FIDES. (i) *Bona fides* (=Latin, *good faith*) is singular: 'His bona fides is in doubt' (not *are*).

(ii) *Bona fide* means 'in good faith'; that is to say, it is, strictly speaking, adverbial in sense, though in English it is more often used adjectivally: *bona-fide enquiries, a bona-fide applicant.* It should never be used as a noun; do not say 'I should question their *bona fide*'. Here *bona fides* is required.

BORN: BORNE. (i) The normal past participle of the verb *to bear* is *borne*. Thus a burden, an insult, a good character, responsibility, the brunt, etc. is *borne*. In other words, if the idea to be expressed has no connexion with birth, use the spelling *borne.*

(ii) A child is *born* (comes into existence as a separate being), and is *born to* its mother; but a woman *has borne* a child. Note also *born of* to denote origin (*born of lowly parents, born of an ailing mother*) and the same word used metaphorically: 'Some people believe that crime is born of poverty'.

BOTH. (i) Should one say *both his sons* or *both of his sons, both the men* or *both of the men, open both doors,* or *open both of the doors?* Neither is incorrect, though the omission of *of* is more usual. When *of* is used the two are thought of individually and separately, when it is omitted they are thought of together. That is why we never have *of* where one cannot exist without the other, or where one implies the other (*both sides, both ends*).

(ii) The same difference exists between *We/you/they both* and *both of us/you/them.*

(iii) 'Such a remark is both offensive, untrue, and likely to cause trouble.' *Both* should not be used if more than two terms are involved. Coleridge (*The Ancient Mariner*), it is true, wrote 'both man and bird and beast', but even Homer may nod; and it is possible to defend Coleridge on the ground that 'bird and beast' is thought of as a single category denoting non-human creatures, as opposed to man.

(iv) *Both . . . and.* (See under CORRELATIVES.)

BOTTLENECK. A useful metaphor, but do not speak of *reducing* the bottleneck when you mean reducing the obstruction.

A reduced bottleneck causes more obstruction, not less. Remember, too, that *severe* and *acute* are not suitable adjectives to apply to a bottleneck. Nor does one overcome, solve or iron out a bottleneck. One can, however, get rid of it.

BRACKETS. Two types are in use, the round and the square, though the former are far more frequent.

  I. **Round Brackets.** Apart from their use with numbers or letters of the alphabet in enumerating a series of subjects, sections or paragraphs, as (i), (ii), (a), (b), (c), etc., round brackets are employed to enclose a parenthesis. This, however, does not mean that they are appropriate for every kind of parenthesis; sometimes dashes or commas are to be preferred. For details, see under PARENTHESIS.

   Care is necessary in punctuating a sentence which includes a parenthesis in brackets. The words within the brackets belong, grammatically, to the part of the sentence which precedes them; thus any stop which would have been placed, had the parenthesis not been there, after the word which immediately precedes the first bracket, is transferred to a position immediately following the second. At the same time the words within the brackets are punctuated according to their own meaning, e.g. 'The new production of *Love's Comedy* (Is it really a comedy ?), in which Mr X.Y. takes the part of the hero, opened last night'. The parenthesis is a question; hence the question mark is placed within the brackets. If there had been no parenthesis the name of the play would have been followed by a comma. This is now transferred so that it follows the second bracket. Similarly, when a parenthesis in brackets occurs at the end of a sentence the full stop will go *outside* the final bracket.

  II. **Square Brackets.** These are used to enclose wholly extraneous matter, chiefly an insertion of the writer's own within a quotation from another writer. E.g. 'He [Heathcliff] stubbornly declined answering for a while'. The name 'Heathcliff' has been inserted in square brackets because it has been supplied by the present writer to explain *he*. To put it in round brackets would have implied that it was Emily Brontë's parenthesis, and therefore part of the quotation.

BRETHREN. An old plural of *brother*. It is now used only in liturgical and ecclesiastical language ('Dearly beloved brethren'), in the name of the sect known as the Plymouth Brethren, and within certain clubs and societies, to refer to their own members.

In ordinary English it has been replaced by *brothers* (for which see below). The title of the novel *Joseph and His Brethren* is, of course, a deliberate archaism, taken from the Old Testament.

BRIM-FULL. So spelt; not *brimful*, though this latter spelling is often seen. The sense is 'full to the brim'.

BRITISHER. American, not British usage. Even in the U.S.A. it is avoided by careful writers and speakers.

BROADCAST. *C.O.D.* recommends *broadcasted* for the past tense, and *broadcast* for the past participle, but most people use *broadcast* for both: *They broadcast his speech. His speech was broadcast.*

BROTHERS. Both *the brothers Wright, the brothers Wesley* and *the Wright brothers, the Wesley brothers* are correct, though there is an increasing tendency to use the latter order. But we always speak of *the brothers Grimm* (perhaps to avoid possible misunderstanding). *Sisters* is always placed after the name: *the Brontë sisters.*

BUFFALO. In the vocabulary of sportsmen the plural is *buffalo*. In ordinary English it is usual to speak of *a herd of buffalo*, but when the animals are thought of individually *buffaloes* is more usual.

BURNED: BURNT. (i) For the adjective always use *burnt* (*burnt paper, burnt sienna, a burnt offering*).
(ii) For the past tense and past participle either *burned* or *burnt* may be used, but the latter is more common in the transitive sense ('He burnt his fingers', 'The acid has burnt a hole in my jacket') and the former in the intransitive ('The fire burned for several days'). *Burned* is also preferred for the figurative use ('A desire for revenge burned within him').

BUS. No apostrophe. *Omnibus* is now used only in official contexts, or to describe a book containing a large number of stories or plays, usually by the same author, or of the same kind.

BUT. (i) *As a Co-ordinating Conjunction.*
(a) On the use or non-use of a comma before *but*, the use of *but* before a relative pronoun (*but who, but which, but that*), and *but* used at the beginning of a sentence, see under AND. The same rules apply to both.

(b) With the correlatives *not only . . . but also* it is perhaps rather pedantic to insist that the *also* must never be omitted. A sentence like the following may be regarded as quite acceptable English: 'Not only beginners, but even experienced craftsmen, may learn much from this book'.

(c) Beware of falling into the error of the redundant *but*, exemplified in the following sentences. (i) *But that, however, is another story.* If *however* is used *but* is not needed : or alternatively omit *however*. (ii) *He tried in vain, but he could not do it.* This implies that if he tried in vain we should expect him to do it, for *but* is an adversative conjunction ; that is to say, it introduces a statement which is opposed to the previous one, or contrasted with it. In the sentences quoted there is no contrast. The correct versions are either 'He tried, but could not do it ', or 'He tried in vain to do it'. (iii) *He is not a native of this town, but he came here from London.* Here, again, the second statement does not contrast with the first : it bears it out and amplifies it. Omit *but* and use a colon instead of a comma, or alternatively retain the comma and omit the second *he*. *But*, however, is correctly used in the sentence 'I am not a native of this town, but I have lived here ever since I was a child of two'.

(d) 'The story is concerned not so much with historical events and political doctrines, *but* with human motives, passions and behaviour.' Another unidiomatic use of *but*, probably through the influence of *not with . . . but with*. *Not so much* must be followed by *as*, not by *but*.

(ii) *As a Pseudo-Relative Pronoun.* Sometimes *but* is used as a kind of negative relative pronoun, with the sense of *who . . . not*, or *which . . . not*, as in Browning's 'No voice but was praising this Roland of mine' (*How They Brought the Good News from Ghent to Aix*). The pronominal element, that is to say, is implied in the word *but* itself ; it must not, therefore, be followed by a further pronoun. 'There was no-one but who admired him' and 'There was no-one but they admired him' are both incorrect. Omit *who* and *they*.

(iii) *As a Subordinating Conjunction.* In sentences like 'It never rains but it pours', 'We ne'er see our foes but we wish them to stay', the word *but* is a subordinating conjunction introducing an adverb clause. A frequent mistake is to use *what* after it : 'We never arrange a game of cricket but what it rains'. Omit *what*.

Most grammarians classify this kind of clause as conditional, perhaps because they nearly always take as the stock example the first one given above, 'It never rains but it pours'; and it does happen that in this particular sentence *but* could be replaced by *unless* without noticeably altering the meaning. But usually it cannot. 'We never arrange a cricket match but it rains' obviously does not mean the same as 'We never arrange a cricket match unless it rains'. The latter would imply that only if it rains do we arrange a cricket match — a manifest absurdity. The former is a complaint that every time we arrange a cricket match — without exception — it rains. In all sentences of this kind we have a case of inverse subordination. What is grammatically the subordinate clause contains the main fact, and the grammatical main clause contains the subordinate fact. It is another, but more forceful, way of saying 'Whenever it rains it pours', 'Whenever we see our foes we wish them to stay', 'Whenever we arrange a cricket match it rains'.

(iv) *As a Preposition.* (a) When *but* means *except* it is a preposition, and therefore should be followed by the accusative case (*everyone but me, everybody but them, all the players but him,* etc.). Usage, however, permits the nominative when it is immediately followed by a verb to which it appears to be (though actually it is not) the subject, so that an accusative would sound strange: e.g. 'Everyone but she knew the answer'. 'The boy stood on the burning deck, whence all but he had fled.' (b) 'We could not help but do it.' A confusion of two constructions: (i) 'We could not but do it' (now rather old-fashioned), and (ii) 'We could not help doing it'. Use the latter.

BY: BYE. By-election, by-way, by-pass, by-product, by-street, bygone times, by and large, by and by (presently): *but* by the bye, bye (at cricket and in other games), bye-bye (colloquial for *goodbye*), bye-byes (childish for *sleep*). *R.C.R.* insists on the spelling *by-law*, which is etymologically the correct one, but in United Kingdom legislation it is always *bye-law*.

By and large has been so overworked during the past few years that it has become something of a vogue expression. It could well be dispensed with. The preposition *by* is not idiomatic in 'That will be all right by me'. Substitute *to me*, or 'so far as I am concerned'.

C

CAFÉ. Do not omit the accent. Pronounced *caffay*. The pronunciations *caff* and *caif* are vulgarisms.

CAN: MAY. *Can* (past tense *could*) denotes ability or potentiality, *may* (past tense *might*) expresses possibility or permission. So long as it is confined to spoken English it is perhaps pedantic to object to the use of *can* and *could* to ask for permission or to make a request ('Can we go when we have finished our work?', 'Could you pass me the newspaper, please?'). In more formal written style *may* and *will* respectively are to be preferred.

CANNOT. (i) American English permits *can not* (two words), but in British English it is spelt as one, except (mainly in verse) when the *not* is to be stressed. Caution is, however, necessary. The following quotation from *The Inquirer* (where *can not* is correctly printed as two words) may serve as a warning of a possible trap for the unwary person whose zeal for 'correctness' may lead him astray.
　　'Family life can not only give security, but also provide children with values and standards with which to face the world.' *Cannot* would be incorrect, for it is the positive, not the negative verb that is used here; the *not* belongs to *not only*, which is correlated with *but also*.
　　(ii) Where the contracted form *can't* is concerned, (a) see that the apostrophe is placed in the right position (a frequent misspelling is *ca'nt*), and (b) avoid the combination *can't seem to* (e.g. 'I can't seem to make him understand'), which is meaningless. The alternatives are (i) 'I can't make him understand', (ii) 'He seems unable to understand'.

CANVAS: CANVASS. The first is the material, the second is concerned with soliciting support. It has a double *s* whether it is used as a verb ('to canvass the members of the committee', 'to canvass votes') or as a noun ('to make a canvass of the neighbourhood').

CAPABLE. 'Capable of doing'; not 'capable to do'. The same applies to *incapable*. Both must be followed by an active, never by a passive voice. We cannot say 'capable (or *incapable*) of being done'.

40

CAPACITY. 'Full to capacity' may pass, but the adjectival use in expressions like 'a capacity crowd', 'a capacity audience' is a piece of journalese which should be avoided.

CAPITAL LETTERS. The general rule is, of course, that capital letters are used for all proper nouns and for adjectives derived from them; but the following points should be noted.

(i) Though words denoting races of people require a capital, those differentiating people by the colour of the skin or other physical characteristics do not: thus *Jew, Jewish, Arab,* but *negro, albino, pigmy.* The importance assumed by the colour question in certain parts of the world in the last few years has led some British writers to adopt what has long been a common American practice, and to use capitals for *Negroes* and *Whites* when the two groups are thought of collectively. This may ultimately become the rule.

(ii) Words which are proper nouns or adjectives by origin but have ceased to be thought of as such, or are no longer closely associated with the place or person in question, have no capitals: *indian ink, indiarubber, plaster of paris, brussels sprouts, a limerick, an aunt sally, tommies* (private soldiers). Similarly vehicles, garments, etc., named after persons or places are written with small letters: *brougham, wellingtons, cardigan, hansom cab.*

(iii) Verbs derived from proper nouns have a small letter: *americanise, anglicise, pasteurise, bowdlerise.* (On the use of *s* in these words, see under Ise.)

(iv) The names of the months, the day of the week, religious festivals, and special secular days or occasions (e.g. Remembrance Day, New Year's Day, May Day) have capitals; but the names of the seasons should be written with small letters, except when personified.

(v) Use small letters for the points of the compass when they merely indicate direction, but capitals when they are the recognised or substitute name for a particular geographical region or area: 'The sun rises in the east and sets in the west', but 'Many years of his life had been spent in the East'. Also, of course, *East Anglia, South Kensington.*

(vi) Capitals are needed for the names of religions, religious denominations or their adherents, and adjectives derived from them; but use a small *c* for *christian name.*

(vii) Names of political parties and their adherents have capitals.

(viii) Words like *channel, straits,* which are normally common nouns, are written with a capital when they mean a particular one and stand as a substitute for the full name: *the Channel* (the English Channel), *the Straits* (of Dover, Gibraltar, etc.), *the Peninsula* (Spain and Portugal).

(ix) Words like *bishop, archbishop, master*, when used alone, usually take a small letter, but they must have a capital when they are part of a recognised title or description : *the Archbishop of Canterbury, the Bishop of London, the Master of Balliol.* A capital is also used when the word stands alone as a substitute for the full title : *The Archbishop said* . . . (e.g. of Canterbury or York). The same applies to *doctor* and *professor.*

(x) Words like *headmaster, vicar, minister, chairman, secretary*, denoting an office or position, normally have small letters, but within the group where the holder of the office has a special status, so that the words are felt to have a more personal signification, a capital may be used. Thus in an advertisement or a public announcement, *the headmaster, the secretary*, but within a school or amongst a board of directors, *the Headmaster, the Secretary, the Chairman.* Similarly names denoting institutions, like *school, college, university, club, association*, may have a capital when they mean 'our' particular institution.

(xi) The names of academic subjects other than languages (which must, of course, have capitals), are normally written with a small letter, but a capital may be used when the word is thought of as the name of a course in a curriculum or a subject in an examination : *A good knowledge of mathematics is essential to an engineer. She is very interested in history.* But *She passed in History but failed in Mathematics.*

(xii) In the names of roads the word *road* should be spelt with a capital if it is part of the actual name, but not otherwise : *(the) Richmond Road, Queen's Road, Harrow Road*, but *the Richmond road, the Harrow road* (the roads that lead to Richmond and Harrow respectively). The use of a hyphen followed by a small letter (*Ebury-street, Brompton-road*) cannot be justified, though it is found in some newspapers.

(xiii) The use of capitals for pronouns referring to God or Christ is best confined to theological contexts ; elsewhere use small letters. Even in theological works, of course, Unitarians and others who do not accept the belief in the deity of Jesus will not use capitals for pronouns referring to him.

(xiv) Use capitals for registered trade-names of commercial products, materials, vehicles, etc. (*Anadin tablets, Biro pen, Zephyr, Wyvern*) but small letters for general or non-trade names : *aspirin tablets, nylon, estate car.*

(xv) When a prefix is hyphenated to a proper noun or adjective the noun or adjective retains its capital letter, but the prefix is not given a capital : *un-English, non-Catholics, non-Christian religions, anti-British feeling, pro-Russian elements. Noncon-formist,* however (in its religious sense) is written as one word and has a capital.

In the titles of literary works, names of organisations, etc., both the prefix and the word to which it is attached must have a capital: *the Anti-Slavery League, The Anti-Jacobin.*

(On the use of capitals generally in titles of literary works, essays, chapter headings, etc., see under TITLES.)

(xvi) In verse the traditional method is to begin each line with a capital letter. Some modern poets, however, use capitals only if the punctuation requires it, as they would do in prose. In quoting such verse the practice of the author must be respected.

CAPITALIST. The stress is on the first syllable. The word should be spelt with a small letter, whether used as a noun, or attributively as an adjective (*capitalists, capitalist countries*). The contrasting term *Communist* is spelt with a capital, since there is a Communist party; but there is no capitalist party.

CARCASS : CARCASE. The former spelling is to be preferred.

CASE. (i) Quiller-Couch's sweeping condemnation of the ex-pression (*in*) *the case of* (see his essay on 'Jargon' in *The Art of Writing*) has had the unfortunate effect of creating a prejudice against its use in any context. There are many legitimate uses of it, apart from law cases, hospital cases, and cases of diphtheria or scarlet fever. Nevertheless it is often an awkward and pointless substitute for a simpler form of expression. The following are a few examples. The suggested corrections are given in parentheses.

In many cases candidates misunderstood the question. (Many candidates misunderstood the question.)

The standard of living of the working class is higher than was the case thirty years ago. (. . . than it was thirty years ago.)

If that is the case (If so).

In that case (If that is so).

(ii) 'We are now able to obtain much better prices than have been the case during the last eighteen months' (from a company report). Incorrect. Amend to 'than *has* been the case'. The subject of the verb is not *prices*, but *the case*, as it also is when the clause is introduced by *as*. The writer might have saved himself from a grammatical blunder if he had simply written 'than at any time during the last eighteen months'.

(iii) The elliptical *in case* or *just in case* (I'll take my umbrella, just in case') is allowable colloquially, but in written English the clause should be completed (*in case it rains*).

CAUSE. 'We shall do our best to find out the cause for the delay'. Incorrect. For *for* substitute *of*. *Cause* is followed by *for*, only when it means *ground* or *justification*: e.g. 'There is no cause for alarm', 'You have no cause for complaint'.

CENTRE (Verb). *Centred on* or *upon*, not *around*.

CENTRE : MIDDLE. In everyday English we need not restrict *centre* to its strict mathematical use. A vase of flowers may be placed in the centre of a table, or a table in the centre of a stage (i.e. roughly equidistant from the four corners), while there are certain traditional combinations where *centre* must be recognised, e.g. *centre-forward* (at football), *centre court* (at tennis), *centre aisle*, *centrepiece*, *the centre of the town*, *the city centre*, but generally the idea of 'mid-way between two other things, groups or extremities' should be expressed by *middle* : the middle of the road, to part one's hair in the middle, the middle shelf, the middle class, etc.

CHAIRMAN. Used for both sexes. *Chairwoman* is not recognised as correct English. A lady chairman may be addressed as 'Madam Chairman'.

CHAR : CHARLADY. *My char* (for *my charwoman*) is a colloquialism, *charlady* a vulgarism.

CHARGE. 'The baby was left in charge of a neighbour.' Incorrect. It was the neighbour who was in charge of the baby; the baby was left in *the* charge of the neighbour. *In charge of* means 'having care of, or authority over' (e.g. 'Drunk while in charge of a car', 'Superintendent Collins is in charge of the investigations'). The idea of 'subject to the care, control or authority of' is expressed by 'in *the* charge of'.

CHECK. (i) *Check up on*. Usually no more than a circumlocution for *check* : e.g. 'Check up on this information, check up on his story'. Use the simple verb whenever possible.
   (ii) *Check one's luggage*. An Americanism, meaning to deposit one's luggage at a left-luggage office and receive a ticket, or check, in return. In British English the only meaning is to go through one's luggage to make sure nothing is missing.

CHEQUE. (i) In British English the word denoting a draft on a bank is always spelt *cheque*. Americans often spell it *check*.
   (ii) In restaurants in some parts of the country a waitress

CURRENT ENGLISH USAGE 45

gives her customers a *check* for their meal. The correct English term is *bill*, though the Americans generally use *check*.

CHERUB. The plural is *cherubim* when used in the strictly Hebraic or religious sense, otherwise *cherubs*. *Cherubims*, a combination of the two, is a solecism.

CHILDISH WORDS. Words like *mum, dad, auntie, dolly* (for *doll*), *granny, grand-dad, pussy,* have their place in childish speech, but should not appear in written English, except, of course, in dialogue when the speech of children, or of adults speaking to children in childish idiom, is being reproduced.

The same applies to what we may call 'dainty words' like *tummy, hanky, pinny* (pinafore), *comfy*.

CHOICE. Purists condemn the construction in which the word *choice* is followed by *of A or B*, insisting that it must be (i) a choice *of* one thing out of several, (ii) a choice *between* one thing *and* another, (iii) a choice *among* three things or more. This may be accepted when *choice* is preceded by the indefinite article, but *of . . . or* would seem justified when the definite article is used: e.g. 'You have the choice of (= you may choose) A or B'.

Between A or B is always incorrect. (See BETWEEN.)

CHRISTIAN NAME. When writing the combination *christian name* use a small letter for *christian*, since most people are no longer conscious of its having any connexion with the Christian Church or the Christian religion. It has come to mean little more than *forename*, as contrasted with *surname*.

CHRONIC. 'My rheumatism is chronic today.' 'I've a chronic headache.' Incorrect. *Chronic* does not mean 'very bad' or 'very painful', but 'of long duration'.

CIRCUMSTANCES. *Under the circumstances* is permissible. *A Deskbook of Correct English*, by Michael West and P. F. Kimber, states that *under* is used when the circumstances affect the speaker, *in* when they do not; but it is doubtful whether so definite a distinction can be made.

CITY. (i) There is a very widely held, but erroneous, belief that in Britain a city must have a cathedral, and that any place with a cathedral is *ipso facto* a city. This is not so. There are cities without cathedrals, and cathedral towns that are not cities. The right of a town to call itself a city is granted by the sovereign; a church is elevated to the status of a cathedral by the Archbishop of Canterbury. Quite frequently, when a town becomes a city, the Archbishop follows the sovereign's lead and raises the oldest, or the principal, parish church to the status of a cathedral; but not always. Cambridge was created a city by King George VI in 1951, but it has no cathedral. Southwell and Guildford both have a cathedral, but neither is a city.

(ii) *A cathedral city (town)*: not merely a city or town which has a cathedral, but one which has grown up around the cathedral, or which owes to its cathedral as its principal public building, e.g. Canterbury, York, Lincoln, Ripon. Birmingham, Manchester, Liverpool and Sheffield all have cathedrals, but we should not call them cathedral cities.

(iii) *The City* (the banking and financial quarter of London) should be spelt with a capital *C. The City Editor* (of a newspaper): the person in charge of that part of the newspaper which deals with banking, the Stock Exchange, and financial matters generally.

CLAD : CLOTHED. Outside poetry, where it survives as an archaism, *clad* is obsolete as a participle, though it is found in certain traditional compounds like *ill-clad*, *well-clad*, *iron-clad*, and expressions like *clad in mail*, where the dress is scarcely thought of as clothing in the ordinary sense. In all other senses *clothed* is the normal word today.

CLAIM (Verb). *M.E.U.* condemns the use of *claim* in the sense of *assert* or *maintain* (e.g. 'He claims that he has broken the record for long-distance flying'), but by now it can probably be regarded as established. Notice, however, that apart from *It is claimed* followed by a noun clause in apposition to *it* ('It is claimed that this discovery will revolutionise surgery'), it can be used only in the active voice. 'This drug is claimed to be a quick cure for colds and influenza' is incorrect. So are sentences containing *it is/was claimed* if the word *it* is not the anticipatory pronoun with a noun clause in apposition, but a pronoun referring to some particular thing or fact that has been mentioned previously: e.g. 'A new kind of synthetic rubber has just come upon the market. It is claimed to be more durable than natural rubber for most purposes.'

Even in the active voice *claim* can be followed by an infinitive construction only when its subject is also the 'subject' of the infinitive, as in 'He claims to have done it', 'She claimed to be the daughter of a well-known business man'. The following sentences, in which the infinitive has its own subject, are all unidiomatic. 'He claimed it to be entirely his own work', 'She claimed the invention to have been made by her late husband', 'He claimed the voting to have been in his favour'.

CLERGYMAN: MINISTER. In America *clergyman* is used of any minister of religion, no matter to what Church or denomination he belongs. In Britain it is usually reserved for ordained ministers of the Church of England. Nonconformist bodies speak of their *ministers*.

Use a small letter for *minister* when it merely denotes the office or vocation, a capital when it is a substitute for the name of a particular person. 'He gave up the profession of surgeon to become a minister', 'The Reverend J. S. Thompson, a retired Methodist minister', but 'Both services next Sunday will be conducted by the Minister'.

CLICHÉS. In French and English the word *cliché* means a metal plate made from movable types, to be used when some set of words has to be printed over and over again, or a similar plate bearing an illustration. In both languages it is also used to denote a hackneyed phrase or expression which a writer keeps ready set up in his mind and puts down automatically without troubling to find an original phrase of his own. Such phrases should, as far as possible, be avoided. At one time they may have been forceful; now they are stale and ineffective.

There are so many clichés that it would be impossible to list them all, but the following are a few examples.

(i) *Conventional Phrases or Expressions*. Hit the headlines; conspicuous by its absence; galvanised into action; food for thought; the arm of the law; the military machine; a raging inferno; last but not least; fast and furious; well and truly; slowly but surely; the happy pair; danger (murder, famine, etc.) reared its ugly head; terror struck again; the young idea.

(ii) *The Conventional Adjective*. A sickening thud; divine discontent; starry-eyed idealists; a hard-headed business man; a bloated capitalist; cut-throat competition; a rasping voice; the bitter end; a piercing scream; a crying shame; the tender mercies of; a crisp five-pound note.

(iii) *The Conventional Verb*. This occurs mainly in magazine stories and third-rate fiction. A detective or a 'hard-headed' business man never merely speaks; he *barks*, or *barks out* whatever he has to say. An attractive young lady, on the other hand, *coos* or *purrs*, while the unpleasant, 'tough' kind of character usually *snarls*. A startling announcement *electrifies* an audience, while emotion *tugs at the heart*. In another kind of writing people never simply *have* a meal; they *partake of* one.

(iv) *The Conventional Adverb*. Bitterly disappointed; passionately fond of; screamingly funny; sadly lacking; fondly imagine; immaculately dressed.

(v) *Circumlocutions*. The succulent bivalve (an oyster); the cup that cheers but not inebriates (tea); [1] devotees of my Lady Nicotine (smokers); disciples of Izaak Walton (anglers).

(vi) *Vogue Words*. Most of these, by their nature, have a short life, so that any list will probably be out of date soon after it is compiled. The following are a few examples of vogue words at the present time: *summit talks/conference meetings, high-ranking officers, fellow-traveller* (in its political sense), *a top-level decision, at the highest level, by and large, rat race*.

(vii) *Hackneyed and Pointless Similes*. To go on for ever, like Tennyson's brook; to ask for more, like Oliver Twist; to grow, like Topsy; to be up early, like the proverbial lark; to sob like a child; to start like a guilty thing.

CLUE. 'I haven't a clue' is a piece of Service slang from the second World War. If it really means what it says, of course, it is good English; it is not if it merely means 'I don't know' or 'I've no idea'.

COCKNEY. Do not use *Cockney* as a synonym for 'Londoner'. Not all Londoners are Cockneys. It is often said that a Cockney is 'one born within the sound of Bow bells', but today the word also connotes certain characteristics of speech, manner and social background.

COHERENCE: COHESION. *Coherence* = the 'hanging together' (literally 'sticking together') of verbal utterance, whether in speech or writing. *Cohesion* = the literal sticking together of two objects or substances, or the metaphorical sticking-together of friends, social groups, nations, etc.

COLLEAGUE. Should be used only of professional people and office workers, not of manual workers, shop assistants, drivers and conductors of public service vehicles, etc.

COLLECT. Often (and wrongly) used nowadays for *fetch*, e.g. 'I called at his office to collect a parcel', 'I will call and collect it on my way home'. Literally the word means 'bring together'. Its legitimate uses, therefore, are: (i) with a plural or a 'class'

[1] Also a misquotation, since Cowper actually wrote 'cups that cheer'.

noun as its object, e.g. *collect stamps, collect the remnants, collect money, collect china, furniture,* etc.; (ii) with singular nouns of substance or material as its object, in the sense of 'cause to accumulate', e.g. 'Curtains and similar hangings easily collect dust'; (iii) with a singular noun as its object, denoting something that is to be put with others of the kind, e.g. to collect the rent, to collect the laundry. With nouns denoting countables *collect* can take a singular object, only when this idea of bringing together with others is present. A tradesman's van may call at our house to collect a television set for repair, but when the repairs are done we do not collect it from his premises, nor does a motorist call at a friend's house to collect his wife, who has been visiting there.

COLLECTIVE NOUNS (Singular or plural?). Four types may be distinguished: (i) What we may call 'class' collectives, like *clothing, furniture, luggage, crockery,* which denote a number of different things that fall into the same general class (*crockery,* for instance, means cups, saucers, plates, dishes, etc. taken collectively). These always take a singular verb and are referred to by a singular pronoun. There is no plural form of the noun, nor can it be preceded by the singular indefinite article: we cannot speak of *luggages* or of *a luggage.*

(ii) Distributive collectives, exemplified in *people, folk, kindred.* These always take a plural verb.

(iii) Generalising collectives (usually referring to professions or occupations), as *the clergy, the police.* These usually take a plural verb and are referred to by a plural pronoun.

(iv) Group collectives, like *committee, congregation, audience, the public.* Many of these have plural forms (*committees, audiences, congregations*), which of course take plural verbs and pronouns; but with most the singular form, for syntactical purposes, can be treated as singular or plural according to circumstances. Generally the singular is to be preferred, but it is not always possible. While we can say 'The audience has already expressed its approval', we cannot say 'The audience is requested to be in its seat by 7.25'; we must use *are requested* and *their seats.* On the other hand, we should probably say 'The committee is (not are) divided on the question', since one thing is divided into two or more parts. But whether we choose to use a singular or a plural, the important thing is that *we must be consistent,* at least throughout the same sentence.

COLON. The chief uses are as follows: (i) To introduce a detailed elaboration of a general term that has preceded the colon. 'The box contained a collection of miscellaneous articles: a few books, some papers of various kinds, odds and ends of photographic apparatus, and an assortment of foreign coins.'

(ii) To introduce a fairly long passage of direct speech, as a comma would introduce a shorter passage.

Introducing the speaker, the Chairman said: (Here follows a verbatim report of his speech, or the relevant parts of it, in inverted commas.)

(iii) Sometimes to divide two antithetical parts of a sentence, balanced one against the other. E.g. 'Speech is silvern: silence is golden'.

(iv) To introduce a rather lengthy quotation from literary or documentary sources. The following are taken from *Georgian Chronicle*, by Betsy Rodgers (Methuen, 1959).

'This note was found among Josiah Wedgwood's papers: "Mrs Barbauld's compliments to Mr Wedgwood . . ."' (and so the quotation continues).

'It was her brother who wrote the couplet she might have written, and for which I ask no apology for repeating as a pious wish:

From the banquet of life rise a satisfied guest, Thank the Lord of the Feast, and in hope go to rest.'

'Lucy wrote an account of their peaceful and contented life to Mr Holland, the Knutsford surgeon: "Our little home is now in all its glory; the garden is as full of flowers and fruit as it can hold . . ."' (So the letter continues.)

(v) A colon followed by a dash is used when the list that it introduces starts on the next line. The dash acts as a kind of 'carry-over'.

The following candidates passed with distinction in one or more subjects :—

J. C. Andrews, W. A. Barsley, J. Charlesworth, P. G. Dutton.

COME. Sometimes misused for *become*, as in the sentence (from a documentary source) 'The matter will be further reviewed when the position comes vacant'.

Come, when followed by an adjective as a complement, expresses the idea of progression from one state to another (usually to one that is desired; *go* is generally used for one that is not desired, e.g. *come clean, come right, come true*, but *go wrong, go bad, go rusty*).

When there is no sense of progression, but merely a statement of the final state or situation that arises, *become* should be used: *become angry, become senile, become anxious*.

COMIC(AL). *Comic* describes the intention, *comical* the effect: *a comic story, paper, costume,* etc., but *a comical appearance, a comical situation.*

COMMA. Of all the punctuation marks, the comma allows more latitude than any other for the personal taste or preference of the writer. There are some circumstances in which it *must* be used, some in which it *may* be used, and others in which it is impermissible to use it. The general tendency is to err on the side of excess. No absolute rule can be laid down, but on the whole it seems a sound principle to omit the comma if it can be omitted.

Bearing in mind that the purpose of all punctuation is two-fold, viz. (a) to make clear the meaning of what is written, and (b) to serve as an aid in reading, by indicating natural pauses, inflexions of the voice, etc., we may distinguish the following uses of the comma.

(1) As a substitute for *and* in the enumeration of a series.

Oats, corn, maize and barley.

He was tall, fair, and rather stout.

He entered the room, locked the door, and seated himself at the desk.

But it does not necessarily follow that because two adjectives stand in series before a noun they should be separated by a comma. Thus though we should write *a black, shaggy-haired dog, a tall, slim girl* (with commas), no commas are needed in *a great big dog, a pretty little girl, a poor old man.* Commas should be used only when the adjectives are co-ordinate, i.e. when they have equal weight and each in its turn qualifies the same noun: in other words, when the conjunction *and* could be inserted between them, as in the first set of examples. In the second set *great big* has the force of a compound adjective, and *little girl* and *old man* that of a compound noun.

Used thus, a comma may separate single words, phrases or clauses, but it cannot be used to separate two grammatically independent statements each of which could, from a syntactic point of view, be a separate sentence. For this purpose nothing less than a semicolon will do, and frequently a full stop is necessary. (See under SEMICOLON.) Nothing so betrays the slipshod or careless writer as sentences like the following:

The British are not a nation of theologians, they are too practical for that.—From a denominational weekly.

Don't jump to conclusions, you may be wrong.—*Ibid.*

If teachers of languages are not prepared to take new information into account in their teaching and their methods,

they are being more than sloppy, they are being dishonest.—
From an educational journal.

Mr . . . is an old college friend of the minister's, he has
preached several times previously in this chapel—From a
chapel calendar.

On the use of a comma before *and*, see under AND.

(2) Between words which are repeated for the sake of
emphasis :

It is a far, far better thing . . .

Hark, hark, the lark at heaven's gate sings.

With exclamations, the exclamation mark takes the place of the
comma. It is incorrect to use both.

(3) To indicate a parenthesis or an interpolation and to
disjoin it from the rest of the sentence. The parenthesis may
consist of a single word or a group of words.

This, however, is certain.

And then, too, there is a further reason.

The story, such as it is, may be summarised as follows.

His conduct, if examined impartially, is inexcusable.

Note that when used for this purpose *two commas are necessary*,
one at each end of the parenthesis ; and care must be taken that
they are correctly placed. It is the very nature of a parenthesis
that it is an insertion ; hence, if it is removed, the remainder of
the sentence should form a natural and coherent syntactic unit.
(See the examples given above.) Faulty placing is most frequent
when the parenthetic words are co-ordinated with a preceding
word-group and both are completed by a word or phrase that
follows the second of them. The following example is quoted
from a weekly magazine :

The immediate cause of, though not the reason, for the
strike . . .

Omit the words between the commas, and we have left *The
immediate cause of for the strike* — obviously not a sentence.
The second comma should have been after *for*.

It must be realised that the introductory and enclitic sentence
adverbs *still, then, now*, etc., stand apart from the main sentence
just as a parenthesis is an insertion in it, and require a comma.
Its omission may lead to confusion with the same words used
as adverbs of time. Note the difference of meaning between
the sentences in the following pairs.

Still, the price is quite reasonable.
Still the price is quite reasonable.

Come, now. Don't waste time.
Come now. Don't waste time.

Did he do it, then?

Did he d_o it then?

There are, too, many people who give only part-time service.

There are too many people who give only part-time service.

N.B.—On the choice between commas, brackets and dashes to mark a parenthesis, see PARENTHESIS.

(4) To mark off a noun or pronoun in the vocative case from the rest of the sentence in which it occurs. (Note that *sir* and *madam*, used to address a person, are vocatives, and therefore need the comma.)

Gentlemen, the time has come when . . .

Is that you, Mary?

Will you come this way, sir?

If the vocative is immediately followed by words that qualify it or form a close group with it, the entire combination is, of course, to be regarded as a vocative group and punctuated accordingly.

Fellow citizens of this great city, I stand before you today . . .

When the vocative occurs internally instead of at the beginning or the end of a sentence it has the force of a parenthesis and therefore needs two commas:

And now, ladies and gentlemen, we come to the most interesting exhibit of all.

(5) To distinguish a non-defining expression from one that defines. This is a very important use, which must be mastered and scrupulously observed.

By a defining expression we mean one that is used to distinguish a particular one (or ones) from others of the same class, or to indicate a particular aspect from which we are to consider the thing or the person mentioned. Thus the sentence 'My brother who is an engineer has gone to Australia' implies that I have several brothers, and the clause *who is an engineer* distinguishes a particular one of them. When we speak of 'the air that we breathe' and 'the sun that ripens the crops', it is true we do not imply that there are several different kinds of air or more than one sun, but the adjective clauses define their antecedents in that they name a particular aspect of them that is relevant to our purpose. A defining expression is *not* preceded by a comma.

Now suppose we write 'My brother, who is an engineer, has gone to Australia'. The adjective clause no longer defines. The implication is that I have only one brother, or that the person to whom the remark is addressed knows of only one, so that there is no need to distinguish him from others. The clause *who is an engineer* supplies an additional piece of information about the brother, but it has not the specifying or selective function that it had in the previous examples. It is therefore non-defining. A non-defining expression must be preceded by a comma, and, if it is interposed within a sentence, so that it has the force of a parenthesis, it must be followed by another.

The types of expressions that may be either defining or non-defining, and which therefore require special care in the use of the comma, are as follows.

(i) A Clause:

The two passengers who were seriously injured were taken to hospital. (Defining)

The two passengers, who were seriously injured, were taken to hospital. (Non-Defining)

In the country where I lived as a boy the people worked long hours. (Defining)

In the country, where I lived as a boy, the people worked long hours. (Non-Defining)

In the afternoons when the heat of the sun made it impossible to work they would retire indoors. (Defining)

In the afternoons, when the heat of the sun made it impossible to work, they would retire indoors. (Non-Defining)

N.B.—(a) The relative pronouns *who* (*whom*, *whose*) and *which* may be either defining or non-defining, but relative *that* can be used only for defining clauses, never for non-defining. Normally, therefore, it cannot be preceded by a comma, unless it introduces one of a series of co-ordinated clauses, where the comma takes the place of *and*: e.g. 'laws that cannot be enforced, that everyone dislikes, and that therefore are completely ineffective'. A variant of this is to be found in the following sentence from an article by the present writer on 'Some Aspects of Conditional Clauses in English', which appeared in the Swedish philological journal *Moderna Språk* (1960): 'There is no point in repeating the obvious things, that have been said again and again, and that can be found in any grammar book'. Most people would probably admit that this reads as perfectly idiomatic English, yet they might find some difficulty in explaining the comma before *that*. Does it mean that, contrary to the rule given above, we have *that* introducing a non-defining clause? At first it might appear so, but second thoughts will show that the clause is a defining one, with *things* (not *obvious things*) as its antecedent. The justification for the comma is that the relative clause is the second of a series of adjectival expressions qualifying the same noun, the first of them being the simple adjective *obvious*. Or to put it another way, *obvious things* is thought of as being equivalent to *things that are obvious*.

Other examples : 'a dastardly crime, that shocked the world'; 'reprehensible conduct, that no-one can excuse'; 'an absurd story, that no intelligent person would believe'.

(b) In a sentence such as the following a comma will be found before a defining clause : 'This is the person, if I am not mistaken, whom we met last Saturday'. This, however, is no violation of the rule laid down above, since the comma belongs to the parenthesis, and is complementary to the one after *person*.

(ii) An appositional expression.

I mean Mr Smith the grocer, not Mr Smith the baker. (Defining)

General Wolfe, the hero of Quebec, was born at Westerham, in Kent. (Non-Defining)

Disraeli the founder of the Conservative Party and Disraeli the novelist were the same person. (Defining)

Disraeli, the founder of the Conservative party, was born in 1804. (Non-Defining)

(iii) An adjective phrase.

The Rev. J. C. White, of Buxton. (Non-Defining)

Mr James Shore, of Tapton Hall. (Non-Defining)

Blight of the *Bounty*, Robert of Gloucester, William of Orange. (Defining)

(iv) Participial or Gerundial Constructions.

Some workmen demolishing an old house came upon a hoard of coins. (Defining)

The policeman, seeing the motorist in difficulties, went to his assistance. (Non-Defining)

The non-defining participial construction often precedes the noun or pronoun that it qualifies, but it must still be separated from it by a comma.

Seeing the motorist in difficulties, the policeman went to his assistance.

(6) Between a continuative clause and the clause that precedes it. A continuative clause is really a non-defining clause used in a special way ; it continues the narrative or description by giving us the next fact. It has the form of a subordinate clause, but notionally it is co-ordinate with the preceding one, the introductory word carrying the sense of a co-ordinating conjunction followed by a pronoun or an adverb.

She gave the letter to the commissionaire, who took it to the manager. (who = and he)

Go to the corner of the street, where you will find a taxi waiting. (where = and there)

(7) Between two words or expressions correlated by *or*, when they represent, not two different things, but alternative names for the same thing.

Constantinople, or Istanbul, was the former capital of Turkey.

Nitre, or saltpetre, is dug from the earth.

But 'I should like to live in Devon or Cornwall', 'Did you say he came from Kent or Sussex?', since here the alternatives are two different places.

(8) To mark off an absolute construction from the rest of the sentence.

Between you and me, I think he knows very little about it.

He leads a very active life, considering his age.

(9) Before a conjunction or conjunctive adverb if it is desired to give weight or emphasis to the statement that follows.

He has a good income, yet he is always in debt.

It is well enough in theory, but it does not work.

(10) To divide quoted (or 'direct') speech from added or interpolated formulae such as *he said, they replied*, etc.

'And now,' he said, 'we come to the greatest treasure of all.'

Note : (a) That the comma adheres to the group of words that precedes it; hence it stands inside the inverted commas if the word-group to which it belongs stands inside, and outside if the word-group stands outside. (For illustration, see the sentence given above.)

(b) That any stop, other than the question or exclamation mark, which would normally be placed at the end of the word-group in inverted commas, is removed to a position immediately after the interpolated words *he said*, etc., and its place in the passage of direct speech is taken by the comma. But the question mark and the exclamation mark, for obvious reasons, retain their original position, and supersede the comma. A comma must *not* be used as well as the question or exclamation mark.

(11) To avoid leading the reader along a false scent. The following, from a schoolboy's essay on Shakespeare's *King Henry IV, Part I*, provides an example.

While Falstaff hides the Prince pacifies the officers who have come to search the inn.

The most natural way to read this is to take *hides* as a transitive verb, with *the Prince* as its object — until we get to the verb *pacifies*; then we realise we have followed a wrong scent. We might have been spared this annoyance if the writer had placed a comma after *hides*. (See also AND (iv).)

(12) As a convenience to the reader, to mark places where he may legitimately pause. This is especially useful when the passage is to be read aloud, but it may also serve a purpose where there is no thought of oral reading. Normally, for instance, a subject should not be separated from its verb by an intervening comma, but if the subject is a long, diffuse or intricate one it is legitimate to insert a comma at the end of it, before we write the verb; it provides a mental pause, and has the effect of gathering up and consolidating the subject. There are cases, too, where a pause or the absence of a pause in speech will determine the meaning conveyed by the sentence. Commas will do much the same in writing. Take the following two sentences:

Would you like John or Henry to go with you?

Would you like John, or Henry, to go with you?

The second sentence asks the person addressed which of the two he would prefer should accompany him, taking it for granted that he wishes someone to do so. The first sentence asks a different question — whether he would like one of them (whichever finds it the more convenient) to accompany him, with the implication 'or would you prefer to go unaccompanied?' The former of the two meanings could, of course, also be expressed by placing Henry's name at the end ('Would you like John to go with you, or Henry?'), but still the comma is needed. Or again:

We did not come early because we thought it would be inconvenient to you.

We did not come early, because we thought it would be inconvenient to you.

The first suggests (or at least might suggest) that the speakers *have* come early, but that their reason for doing so was not that they thought it would be inconvenient to their host. The second implies that they have *not* come early, and then proceeds to give the reason why they have not. A nice point, perhaps, but an important one.

Commas Misused. We append here a few examples of the misuse of the comma, or of neglect to use it where it is required. All come from printed sources, though the journal concerned should not necessarily be held responsible, since all the sentences quoted are from signed articles or letters.

(i) For the expression of the heart's secret the axiomatic or polemical is secondary or futile. Given that the secret is expressible, when the heart's feeling surges or rises from its pent-up places; it calls for that which, as Milton taught, is 'simple, sensuous and passionate'.—A theological journal.

It is not very easy to see what the second sentence was intended to mean. As it stands it means nothing, and it is quite indefensible grammatically. The semicolon certainly should not have been used. Either the comma should stand as it is at present, after *expressible*, and there should be no stop at all after *places*, or the comma which at present follows *expressible* should be removed from that position to take the place of the semicolon, or (a third possibility) a comma should be substituted for the full stop after *futile*, the second sentence made to begin at *when*, and the semicolon removed after *expressible*. It depends on the meaning the author intended to convey.

(ii) Finally — it may not be too much to say — that out of prayer is born conscience, and out of conscience the good life. Or, as the Hindu might put it; out of meditation Selfhood is born and out of Selfhood, union with the Supreme.—*Ibid.*
To treat the words between the dashes as a parenthesis is to make nonsense of the rest of the sentence. They are not a parenthesis at all; they are the main clause. *Finally* should have been followed by a comma, and no stop at all should have been used after *say*. In the second sentence the opposite kind of mistake has been made. The words 'as the Hindu might put it' are parenthetic, though the writer does not seem to have realised it; consequently the comma which precedes them should be balanced by a complementary comma at the other end. The semicolon does violence to both syntax and sense. The comma after *Selfhood*, too, is misplaced; it should have been inserted between *born* and *and*.

(iii) A North Staffordshire man, he had, when young, greatly appreciated the university extension courses, which he attended in the Potteries.—*A daily newspaper.*
The clause 'which he attended in the Potteries' is clearly a defining clause, but it has been punctuated as though it were non-defining. No comma should have been used.

(iv) Professor Cole cannot know what is happening today in industry otherwise he would have realized that it is the unions who are keeping the question of joint consultation alive, and, as a matter of fact, the T.U.C. has had to press continually through the National Joint Advisory Council for a resuscitation of the production committees which had fallen into disuse after the war.—*An educational journal.*
A discreet use of commas might have done much to simplify (and clarify) this long, unwieldy sentence. A comma is desirable after *industry*, though it is not obligatory; those after *and* and *matter of fact* are not really needed, but some kind of stop is necessary before *and*. A comma might serve, though a semi-

colon is to be preferred. The unstopped group 'the T.U.C. . . . National Joint Advisory Council' lays a false scent which could have been avoided by placing a comma after *continually* and another after *Council*. One suspects, too, that the final clause was intended to be non-defining, in which case it should have been preceded by a comma.

(v) The social scientist aims to test to what degree people segregate themselves and at a later stage, overcome their divisions, as they re-group themselves into new strata.—*Ibid.*
For the moment we may leave aside the unidiomatic *aims to test* (see under AIM). There should be no comma after *division*. There is really no need for one in the whole of the sentence, but if any phrase is to be treated as parenthetic it can only be *at a later stage. Overcome their divisions* is certainly not a parenthesis, and to print it as though it were makes nonsense of the sentence.

(vi) I should like to plead with some of those men who now feel ashamed to join the Colonial Service.—A daily newspaper. More false scent, though this time the blame is to be laid upon the compositor, not the writer of the letter (the Bishop of Gambia), who wrote a few days later protesting (quite rightly) that 'the omission of a comma makes me seem to suggest that men might feel ashamed of joining the Colonial Service'. The comma should, of course, have appeared after *ashamed*. The men with whom the Bishop wished to plead were not those who were ashamed to join the Colonial Service, but those who were ashamed of the state of affairs in West Africa.

(vii) For all this wealth of literary output, Mr Belloc deserves the thanks that are due to a man who has faithfully practised a great craft for more than half a century.—A literary weekly.
Not very complimentary to Mr Belloc, for with the sentence punctuated as it is we can only read the phrase from *for* down to *output* in a depreciatory sense (*for all*=in spite of). The comma should have been omitted.

Excessive Use of Commas. At the beginning of this article a warning was given against the excessive use of commas, which produces a 'chopped-up' impression. The following examples are taken from H. W. and F. G. Fowler's *The King's English.* They speak for themselves.

Jeannie, too, is, just occasionally, like a good girl out of a book by a sentimental lady novelist.—*The Times.*

Thus, their work, however imperfect and faulty, judged by modern lights, it may have been, brought them face to face with . . . —T. H. Huxley.

Shakespeare, it is true, had, as I have said, as respects England, the privilege which only first-comers enjoy.—J. R. Lowell.
A sound rule is to see that one uses sufficient commas, but
no more than are necessary to render the meaning perfectly
clear and to make for easy reading. An excessive use of them
may defeat both ends.

COMMANDO. Strictly, a small body of soldiers operating inde-
pendently, but since the war of 1939–45 also used of a single
member of such a body. This latter use is now recognised. Cf.
a Wren, a Waaf, where a similar development has taken place.

COMMENCE. See BEGIN.

COMMERCIAL JARGON. There is no reason why a business
letter should not be written in normal English. The following
are some of the commoner pieces of commercial jargon to be
avoided : *Inst., ult., prox.* (name the month); *same* (it, them);
enclosed please find (I enclose); *your esteemed favour* (your letter,
order, enquiry); *your good selves* (and even worse, *your good-
selves*); *further to your letter, to our conversation* (use *with
reference to,* or re-word the sentence); *your communication to
hand* (we have received your letter); *I beg to inform you, I beg
to remain* (see under BEG).

COMMONSENSE. Does such a word exist ? It should always be
written as two separate words when used as a noun ('Use your
common sense'), and as a hyphenated compound rather than
as one word when used adjectivally (*common-sense precautions*).

COMPARATIVES. (i) The comparative degree is used when
two things are compared, the superlative for more than two.
It is incorrect to say 'Which is the better of the three methods ?'
Amend to 'Which of the three methods is the best ?' The superlative instead of the comparative, however, is allowable where
in actual fact only two things are concerned but where more than
two might have been. ('I shall go by the cheapest route').
'Which do you like best ?', for 'Which do you prefer ?' has
become a set phrase invariable in form, whether applied to two
or to more than two things. We should never say 'Which do you
like better ?' Similarly 'I like that one best', 'I will have the one
that costs least'. The combinations *like best* and *cost least* express
the general idea of preference and cheapness respectively, irrespective of number. The fact that in a particular case only two
things may be concerned is purely coincidental.

(ii) 'This box is three times heavier than the other.' Incorrect. Amend to *three times as heavy as*. Since the comparative indicates merely superiority, and is not in itself confined to any definite limit, there cannot be multiples of it. It can be modified only by adverbs of degree, like *much, little, rather, scarcely, barely, far*, or by a statement of a definite amount, as *five pounds heavier, fifty pence dearer*.

(iii) Adjectives like *unique, dead, blind, dumb*, which express an absolute idea of which there cannot be degrees, obviously cannot have a comparative. One thing cannot be more unique than another or one person more dead or more dumb than another. But words like *full, perfect*, etc., which express completeness may be used in the comparative to denote a nearer approach to the complete notion: e.g. 'A fuller account will appear next month'. 'We could not have had a more perfect day for the garden party.' Some words which normally belong to the first group fall into the second when they are used figuratively: 'Nothing is more dead than the centre of a large city on a Sunday morning.' (See also MORE.)

COMPARATIVELY. Should not be used in the sense of 'rather' or 'fairly'. *Comparatively easy* does not mean 'fairly easy', but 'easy in comparison with something else'.

COMPARE TO: COMPARE WITH. *Compare to* = state a resemblance between (*Shakespeare compared the world to a stage*); *compare with* = place side by side, noting the resemblances and the differences (usually with the stress on the differences): 'Compare this with that, and you will see which is the better'. 'Most working people are well off compared with what they were in the 1930's' (not *compared to*).

By comparison and *in comparison* are usually followed by *with*.

COMPLACENT: COMPLAISANT. *Complacent* = self-satisfied; *complaisant* = ready to oblige.

COMPOUND ADJECTIVES. While there is no objection to such compounds as *an out-of-the-way place, a give-and-take policy, a take-it-or-leave-it attitude, a couldn't-care-less philosophy*, others, like *an on-the-spot account*, sound very inelegant and awkward. No rule can be laid down. Perhaps the best advice is to avoid compounds of this kind wherever possible.

On the use of hyphens, see under HYPHEN.

COMPRISE. 'The delegation was comprised of the following persons.' Wrong. (*Is*/*was*/*will be*) *comprised of* is always incorrect. The alternatives are (i) was *composed* of the following persons, (ii) *comprised* the following persons.

CONFIDE. Confide *in* a person: confide information, documents, a secret, etc. *to* a person.

CONFRONTED. When *confronted* is used adjectivally, to denote the situation that one is in, it is followed by the preposition *with*: 'We are confronted with a difficult task' (cf. *covered with*, *surrounded with*). When it is a participle forming part of a passive voice *by* is used when the noun that follows denotes the person or the thing that actually confronts one ('As he entered the room he was confronted by a policeman/by a scene of disorder'), *with* when it represents the person or the thing that is placed or brought before one: 'He was confronted with a bill for over twenty pounds/with a demand for his resignation/with the person to whom he had paid the money'.

CONGRATULATE. Congratulate someone *on* something. (Not *for* or *at*, both frequently, though wrongly, used before a gerund.)

CONNECTION: CONNEXION. The latter spelling is the more correct etymologically, and is preferred by the Oxford Dictionary and by *R.C.R.* American usage favours *connection*.

CONNIVE. Followed by *at*, not *in*. (Connive at a subterfuge.)

CONSCRIPT (Verb). The insistence of *The Times* on *conscribe* is merely pedantic, though correct from an etymological point of view. *Conscript* (with stress on the second syllable) has long been admitted as a verb, and is now the accepted English word.

CONSEQUENT ON: SUBSEQUENT TO. Note the prepositions. *Subsequent to* merely means *after*; *consequent on* means 'following from, as a result or consequence'.

CONSIDER. 'I consider it a good thing' (not '*as* a good thing'). The infinitive *to be* is understood after *it*. Similarly 'You may consider the matter settled' (not '*as* settled'); but 'We will consider *Hamlet* as an example of a Shakespearian tragedy', 'The Board are considering a young man from London as a possible successor to Jones', since here *consider* has a different meaning (= think about, give one's mind to) and the phrase introduced by *as* signifies the capacity in which the play or the person is to be considered.

CONSIDERATION. Do not say that something is 'under active consideration'. The adjective *active* is pointless (though it seems to have become firmly established in officialese), and in any case it is better to write or say 'is being considered' than 'is under consideration'.

CONSIST OF: CONSIST IN. *Consist of* = 'be composed of, or made up of' ('The drink consists mainly of water, with a little flavouring added'). *Consist in* = 'have as an essential element' ('Courage consists in overcoming one's fears').

CONTACT (Verb). Sir Ernest Gowers (*Plain Words*) is willing to accept *contact* as a convenient verb to cover all methods of communication with a person, but it is difficult to see what merits it has for this purpose over *communicate with*, or *get in touch with*. Even if we accept it as a comprehensive term, there is no excuse for using it when only one means is concerned. A person who writes in a letter, 'As the situation has changed since we last discussed the matter, I thought I had better contact you at once' is going out of his way to use a piece of jargon when he could have said quite simply 'I thought I had better write to you at once'.

CONTEMPORARY. (i) Few words have been so much misused during the past two decades as *contemporary*. One example, from a theological journal, will suffice, though it could be matched with scores of others from magazines, the daily press and advertising: 'St. Paul, it is true, did not live in the contemporary world, but it is remarkable how applicable much of his teaching is to contemporary problems.' What world did St. Paul live in, then? He could live in no other than the contemporary world. Quite clearly, the author of the sentence means the modern, or the present-day, world, and modern, or present-day, problems. But *contemporary* does not mean this: it means 'Living, existing or occurring at the same time'. It is synonymous with *modern* or *present-day*, only if no other time or person is mentioned, when it means contemporary with ourselves (as 'contemporary designs in wall-papers' or 'an exhibition of contemporary paintings'), and even then it is often a mere vogue word substituted for something simpler. If it is used in conjunction with the name of a particular person or a particular period of time, it means contemporary with those.

Tennyson and Browning were contemporary poets, but they are not modern poets. 'Elizabethan plays presented in contemporary costume' means 'in Elizabethan [not in modern] costume', 'Matthew Arnold's reputation with contemporary critics' means 'with critics of his own day', not with those of the present time, and when 'the contemporary world' is mentioned in conjunction with the name of St. Paul, it means the world of St. Paul's day, not of ours.

(ii) One person is *contemporary with* another, or *the contemporary of* another. *Contemporaries of each other* is pleonastic: *contemporaries* alone is sufficient.

CONTEMPTIBLE : CONTEMPTUOUS. *Contemptible* means 'deserving of contempt', *contemptuous* 'showing, or expressive of, contempt'. In August 1914 the Kaiser was alleged to have spoken of 'Britain's contemptible little army'. His remark was a contemptuous one.

The correct preposition to follow *contemptuous* is *of*, not *about*: 'The Kaiser was contemptuous of Britain's army'.

CONTRIBUTE. Stress on the second syllable, not the first.

CONTROVERSY. The pronunciation with the stress on the second syllable, at one time considered a vulgarism, seems to be gaining ground, but Standard English recognises only *cóntroversy* (stress on the first syllable).

CORPORAL : CORPOREAL. *Corporal* = pertaining to the body (e.g. corporal punishment). *Corporeal* = bodily as opposed to spiritual : having bodily substance. ('A ghost has no corporeal existence.') The pronunciation rhymes with *memorial*.

CORRELATIVES. The name given to pairs of conjunctions or conjunctive expressions which always go together, like *either . . . or, neither . . . nor, both . . . and, not only . . . but also*. The points to notice are :

(i) Each initial correlative must have its correct complementary one. The following is a typical violation of this rule : 'An illiterate person is one who can neither read or write'. *Neither* must be followed by *nor*, not by *or*.

(ii) *Not either* is followed by *or*, not *nor*, since *not* applies to both correlatives : 'If it is not either useful or ornamental . . .' (not *nor ornamental*).

(iii) *Neither* is used for other purposes than that of correlation. The rule stated under (i) above applies only to the correlative use. A writer who blindly follows up *neither* by *nor* as a matter of course, under the impression that he is being correct, may

unwittingly commit the very mistake he is anxious to avoid.
Here is an example where this has occurred:

> He is neither hero nor saint. Neither is he sadist nor
> criminal.—*The Inquirer*.

The first sentence is correct, but in the second one *nor* should be
or. It is not correlated with *neither*, which is merely used to
link and contrast this statement with the preceding one. What
the writer, in effect, is saying is 'But he is not sadist or criminal,
either'. *But . . . not . . . either* becomes the introductory
neither. And besides, its position in the sentence precludes it
from correlating *sadist* with *criminal*. (See the point that follows.)

(iv) Care must be taken that the correlatives are correctly
placed. Mistakes very frequently arise here. The rule is that
all words that apply to both the correlated terms must precede
the first of the correlatives. The following violation of this
rule is quoted by Gowans Whyte (*An Anthology of Errors*):

> She had noticed nothing either to cause her the least doubt
> or the faintest anxiety.

The two terms correlated are *the least doubt* and *the faintest
anxiety*. The word-group *to cause her* applies to both, and
should therefore stand outside both, being placed before *either*
(*. . . to cause her either the least doubt or the faintest anxiety*).
Here are some further examples of wrong placing. The corrections are given in parentheses.

> You will either carry out my instructions or I will give the
> work to someone else. (Either you will carry out . . .)

> We have neither had a visit from him nor has he written
> to us. (We have not had . . .)

> He was not only insolent, but he also threatened us. (Not
> only was he insolent . . .)

> His speech neither brought credit to him nor prestige to
> his party. (Brought neither credit to him . . .)

CORROBORATE. See *Verify*.

COULD. (i) 'We climbed up an electricity pylon. It was a
foolish thing to do, for we could have been killed.'—From a
schoolboy's essay.
Substitute *might* for *could*. Possibility is expressed by *might*:
could denotes potentiality.

(ii) 'Could you lend me twenty pence?' Acceptable as a
more courteous way of making a request than *would you?* or
will you? Similarly, 'Could you close the window, please?'

COUNCIL: COUNSEL. *Council* = an assembly: also attributively, as 'a council house', 'a council estate', 'a council

school'. *Counsel* (verb) = advise: (noun) = advice: also one who gives advice (usually a barrister), as *counsel for the defence*, *take the opinion of counsel*. *Queen's Counsel* has the same form for the plural as for the singular (*several eminent Queen's Counsel*), but the abbreviated form is *Q.C.s*.

COVERED IN: COVERED WITH. Both prepositions are permissible, though *in* is used only when *covered* has the force of an adjective used predicatively, rather than a participle. ('His boots were covered in mud.') The strict participial use must be followed by *with*. ('The table was covered with a white cloth.' 'The fruit should be put into a pan and covered with water.')

When *covered* means 'hidden' or 'submerged', and the word following the preposition is thought of as the agent, then the correct preposition is *by*. ('The pathway was completely covered by the dense foliage.' 'The plates of the battery should be just covered by the electrolyte.') These are the passive forms corresponding to 'The dense foliage completely covered the pathway' and 'The electrolyte should just cover the plates of the battery'.

CREDIBLE: CREDITABLE: CREDULOUS. *Credible* = believable (*a credible story*), *creditable* = bringing credit or honour to one: deserving of credit (*a very creditable achievement*). *Credulous* = ready to believe anything (*a credulous person*).

CRESCENDO. 'The applause rose to a crescendo.' Incorrect. *Crescendo* is an Italian word meaning *growing*. As used in music it denotes a gradual increase in volume, not the point at which the greatest volume is reached. 'A crescendo of applause' is acceptable, but applause rises to a climax.

CUI BONO? (Latin). Not, as is sometimes supposed, 'What good is it?', but 'Whom will it benefit?' (literally, 'For a good to whom?'). Roman lawyers held that very often, if you could not find the person responsible for a crime, a fruitful line of inquiry might be to ask who was likely to have benefited from it.

CURB: KERB. *Curb* is always used as the verb, and also as the noun when it has to do with checking or restraining: e.g. place a curb on one's expenditure. The metaphor comes from the strap that passes under the jaw of a horse.

For the edge of the pavement or the raised edge round a hearth, British English usually uses the spelling *kerb*, though *curb* is not incorrect. It is, indeed, the older form, and is still used in America. Similarly *kerbstone* or *curbstone*.

D

DAINTY WORDS. See ABBREVIATIONS, VI (ii).

DARE. (i) When *dare* = 'challenge' it is followed by a personal
object and the infinitive with *to*: 'I dare you to do it'. The
past tense and the past participle are *dared*. Third person
sing., pres. tense: *he dares*.

(ii) When it means 'have the effrontery' it is also followed by
the infinitive with *to*, but has no personal object: 'He dares to
accuse me of dishonesty'. Pres. tense, third person sing.: *he
dares*. Past tense and past participle: *dared*.

(iii) When it means 'be bold enough' or 'have the courage'
it takes an infinitive without *to*. Third person sing., pres.
tense: *dare* ('He dare do all he says he will.' 'She dare not
say what she thinks.'). Past tense and past participle: *dared*,
though the past tense *durst* is sometimes used colloquially,
especially with *not*.

DARE SAY. Should be written as two words ('I dare say he
will come), though it is sometimes printed as one when the
stress is on *say*, 'He's a pleasant sort of fellow' — 'I daresay,
but I don't trust him'. Used only in the first person and the
present tense.

DASH. The dash is used:

(i) To separate a parenthesis from the main body of the
sentence (see under PARENTHESIS), or to attach an afterthought
to the end. For a parenthesis two dashes are needed, one at
each end. For an afterthought the dash is appropriate only
when what follows it is not a complete clause.

Of the young men called up for the forces each year, about
two thousand can scarcely write their name or read a simple
sentence of English — a sad commentary upon our educational
system.

(ii) To attach a final summing-up to a sentence. Here the
words that follow the dash may, and usually do, constitute a
complete clause, or even several clauses.

Friends, money, power, position — all these he had before
he reached middle age.

(iii) To denote an abrupt change of subject, or a sudden
bandonment of one construction and the substitution of another.

You take the pin in the fingers so, and — but perhaps this doesn't interest you? (A. A. Milne, *The Boy Comes Home*.)

(iv) To show that a sentence is unfinished or has been interrupted.

A: I was about to say—

B: I am not interested in what you were about to say.

(iv) To give warning that something startling or unexpected is about to follow.

After I had resided at college seven years my father died and left me — his blessing.—Goldsmith.

This use is not generally to be commended. It rather reminds us of the public speaker or the comedian who pauses to invite applause; and often the *imprévu* or the anticlimax is more effective if it comes unheralded and without any warning.

(v) To denote a pause between words or hesitancy in speaking.

One — two — three — go!

I — er — should like to say — er — how much we appreciate — er — this — er — generous offer.

Note: (i) A comma is never used together with a dash. When the dash is employed it supersedes any comma that would otherwise have been used.

(ii) A dash separates, where a hyphen joins; consequently stammering is usually indicated by hyphens, not by dashes.

(iii) On the use of a dash with a colon, see under COLON.

DATA. Really a plural, meaning 'facts given' (the singular *datum* is rarely used), and a plural verb is therefore to be preferred ('What are the data?'), but in certain contexts it is permissible to treat the word as a collective denoting a single body of facts rather than a number of individual points (cf. *agenda*) and to use a singular verb: 'Is that all the data we have?' 'The data is rather meagre.'

DATE. *Date* for *appointment* or *engagement* is not recognised as good English.

DATES. (i) Use figures, not words. Thus 'the year 1800', not 'the year eighteen hundred' and 'on May 25th', not 'on May the twenty-fifth'. (See, however, point (iii) below for exceptions.)

(ii) At the head of letters either 17 July, 1961, or July 17th, 1961 is acceptable, though the former is to be preferred. Note the comma before the number of the year. 17/7/61 is not recommended. (Incidentally, to an Englishman 2/6/61 means June 2nd, 1961; to an American it means February 6th.)

(iii) In a sentence July 17th is to be preferred. Dates that have a special significance and have become something of institutions, however, may be written in words when their significance is the relevant point: *the first of April, the fourteenth of July*. Note that when merely the month and year are mentioned, without a definite day, no comma is used: *June 1927*.

(iv) Write *from 1753 to 1785*, or *1753–1785*, but not *from 1753–1785*.

(v) B.C. follows the number of the year, but A.D. should precede it, since the letters stand for *Anno Domini* (in the year of Our Lord), and we should say 'in the year of Our Lord 1959', not '1959 in the year of Our Lord'.

(vi) For the plural of dates use the apostrophe if the date is written in figures (*the 1850's*), but no apostrophe if it is spelt as a word (*the fifties of the last century*). When the hundreds are omitted from the number of a year, and are assumed as understood, use an apostrophe (*the General Strike of '26*).

(vii) Write *nineteenth century*, not *19th century*. When used attributively, the name of a century needs no hyphen (*nineteenth century poetry*), though it is not incorrect to use one. Some publishing houses prefer it.

DAYS OF THE WEEK. The adverbial use without the preposition is normal when the name of the day is preceded by *last* or *next* (i.e. *I saw him last Friday*), but otherwise *on* must be used. *I will come Friday* is a vulgarism.

DÉBUT. Note the accent.

DECIMATE. To kill one in every ten, not to reduce to one-tenth.

DEFENSIBLE : DEFENSIVE. *Defensible* = that may be defended : *defensive* = intended, or serving, to defend.

DEFER. *Defer* (= put off, postpone) gives the noun *deferment*; *defer to* (= give way to, show respect for) gives the noun *deference*. The adjective is *deferential*.

DEFINITE : DEFINITIVE. A *definite* proposal is one made in clear and unmistakable terms ; a *definitive* proposal is a final one, that will not be modified, and therefore must be accepted or rejected as it stands.

DEFINITELY. A very much overworked word, often used unnecessarily, and sometimes wrongly.

Correct: The meeting is definitely fixed for July 25th (as opposed to *provisionally*).

Are you definitely leaving at the end of this month? (implying 'or is there still some doubt?')

Not incorrect, but unnecessary: He is definitely the better qualified of the two candidates. The weather is definitely warmer today.

Incorrect: She looked definitely ill. I was only dozing; I was not definitely asleep. You must definitely finish the work tomorrow.

DELUSION: ILLUSION. *Delusion*: a false belief which is accepted as true, and which therefore deceives. *Illusion*: something which appears to be other than it really is, though the false appearance is not necessarily accepted. A person who is convinced that he has seen a ghost is suffering from a *delusion*; if we suggest that the 'ghost' was really a perfectly natural phenomenon which, in the particular circumstances, gave the impression of a ghost, we are explaining it as an *illusion*.

There may be no basis whatever for a delusion (an insane woman, for instance, may be under the delusion that she is the Queen, Joan of Arc, or the widow of Captain Cook); for an illusion there must be some basis.

DEMOTE. A recent coinage by analogy with *promote*. It looks like being accepted.

DEMUR. Followed by *to*.

DEPEND (ON). Sir Ernest Gowers (*An A.B.C. of Plain Words*) objects to the omission of *on* in such sentences as 'It depends what you mean', 'It depends whether they come', but this seems pedantic. The omission is justified by usage. The *on* must be inserted, however, if the subject is any other word than *it*: e.g. 'Are we going away for a whole month this year?' — 'It depends whether we can afford it', but 'That depends on whether we can afford it'.

It all depends (without any further specification of what it depends on) may be acceptable in conversation but should not be used in writing.

DEPRECATE: DEPRECIATE. A common mistake is to use *deprecate* when *depreciate* is required. *Deprecate* = express disapproval of or, more strictly, to pray against ('He deprecated the use of such extravagant language'). *Depreciate*=belittle, lessen

('Those who were jealous of his success always depreciated his achievements').

DESPITE. Followed by no preposition. *Despite of* is incorrect. The idiomatic expressions are 'in spite of repeated warnings' and 'despite repeated warnings'.

DETOUR. Has no acute accent.

DEVELOP. No *e* at the end. Similarly *development*. No doubling of *p* before a suffix: *developed, developing, developer*.

DICE. See next entry.

DIE: DYE. *Die* = expire: *dies, died, dying*. *Dye* = colour: *dyes, dyed, dyeing*.
  Die, the old singular of *dice*, is now used only in the expression *the die is cast*. In other contexts *dice* is used as both singular and plural. *Die* meaning a stamp for embossing paper, or making a coin or medal, has the plural *dies*.

DIFFERENT(LY). (i) Followed by *from*, not *to* or *than*. *Different to* is often heard in speech and sometimes seen in print, and it has even found qualified approval from such authorities as Fowler and the Oxford Dictionary, but it is generally regarded as a solecism. Before a clause, *from what* is required ('different from what it used to be', not 'different than it used to be'.
  (ii) *Different* stands apart from most other adjectives in that, though it is grammatically of the positive degree, the idea it expresses implies a comparison. This gives rise to certain syntactic peculiarities. In the first place, when used predicatively it can be preceded by the adverb *no*, which can be added only to the comparatives of other adjectives and adverbs. 'The position today is no different from what it was two years ago.' 'I shall treat her no differently from anyone else.' (*No good*, in such sentences as 'It's no good doing that', 'These shoes are no good for wet weather', is not a parallel case, since *good*, used in this way, is by origin a noun, with the meaning 'advantage'. Cf. 'What's the good of doing that?' and the expression 'five pounds to the good'.) Secondly, though in affirmative statements, like other adjectives of the positive degree, *different* may be modified by *very* ('a very different state of affairs', 'Things are very different now'), in negative statements and in questions, though *very* is not impossible, it usually follows the comparative degree of other adjectives and

adverbs, and takes *much*. 'The weather today is not much different from what it was yesterday.' 'Is the position today much different from what it was six months ago?'

(iii) 'A Cockney speaks different from a Yorkshireman.' Amend to *differently*. *Different* is not recognised as an adverb, though some defence of the sentence might be put up on the grounds that here the word is half adjectival, in that we have in mind, not merely a different manner of speaking, but a different kind of speech. And certainly a strong case could be made out for saying 'He talks very different now from what he did when I first knew him' if we mean, not that he speaks better, or more clearly, or more grammatically, but that he expresses different views. *Think different*, when it means, not think in a different way, but have different thoughts, is certainly correct: 'I used to hold that opinion, but now I think different.'

DIPHTHERIA. Notice the *ph* in the spelling. Pronounce *dif-*, not *dip-*.

DIPHTHONG. (i) Pronounce *dif-thong*, not *dip-thong*. (Note the *ph* in the spelling.)

(ii) Do not call the vowel ligature *æ* (as in *Julius Cæsar*) a diphthong. It should be called a digraph (i.e. two letters written as one). In pronunciation it has the value of a simple vowel, like that in *me*, *tea*, etc. *Diphthong* is a phonetic term; that is to say, it refers not to written symbols, but to sounds, and is used to describe two vowel sounds which are pronounced so rapidly one after the other that they merge together. Thus the sound in *mouse* begins with the same vowel sound as that in *far* or *master*, and finishes with that in *do*. The plural *mice*, again, begins with the same vowel sound as that in *far* or *master*, but finishes with that in *ease*. In spelling, a diphthong may be represented by two separate letters (as in *mouse, house, chair*), or by only one (as in *mice, fame, cake*).

N.B.—R.C.R. prefers 'ligatured digraph' for æ and œ, since it would regard two letters written separately, but pronounced as a single sound (e.g. *ph, ch, sh*, and the oe in *Phoebe*), also as digraphs.

DISASSOCIATE. Use *dissociate* as the opposite of *associate*.

DISGUSTED. We are disgusted *with* a person and disgusted *at* or *with* a sight, a fact or an occurrence; *at* represents the immediate reaction, *with* a more permanent feeling or attitude of mind. *Disgusted by* is also used.

DISINTERESTED: UNINTERESTED. 'At one time he was an enthusiastic worker for our cause, but lately he seems to have become disinterested.' Incorrect. The word required is *uninterested*. *Disinterested* = having no personal advantage to gain. *Uninterested* = unwilling to give attention to: bored. A judge should be disinterested in a case he is trying: he should not be uninterested.

DISPERSAL: DISPERSION. *Dispersal* = the act or process of dispersing: *dispersion* = the resultant state or situation. We speak of the *dispersal* of a crowd by the police (i.e. the scattering or breaking up), but 'It was difficult to trace all the members of the family, owing to their dispersion over various parts of the country' (i.e. the fact that they lived dispersed).

DISPUTE. Stress on the second syllable for both verb and noun.

DISTINCT: DISTINCTIVE. *Distinct* = clearly perceivable: *distinctive* = peculiar to, or characteristic of, one particular thing. 'A distinct smell of petrol', but 'Petrol has a distinctive smell' (i.e. one which distinguishes it from anything else).

DISTINGUISH: DISTINGUISH FROM/BETWEEN. (i) When *distinguish* means 'tell apart' or 'discern a difference' the construction is either *distinguish* followed by a plural object, or 'distinguish one from the other': e.g. 'The twins were so much alike that you could scarcely distinguish them' (or 'could scarcely distinguish one from the other').

(ii) *Distinguish between* is used when the verb means 'make a distinction'. 'Courts of law should not distinguish between persons on account of their race, colour or religion.' 'You must distinguish between those private schools which are run primarily for profit, and are therefore really business concerns, and those which are supported by religious bodies or philanthropic institutions.'

DISTRIBUTE. Stress on the second syllable, not on the first.

DO. (i) As a 'substitute verb' (i.e. one standing in place of some other verb which has been used previously), *do* can be used only after an *active* voice, never after a passive. The following sentences are accordingly incorrect. 'He was told that the money would have *to be paid back*, but he refused *to do so*.' 'Many nineteenth-century novels *were published* in monthly numbers, as Dickens *did* in the case of *The Pickwick Papers*.'

(ii) Closely allied to this error is the use of *do* to refer back to a verb which the writer imagines he has used, but which actually he has not : e.g. 'The landlord asked for the payment of a week's rent in advance, and the tenant agreed *to do so*'. By the time he gets to the end of his sentence the writer has forgotten the beginning. He is under the impression that he has used the verb *to pay*, but he has not ; he has used the verbal noun *payment*.

(iii) 'I prophesied he would fail, and he *did do*.' Omit *do*. Here *did* is not a substitute verb ; it is the emphatic *did* (short for *and he did fail*). With compound tenses, if the non-finite part can be understood and carried over from the previous verb, there is no need to use the substitute *do* : e.g. 'Anyone who has lived in a large industrial town, as I have' (not as *I have done*).

(iv) If it is necessary to use a full compound tense of the substitute *do*, it should be remembered that it can never refer back to the verb *to be* : e.g. 'Anyone who has been over twenty years in India, as I have done . . .', 'Those who have been down a coal mine, as several of us here have done . . .' In both these cases substitute *have been*, or merely *have*. The mistake is most frequent when 'being' or 'having been' somewhere is thought of as meaning going, living, staying, travelling, visiting, etc.

(v) Another illegitimate use of *do* is in inverted constructions of the type 'If war comes, as come it may do'. Here *do* is redundant, as it merely duplicates *come*, the clause *as come it may* being an inversion of *as it may come*. To use *do* as well as *come* is like saying 'as come it may come'.

(vi) On *do have*, in such sentences as 'Do you have any brothers or sisters ?', 'He said he didn't have any money', see under HAVE.

DOCTOR : DR. Use the abbreviation *Dr.* only before a personal name, as *Dr. Johnson*. Do not write 'They sent for the Dr.' When the word is used as a substitute for the person's full name, and not merely to denote his profession, spell it with a capital : 'We must thank the Doctor for his interesting lecture', i.e. Dr. So-and-so.

If *Dr.* is prefixed to a person's name the doctor's degree should not also be written after it. Write *E. J. White, Esq., M.A., D.Sc.* or *Dr. E. J. White, M.A.*, but not *Dr. E. J. White, M.A., D.Sc.*

Some purists contend that the only 'Reverend Dr.' is a Doctor of Divinity, and that a clergyman or minister who has any other doctor's degree should be described as 'Dr. the Reverend', but the distinction is not generally observed, and in any case the logic behind it seems questionable.

DONATE. 'The Young People's Club have donated £20 towards the cost of the new floor in the Church Hall.'—From a church magazine.

Why not 'given' or 'contributed'? *Donate* is an ugly back-formation from *donation*, and should be avoided.

DOOMSDAY: DOMESDAY. *Doomsday* for the day of judgement, but *Domesday Book*.

DOUBLE ENTENDRE. Actually a mistake for *double entente*, but now the accepted form. To revert to *double entente* is pedantic.

DOUBLE NEGATIVE. (i) Few will be guilty of perpetrating the more obvious type of double negative, like 'I haven't never been there'; more are likely to be ensnared by the semi-negative adverbs *hardly*, *scarcely*, *barely*, which, like the full negatives, cannot be combined with another negative word: e.g. 'They have not been here for hardly an hour'. 'There was no one, scarcely, who could hear what he said.' Amend to 'They have been here' and 'There was scarcely anyone'.

(ii) Certain double negatives, however, have become recognised idioms: 'I shall not stay unless I can help it'. 'I should not be surprised if it doesn't rain before the day is out.' (See under SURPRISE.)

(iii) In the past few years some writers (e.g. George Orwell, in his essay *Politics and the English Language*) have condemned pretty severely the expression of a positive idea by *not* followed by a word with a negative prefix, as *not unnaturally*, *not unlike*, *not unlikely*, *not unknown*. Many of these combinations are to be condemned, but some can be defended. To say that something is 'not unlikely' is not quite the same as saying it is likely. The test is whether the *not un-* expresses an idea different from that of the simple positive word.

DOUBT. (i) Verb: I doubt *whether* (or *if*) he is honest. (Not *that*; nor *as to whether*.)
(ii) Noun: There is no doubt *that* . . . I have no doubt *that* . . .
I have my doubts *about* it/*about* his honesty.
I have my doubts *whether* he is honest. (Not *as to whether*.)

DOUBTFUL. It is doubtful *whether* he can do it (or 'if he can do it').

I am doubtful *about* doing it.

I am doubtful *of* the outcome.

DRAFT : DRAUGHT. *Draft* : a draft of money, of soldiers, etc. ; make a rough draft ; to draft a bill, a document, etc.

Draught : a draught of water (or any other kind of drink); the draught of a ship ; beer sold on draught ; a draught of fishes ; to exclude the draught (from a room, etc.) ; play draughts ; a draught-horse ; a draughtsman.

DRAMA. Correctly used to denote plays of all kinds (comedy, tragedy, tragi-comedy, farce, etc.) collectively, as in *A History of English Drama*, a course of lectures on eighteenth-century drama. Incorrectly (though popularly) used to describe a play characterised by sensation, thrills and strong emotional appeal. This last should be called a *melodrama*.

DRAUGHT. See DRAFT.

DREAMED : DREAMT. *Dreamt* is the more usual for both past tense and past participle. *Dreamed* is still seen in print, but is almost archaic.

DRUNK. The past participle of the verb *to drink*, but not the past tense, which is *drank*. 'He drunk the lemonade' is incorrect. The correct verb forms are (i) 'He has drunk', (ii) 'He drank'.

As an adjective *drunk* is used only predicatively ('They were drunk'). *Drunken* is the correct word for the attributive use ('drunken fellows').

As a noun *drunks* (people who are drunk) is permissible colloquially, but not in writing except of the most informal kind. The singular *a drunk* is not often heard.

DUE TO. It is incorrect to use this combination as a compound preposition to introduce an adverb phrase of reason, as is done in the following sentences.

Due to illness, he was unable to go on his holiday.

Many trains were late, due to the fog.

Due to the state of the ground, the match has been postponed.

Either *owing to* or *because of* should have been used.

Due is an adjective ; therefore *due to* can be used only :

(i) Predicatively: i.e. as a complement to a verb, usually some part of the verb *to be*:

His absence *is due* to illness.

The accident *was due* to the driver's failing to give a signal.

(ii) Following a noun, and introducing an adjectival construction which qualifies that noun.

Mistakes *due to carelessness* may have serious consequences.

A power failure, *due to a fault in the cable*, brought all the machinery to a standstill.

These may be regarded as ellipses of 'which are due to carelessness' and 'which was due to a fault in the cable' (i.e. of adjective clauses) and are therefore really another form of the predicative use.

A person is *entitled*, not *due*, to something to which he has a right: e.g. 'You are entitled to one new share for every two that you already hold', 'I am entitled to another week's holiday' (not 'you are due to one new share', etc., 'I am due to another week's holiday.').

Due for is recognised as idiomatic in sentences of the type 'Our salary scales are due for revision in the New Year', 'I am due for promotion to a higher grade in September'.

DUMB. In the sense of 'stupid', an Americanism, not recognised in British English. Etymologically it has no connexion with the normal English word *dumb*. It is the German *dumm* (= stupid), introduced into America in the speech of German immigrants in the latter part of the last century, and then spelt *dumb* by analogy, or confusion, with the word meaning 'unable to speak'.

DYE. See DIE.

E

EACH. (i) When used as an adjective, *each* is singular; the noun it qualifies must therefore be referred to by a singular pronoun or possessive adjective, and when it is a subject it takes a singular verb: 'Each person has a special seat allocated to him, hasn't he?' (not *them . . . haven't they?*)

(ii) When it is a pronoun it is always singular if it has no antecedent ('Each has his own ideas on the subject'), but if it refers back to an antecedent it may be either singular or plural, according to circumstances, viz.:

(a) When the antecedent is plural, *each* is also plural: 'The children each have a special task allotted to them'.

(b) When the antecedent consists of two or more singular nouns which *each* individualises, the verb is usually plural ('My wife and I each subscribe a pound a year'), but, though condemned by Fowler (*M.E.U.*), a singular verb is not impossible if the intention is to differentiate: 'The rural south and the industrial north each has its attractions for the tourist'.

(c) When the antecedent consists of two plural nouns, each of which is referred to separately and individually, then *each* is plural: 'The French and the Germans each claim the territory'.

(iii) When *each* is used in a partitive sense (*each of us/you/them/the passengers,* etc.) special care must be taken. The singular is still necessary in the sentence proper ('Each of the men has been given his instructions', 'Each of the successful candidates was presented with a certificate'), but an appended 'tag' question may be either singular or plural. If *each* individualises, it is singular ('Each of the successful candidates was presented with a certificate, wasn't he?'), but if it is collective it takes a plural tag: 'Each of us put ten pence in the collection, didn't we?'

(iv) When *each* follows the pronoun (*we each, you each, they each*), verbs, pronouns and possessive adjectives, in both main sentence and tag, agree with the plural pronoun: 'We each have our problems, haven't we?'

(v) On the incorrect *between each*, see under BETWEEN.

EACH OTHER. (i) The one-time 'rule' that *each other* can refer only to two, and that for more than two *one another* must be used, is no longer strictly observed. 'The three men distrusted each other' is now accepted as idiomatic.

(ii) The genitive always has the apostrophe before the s (*each other's*). The noun that follows the genitive is singular if each of the persons in question has only one of the things concerned : 'They stayed at each other's house, borrowed each other's car, took each other's photograph', etc.

(iii) *Each other* may be used as the object or the indirect object of a verb ('They saw each other', 'They gave each other a present'), or it may be governed by a preposition ('They have a high regard for each other', 'They write to each other every week'), but it cannot be used as the subject of a verb. 'They had no idea that each other knew the secret', 'We thought each other was joking' are incorrect. Amend to 'They each had no idea that the other knew the secret', 'We each thought the other was joking'.

Similarly it is quite idiomatic for *each other*, when used as the object of a verb or a preposition, to be followed by an infinitive with an adverbial function ('They helped each other to mend their bicycles'), but it cannot be followed by an infinitive to which it is the subject : e.g. 'They waited for each other to go first'. Amend to 'Each waited for the other to go first'. The reason is that within the combination *each other*, *each* is a nominative, in apposition to the subject, and *other* an accusative. In such a sentence as 'They knew each other', *each* individualises the subject *they*, and the object is *other*. Hence the entire combination cannot be used in such a way as to give *other* a non-accusative function.

(iv) *Each* must always refer back to a plural noun or pronoun. We cannot, therefore, say 'Neither of them saw each other', since *neither* is singular. Amend to 'Neither of them saw the other'.

(v) 'The two cars were following each other.' Incorrect ; only one was following. *Each other* is reciprocal, *one another* is not ; there is not, therefore, the same objection to *following one another* if several are concerned : one can follow *an*other, but each cannot follow *the* other. ('The cars followed one another in quick succession.')

(vi) 'There was no love lost between each other.' *Between each other* is always incorrect (see under BETWEEN). Amend to *between them*.

EARLIER ON. Often heard, but incorrect. It has probably arisen by analogy with *later on*; but *later on* is logical, *earlier on* is not, since *earlier* is 'back', not 'on'. Usually *earlier* alone will suffice, without any additional adverb.

With the positive degree *early*, the appended *on* can be justified (e.g. 'Quite early on in the match it became apparent that our team would lose', i.e. at an early stage as the match went on); but even here it is unnecessary, and is best omitted.

EASY : EASILY. The usual adverb is *easily*, as in 'I can do that easily', 'We found the house quite easily'. *Easy*, however, is idiomatic in the expressions *go easy* and *take things easy*, and in compounds with a participle, like *an easy-going attitude, easy-earned money, easy-fitting shoes* (cf. loose-fitting, tight-fitting, close-fitting, etc.).

EATABLE : EDIBLE. Mushrooms are edible, toadstools are not; but even things which are edible may sometimes be un-eatable because of their condition, e.g. mushrooms which have been burned in the cooking, meat which is tough, or bread which has become stale. *Eatable* refers to palatability, *edible* to what may, normally, be eaten.

EATS. *Eats*, for *food*, is a vulgarism.

ÉCLAIR : ÉCLAT. Do not omit the accent.

ECONOMIC : ECONOMICAL. *Economical* has to do with saving (*the most economical method*); *economic* means 'pertaining to the science of economics : relating to trade, commerce, the production and distribution of wealth, etc.' (*economic problems, a period of economic expansion*).

EDIFICE. A rather pretentious word. In all ordinary contexts use *building*. Permissible figuratively if the suggestion is slightly scornful or derogatory : 'Hitler's elaborate edifice of the Third Reich'.

EDUCATIONAL : EDUCATIVE. *Educational work* = work in connexion with education (it may be administrative, organising or actual teaching). *Educative work* = work which educates those who undertake it. An *educational* tour = one arranged for the purposes of educating. An *educative* tour = one that results in educating those who take part in it, though it may not have been arranged with that object in view. An *educational* (not *educative*) organisation, body, institution, system, etc. : *educational* (not *educative*) reforms : an *educative* (not *educational*) experience.

EDUCATION(AL)IST   Use *educationist*.

E'ER : ERE. *E'er* is short for *ever*: *ere* means *before*. Neither word has any place in modern prose, except as an archaism or for facetious effect.

EFFECT. See AFFECT.

EFFECTIVE : EFFICACIOUS : EFFICIENT. *Effective* = capable of effecting (i.e. bringing about) a desired result, as *an effective method of preventing smuggling*. *Efficient* = giving satisfactory results, as an efficient heating system. *Efficacious* is used only of remedies, medicines, medical and surgical treatment, etc. (efficacious in cases of fever).

E.G. See under I.E.

EGOIST : EGOTIST. *Egoist* = a selfish person : one who puts his own interests first. *Egotist* = a self-centred person : one who is continually speaking of himself, or trying to attract attention to himself.

EITHER. (i) *Either of them/us/you* can be used only of two, and it always takes a singular verb even if the two groups concerned are each plural : 'If either of you cares to call, I shall be in this evening'. 'Both the employers and the men have so far remained obdurate, but the Minister is always ready to use his good offices if either of them *requests* him to do so.'

(ii) With *either . . . or* the verb is singular if the correlated terms are singular, plural if the correlated terms are plural. If each of the terms requires a different verb, either in number or person, then it is usual to use the form that will go with the second of them : 'Either he or I *am* to go'.

(iii) On the correct position of *either . . . or*, see CORRELATIVES.

(iv) *Either* in the sense of 'one *and* the other' differs from *both* in that it thinks of each separately (and therefore, if used as a subject, takes a singular verb), where *both* thinks of them together. Its use is restricted to those things where the two are complementary, the existence of the one implying the existence of the other, as *either side, either end, either hand*. We cannot say 'Either son distinguished himself'.

EKE OUT. The correct meaning is 'to make something, of which there is an insufficient supply, go further by adding something else to it or by supplementing it with something else'. If there is insufficient butter we may eke it out with margarine. The points to notice are :

(i) The subject of *eke* is always a personal one; it cannot be the name of the thing that is added; e.g. the margarine does not eke out the butter.

(ii) The object must be the thing that is insufficient, and is added to or supplemented.

(iii) *Eke out* does not mean 'use frugally' or 'stretch (something) with difficulty further than it will conveniently go'. If we have only enough milk for twelve cups of tea we do not *eke it out* amongst twenty by putting less in each.

ELDER, ELDEST. (i) Used only of close family relations, e.g. sons, daughters, sisters, brothers. It cannot be followed by *than*, and if used predicatively must be preceded by *the*: 'He was the eldest of the three sons', 'She is the elder of the two', but not 'Of Jane and Susan, Susan is elder', or 'Susan is elder than Jane'.

(ii) There are also the expressions *an elder statesman* (one respected on account of his long experience) and, in the plural, *one's elders*, implying a considerable difference in age (usually as between children and adults).

(iii) The noun *elders* denoting certain officers in the Presbyterian church is no longer thought of as having any connexion with age, but rather with seniority of status.

ELEVATOR. British English speaks of a grain elevator, but a lift for passengers. Americans use *elevator* for both.

ELIGIBLE. Stress on the first syllable.

ELIMINATE. (i) *Eliminate* does not mean 'destroy', 'kill', or the various associated senses that have been given to it in recent times (e.g. 'Stalin eliminated anyone who opposed his policy'). It means 'to thrust out', or 'to get rid of', but not by killing. Of the competitors who enter for a race, a certain number are eliminated in the preliminary heats, and we eliminate from a list those names or items which we no longer wish to consider. Cf. also the expression 'to arrive at the answer by a process of elimination'.

(ii) *Eliminate* is sometimes misused for *exclude*. *Exclude* means 'to shut out'. *Eliminate* comes from a Latin root which means 'to thrust out over the threshold', and you cannot thrust a person out of a room until he is in it. People who are deliberately left out of a football team from the first are excluded; those whose names are admitted to a preliminary list but then deleted are eliminated.

ELSE. (i) Followed by *than*, not *but* : 'nothing but' and 'nothing else than' are the alternatives. 'Nothing else but' is an unidiomatic combination of the two.

(ii) Genitive = *anyone else's, no-one else's, someone else's, everyone else's*, etc., not *everyone's else, anyone's else*, though *whose else* is generally used in preference to *who else's* when it occurs predicatively (e.g. 'Whose else should it be?'). The attributive use is best avoided, but on the few occasions when it is necessary it must be *who else's* : e.g. 'Who else's house have you called at?' 'Whose house else' is to be deprecated.

(iii) For the accusative the tendency is to use *who* rather than *whom* : 'Who else did you see?', 'To who else have you given the information?'

(iv) 'We shall have to hurry, else we shall miss the train.' Incorrect. *Else* is an adverb, not a co-ordinating conjunction. In sentences of this type *or else* (or simply *or*) must be used.

ELUSIVE. Sometimes misused for *illusory* (for which see under *Delusion, Illusion*). *Elusive* is the adjective which comes from the verb *to elude*, and means 'not easily apprehensible' or 'constantly eluding one'. Cf. the title of Baroness Orczy's novel *The Elusive Pimpernel*.

ELY (Place name). Pronounced to rhyme with *mealy*, not with the name of the Old Testament High Priest *Eli*.

EMEND. See under Amend.

EMOLUMENT(S). When the pecuniary rewards of an office or position come from various sources and are of various kinds, they may be correctly referred to collectively as the emoluments of the office. Used merely as a substitute for *salary* or *stipend*, the word is pretentious.

END UP. *End up* should be used (if it is used at all) only when the reference is to the final stage of a progression or series : e.g. 'He entered the army as a private and ended up a Brigadier', 'He started as an office boy and ended up as a director of the firm', 'If you go on like that you'll end up in prison'. But 'The story ends (not *ends up*) with the discovery of the lost heir, and his marriage to the heroine', 'The concert ended with the playing of the National Anthem', 'The discussion ended in a deadlock.'

ENDOW : ENDUE. *Endow* can be used of material and of non-material things ('He was endowed with wealth, wisdom and compassion'), *endue* of non-material things only ('Endue us with wisdom, patience and compassion', 'Endue thy ministers with righteousness'). (From the Book of Common Prayer.)

ENHANCE. When used in the active voice, *enhance* must have an abstract noun for its object, and when in the passive voice for its subject. 'This discovery has enhanced his reputation', and 'His reputation has been enhanced by this discovery' are both correct. The following are incorrect: (i) 'has enhanced him in reputation', (ii) 'He has been enhanced in reputation'.

ENQUIRE: INQUIRE. The verb is now usually spelt *enquire*. *Enquiry* = request for information (more often used in the plural, as 'All enquiries to be made at the office). *Inquiry* = investigation, as 'a court of inquiry', 'an inquiry into the causes of an accident'.

The agent-noun is usually spelt *enquirer*, but the oldest Non-conformist weekly is *The Inquirer*.

ENSURE: INSURE. We *ensure* (i.e. make certain of) the success of an undertaking, and take measures to *ensure* that instructions or regulations are carried out. We *insure* our lives, property, etc., and *insure against* death, accident, fire, loss of income, etc.

ENTERTAIN. We entertain a person *to* a meal, but *at* a hotel or restaurant.

ENTHUSE. The use of this verb (a back-formation from *enthusiasm*) is to be deprecated.

ENTRÉE. Do not omit the accent in writing. Pronounce in the French way.

ENVELOPE. (Noun). The anglicised pronunciation of the first syllable (to rhyme with *pen*), regarded as a vulgarism a generation ago, is now accepted, though the French pronunciation is still to be preferred. The verb: *envelop* (no *e* at the end: stress on the second syllable).

EQUALLY. (i) Two things are *as good as* each other, or they are *equally good*, but not *equally as good*.

(ii) A garment is equally useful for country *and* city wear (not *or*). But *or* is correct in the following sentence: 'I shall be equally pleased, whether you accept this offer or the other'.

(iii) Though it is absurd to say that some people are more

equal than others, there is no objection to 'a more equal distribution of wealth', or 'Wealth is now distributed more equally than it used to be'. Here *more equal(ly)* means 'approaching nearer to the idea conveyed by *equal(ly)*'. Cf. *a fuller account*.

EQUITABLE. Stress on the first syllable.

ESKIMO. This spelling (plur. *-oes*) has now superseded the older *Esquimau(x)*.

ESPECIALLY. (i) *Distinction between 'Specially' and 'Especially'*. *Specially* means 'for this special purpose, or to this special end, and no other'; *especially* means 'to a degree beyond others'. Both the following sentences, therefore, are incorrect: 'I went there especially to see him', 'There is a shortage of well qualified teachers of most subjects, but specially of science and mathematics.' In the first sentence *specially* is needed, in the second *especially*.

(ii) *Especially* specifies or particularises within the category that precedes it; what follows *especially* must therefore be included in this more general category, and not something additional to, or quite distinct from it. 'Many alterations will have to be made to the house, especially to the kitchen.' This is correct; the kitchen is part of the house. But the following, from an examination candidate's essay on 'Some Inventions that are Needed', is wrong: 'Inventions are needed to lighten the work in the home, especially on the farm'. The term *in the home* does not include the farm.

ESQUIRE. Use the abbreviation *Esq.* (followed by a full stop) in an address on an envelope; but remember (a) *Mr* must not be used as well, (b) *Esq.* must not be used unless the christian name or the initials precede the surname. If they are not known write *Mr Johnson*, not . . . *Johnson, Esq.*, (c) Any letters denoting degrees, honours, etc. follow the *Esq.* (J. C. Smith, Esq., M.A.; R. A. Mitchell, Esq., O.B.E.).

At one time *Esq.* was very restricted in its application; then it became a courtesy mode of address for anyone (of the male sex, of course) above the social grade of a manual labourer. Thirty or forty years ago a middle-class person might have felt affronted, or considered his correspondent guilty of a breach of etiquette, if he had received a letter addressed to *Mr* . . . There is not the same feeling about it today. *Esq.* is still felt to be the more formally courteous, but *Mr* . . . is much more widely used than it used to be. It should certainly be used in preference to *Esq.* in announcing a person on a printed notice: 'The bazaar will be opened by Mr E. H. Watson, O.B.E.' (not 'by E. H. Watson, Esq., O.B.E.').

EUPHEMISM: EUPHUISM: EUPHONY. 'You committed the sin of euphuism: you called it, not fat, but weight'.—H. G. Wells, *The Truth About Pyecraft.* Wells (or the character in his story) has confused two words. Pyecraft had not committed the sin of euphuism, but of *euphemism* (if that is a sin), i.e. the use of a more pleasant term for something that might be offensive or distressing if referred to by its real name. *Pass away* and *depart this life* are well-known euphemisms for *die*, *toilet* is a modern euphemism for *lavatory* (which in the first place was itself a euphemism, since literally it means a washing-place), and many of the milder forms of oaths are euphemisms for swear words, or to avoid the profane use of the names of God and Christ. We are using a euphemism again when, instead of saying 'Go to Hell', we say 'Go to blazes' (Hell fire), or 'Go to Hades' (the Greek underworld).

Euphuism is an affected and artificial style of writing like that adopted by John Lyly in his work *Euphues* (1579). It is characterised by alliteration, antithesis, and frequent allusion to natural history and mythology. It had something of a vogue in the late sixteenth and early seventeenth centuries.

Euphony, a term sometimes confused with one or the other of the foregoing, means 'pleasantness of sound'. We avoid combinations of words like 'confirmation of this information' on grounds of euphony.

The adjectives are *euphemistic*, *euphuistic* and *euphonious* respectively, though *euphony* also gives the adjective *euphonic*. *Euphonious* means 'characterised by euphony' (a euphonious combination of words, a euphonious sentence, a euphonious style). *Euphonic* means 'relating to euphony' ('We avoid certain combinations of words or sounds for euphonic reasons.')

EVENT. Wherever possible, use *if* instead of *in the event of*, which is usually just official jargon.

EVENTUATE. A word to be avoided. Use *happen* or *occur*.

EVER. (i) Do not use such combinations as *the biggest ever*, *the best ever*, etc., as 'This year's radio show will be the most remarkable ever'. Write instead, 'the most remarkable there has ever been', or 'the most remarkable ever seen'.

Even more objectionable than the predicative use is the attributive, as in the following, from *The Observer*: 'France is planning to stage shortly the biggest-ever offensive against the Algerian rebels'. Substitute 'the biggest offensive it has ever launched'.

(ii) In expressions like *ever so much*, *ever so small*, etc. the combination *ever so* (which must always be written as two words) has become a compound adverb modifying the adverb or adjective that follows it; it cannot be used by itself to modify a verb. 'I enjoyed my holiday ever so' is incorrect, for there is nothing for *ever so* to modify. Write (and say) *ever so much*, or, better still, *very much*.

(iii) *Whoever, whichever, whatever, whenever, wherever, however* are written as one word, only when -*ever* is generalising: 'Whoever wants it may have it', 'Take whichever you like', 'I know nothing whatever about it', 'It is going to be difficult however we do it'.

When *ever* is emphasising (i.e. when the expression means something like 'what on earth', 'how on earth', etc.) two separate words must be used: 'Who ever told you that?', 'What ever shall we do?'   'Where ever have you been?', 'How ever shall we do it?', 'Why ever did you say that?'.

EVERY. Singular. It therefore takes a singular verb and must be referred to by a singular pronoun or possessive adjective. 'Every person brought his lunch with him' (not *their . . . them*).

EVERY DAY: EVERYDAY. Use *everyday* (one word) only when adjectival, as *an everyday occurrence*, *our everyday life*. In all other senses, use two words: 'He comes here every day', 'I have seen him every day this week', 'Every day somebody dies'.

EVERYBODY, EVERYONE, EVERYTHING. (i) Like *every*, all these words are singular. They therefore take a singular verb and must be referred to by singular pronouns and singular possessive adjectives. ('Everyone/everybody promised he would keep his word'—not *they . . . their*).

(ii) In 'tag' questions, however, the plural is permissible for *everyone* and *everybody* when the statement that precedes it has a collective rather than a distributive sense: e.g. 'Everybody can't be clever, can they?', 'Everyone present made a wild rush for the door, didn't they?'. The tag for *everything* must always be singular: 'Everything looked beautiful, didn't it?', 'Everything has gone wrong today, hasn't it?'.

(iii) The compound *everyone* can be used only to refer to people. For things, two words are necessary: 'She dusted the books and put every one back in its place', 'She bought a dozen eggs, and every one was bad', 'I've looked at six houses so far, and found something wrong with every one of them'. Even for people two words must be used when the sense is 'every single one': e.g. 'Every one of these pupils has passed', 'He had five children, and every one of them has done well in the world'. In such cases *one* is usually stressed in speech.

EVIL. The vowel of the second syllable is pronounced to rhyme with *fill*, not with *full*.

EX-. Pronounced *eks-* in *exercise, exhume, exigent, exile, exit, extol, extraordinary, exude.* The pronunciation *egs-* in some of these words is a regional one.

EXCEPT: EXCEPTING. (i) *Except* is a preposition, and is therefore followed by the accusative: 'Everyone except me has been informed' (not except *I, he, she,* etc.).

(ii) *Except* in the sense of *unless* ('Except the Lord build the house, their labour is vain that build it') is now archaic. Do not say 'I cannot do it except you help me'. Use *unless*.

(iii) *Except* excludes a particular one, or particular ones, from a group or a more general category (*everyone except me, all the girls except Vera, soft fruits except cherries*). If we wish to modify a whole statement by making a reservation, then *except for* is used. It may be placed either before or after the statement: 'Except for a few small firms, the whole industry is participating in the scheme', 'I am quite well now, except for a slight cold'. But 'Except for your help we should have been in a difficult position' is incorrect. Here the word required is either *but for* or *without*.

(iv) *Excepting* is used as a preposition, only when it is preceded by *not, always* or *without* ('not excepting the police', 'without excepting even the highest-placed officials,' 'always excepting the officers'). In such a sentence as 'We have won every match excepting that against Redcoates', *excepting* is wrongly used for *except*.

EXCLAMATION MARK. A. *Uses.* (i) After interjections, words or phrases that have the force of interjections, and certain onomatopoeic words which are meant to imitate a sharp, sudden sound: *Ah!, Oh!, Good Heavens!, Dash it all!, Only imagine!, What a stupid thing to say!, Bang!, Pop!, Crash!*

Note, however :

(a) When words like *crash* and *bang* are used as ordinary nouns and are part of the normal syntax of the sentence, no exclamation mark is used : 'Startled by the bang, the dog dashed out of the gate', 'There was a sudden crash as the trayful of crockery fell to the floor'.

(b) After an imperative verb the exclamation mark is used only when the word is uttered in an exclamatory tone (*Stop !*, *Halt !*). It is incorrect to use it after an ordinary imperative, like 'Open your books', 'Come here', 'Sit down'.

(c) Not every sentence which is an exclamation grammatically needs an exclamation mark — only those which are felt to be exclamations vocally. Thus 'What a fool that fellow is !' will need one, but there seems no case for using one after 'What a pity you did not let me know before'.

(ii) After the device known as apostrophe (i.e. invocation) :

Milton ! thou shouldst be living at this hour.

This must be distinguished from the ordinary vocative case, which needs only a comma :

Caesar, beware of Brutus ; take heed of Cassius ; come not near Casca ; have an eye to Cinna.

(iii) Occasionally at the end of a sentence to denote surprise, astonishment or sarcasm, or even to convey the notion of finality. For this purpose, however, it should be employed very sparingly, and it should never be used — as it sometimes is — when the sentence is actually a question : e.g. 'What on earth is that !', 'And did you actually stand by and do nothing !'. In both of these the question mark is needed.

On the other hand, the inverted verb-subject sequence, normally associated with the question, may also occur in an exclamatory sentence, in which case the exclamation mark, not the question mark, must be used. Notice the difference between 'How mischievous are the effects of war !' (the example given by *R.C.R.*) and 'How mischievous are the effects of war ?', or between 'And he actually stood by and did nothing !' (a statement where the exclamation mark is used to express surprise or disgust) and 'And he actually stood by and did nothing ?' (a question without inversion).

B. *Abuse.* For a certain class of writer the exclamation mark seems to have a strange fascination ; he sticks it at the end of plain and very ordinary statements, perhaps in the belief that it lends force to what he is saying, until it begins to assume the character of what has very aptly been called 'the mark of admiration'. Not surprisingly, the effect is usually the opposite of that intended, and often approaches near to bathos. A particularly bad example comes from a well-known Free Church weekly :

'I have always felt it a reproach to our movement that we should devote less time to resolutions than some of the larger orthodox Nonconformist bodies ! Think of the issues at stake : Federal Union, Blood Sports, Public Control of the Drink Trade, Conscription, the Closed Shop, to name only a few, the last two intimately connected with our hardy annual on civil liberties ! It might be a good idea to make the 'resolutions' meeting the public meeting. It would show the public we were alive ! It would be far better than holding a public meeting on the social implications of our faith without allowing any opportunity for discussion ! The first speech alone at the last public meeting would have provided us with ample material for the rest of the evening !'

Of all these exclamation marks, the one at the end of the penultimate sentence *might* be justified (assuming that the writer wished to express indignation or astonishment); the others certainly are not.

C. *The Exclamation Mark and other Stops.* (i) When an exclamation mark occurs at the end of a sentence, it takes the place of the full stop ; when it is used within a sentence it supersedes any comma or semicolon that otherwise would have been necessary in the same position.

(ii) Unless at the end of a sentence, it is followed by a small, not a capital letter :

Ethereal minstrel ! pilgrim of the sky !

(iii) On its position in relation to the inverted commas in direct speech, see under INVERTED COMMAS.

EXHAUSTING : EXHAUSTIVE. *Exhausting* work exhausts the person who does it ; *exhaustive* work exhausts (i.e. says all there is to be said about) the subject. Thus if the sense to be expressed is 'very thorough', 'leaving no stone unturned', use *exhaustive* : exhaustive inquiries, exhaustive research, etc.

EXTEMPORARY. 'Some of the speech seems to have been delivered extemporary.'—*The Observer*, March 1st, 1959. Is there such a word ? Several dictionaries give it, as an adjective, with an adverbial equivalent *extemporarily*, and if either is to be used it is the adverb which is required here. But there is really no reason for either of them, since *extempore* can be used both adjectivally (*an extempore speech*) and adverbially (*he spoke extempore*).

EXTEMPORE. See the preceding entry. Note also the pronunciation, as four syllables (ex- tem- por- ay). *Ex-tem-por*
(three syllables) is an illiteracy.

An *extempore* speech is one which the speaker has not prepared
beforehand, but makes up as he goes along. An *impromptu*
speech is one of which the speaker has received no previous
notice, or which he had not contemplated making. An impromptu
speech is necessarily extempore, but an extempore speech may
not be impromptu.

EXTERMINATE. Means '`to destroy utterly`', and can be
applied only to the destruction of a whole race or species in a
particular locality, not to the killing of one person or even of
a few. We cannot say that a tyrant exterminated anyone whom
he regarded as a rival, or that a considerable number of rabbits
have been exterminated.

EXTRA: EXTRA-. (i) When the word is an adjective meaning 'additional' write as a separate word (*two extra copies*):
when it is an adverb, meaning 'beyond the normal', use a
hyphen if it might be mistaken for the adjective, but not otherwise (e.g. *an extra-thick blanket*, which means something different
from *an extra thick blanket*). But no hyphen is needed in *The
blanket is extra thick*, *He worked extra hard*, since no ambiguity
results from its omission.

(ii) Except for recognised compounds which are written as
one word, use the hyphen if the adjective or adverb that *extra*
modifies is not normally used alone: e.g. *extra-curricular*,
extra-mural (though there is a growing tendency to write the
latter as one word when it refers to a university department).

F

FACE UP TO. *Face* alone is generally sufficient (*face the facts, face a difficult task*), but *face up to* may occasionally suggest determination, and then it seems justifiable. (*He is a person who will face up to the most difficult task.*)

FALSEHOOD; FALSITY; FALSENESS. *Falsehood* = untruth, in the abstract and general sense ('In the long run truth will vanquish falsehood'). *Falsity* = the false nature of a particular thing ('to expose the falsity of a charge or accusation'). *Falseness* = disloyalty, treachery ('the falseness of his supposed friend', 'falseness of heart', 'falseness to one's trust').

FAMILIAR TO: FAMILIAR WITH. *Familiar to* = known to (by), as 'His face is familiar to me': *familiar with* = having a fairly good knowledge of, as 'I am familiar with the countryside'.
    He was familiar to me = I recognised him as someone I had often seen. *He was familiar with me* = he treated me as though he knew me well. (Usually with a deprecatory sense.)

FANTASY: PHANTASY. Use the spelling with *f*.

FAR. (i) *Far better*, but *better by far*, *by far the better*, *by far the best*.
    (ii) *Far and away the best/the better of the two* is an accepted colloquialism. The plain comparative or superlative cannot be used; it must always be preceded by *the*.
    (iii) On *few and far between*, see under that heading.
    (iv) *As far as: so far as*. *As far as* denotes a destination or stage of progress: 'They went with us as far as Bedford'; 'I have considered having a car, but I haven't got as far as buying it yet'. *So far as* denotes the limits within which a statement holds good, or is to be understood: 'You may do it so far as I am concerned'. The two should not be confused.
    (v) *In so far (as)* is three words. Do not write *insofar as*.

FARTHER: FURTHER. Always use *further* (i) when the sense is 'additional' (*further information, further evidence*), or 'in addition' ('Have you anything further to say?' 'Further, the committee are of the opinion that the time is inopportune'), and (ii) when it is a verb meaning 'advance', 'promote' ('to further one's own interests').

As adjective or adverb denoting distance, *farther* is the more strictly correct, but *further* is also allowable, and is probably now more common, though in the superlative *farthest* is commoner than *furthest*.

FAVOURITE. Do not omit the *u*. The spelling *-or* is American.

FEASIBLE. Often misused as though it meant 'possible' or 'probable': e.g. 'It is quite feasible that within the next fifty years travel to the moon will be a commonplace thing'.

It means *possible* only in the restricted sense of 'able to be done': e.g. 'Your suggestion is feasible, though it might be rather costly', 'Travel to the moon may become feasible by the end of this century'.

FEATURING. 'My favourite Shakespeare play is *The Merchant of Venice*, featuring Shylock, Antonio, Bassanio and Portia' (from a schoolboy's essay). A term from film advertisements, and even there it is used of the actors, not the characters in the play. It is a piece of jargon which should be avoided in normal English.

FED UP. At best a colloquialism, which should not appear in written English. If it is used, the idiom is *fed up with*, not *of*.

FEINT. Use this spelling only when the meaning is *pretence* or *show* (make a feint of doing something: cf. the verb *to feign*). As an alternative spelling of *faint* it is a stationer's term, not recognised by the dictionaries. (*Notepaper ruled feint* = with faint lines.) Use the normal English spelling.

FEMALE: FEMININE. (i) As a synonym for *woman*, *female* is a vulgarism ('Females under the age of twenty-five are eligible for the post'). Say *women*.

(ii) *Female* denotes the sex of the creature to which it is applied (*the female of the species*, *a female swan*) or some physical part of such a creature (*the female form*, *female organs*, etc.) which has sexual characteristics. *Feminine* means pertaining to, or such as one associates with, a woman: *feminine charms*, *a feminine style of writing*. (Charms and writing have no sex, so *female* cannot be used.)

(iii) Say that a person is 'of the female sex', not 'of the feminine gender'. Only words have gender. (See *Gender*.)

FEMININE FORMS. The use of unnecessary feminine forms of nouns should be resisted. Generally speaking, unless there is a point in stressing the sex, the masculine form should be used as a common gender. A woman who conducts, whether it be a bus, an orchestra or a party of tourists, is doing precisely the same as a man in a similar position, so why not use the same word — *conductor*? The question of sex is irrelevant; and in cases where it is necessary to distinguish we can always say *woman conductor*, as we say *woman teacher* and *woman doctor*. *Actress, hostess, stewardess* and *mayoress*, on the other hand, are justifiable, for an actress usually acts female parts and an actor male ones, while a hostess, stewardess or mayoress fulfils a social rôle complementary to that of the host, steward or mayor. *Heroine*, similarly, is appropriate in a play or novel where there is also a hero, but there seems no reason why a woman who performs an heroic act should not be called a hero, just as the mistress of a household may be the master of a situation or a skill. *Waitress* and *manageress* are probably too firmly established to be uprooted now, though the latter is generally used only in certain kinds of business (mainly shops, cafés and laundries), but there is no justification for *directrice, benefactress, inspectress, murderess, proprietress, poetess* and *authoress* (the last two, indeed, nowadays have a depreciatory suggestion about them), while *executrix* may be left to the lawyers.

FETCH. 'The birds have fetched most of my raspberries.' A common misuse of the word in certain parts of the country. Correct to *taken*. *Fetch* means 'go and get, and then bring back here', as in the sentence 'Will you please fetch me my coat?' But there is, of course, no objection to our asking a firm of carriers to call at our house to fetch a parcel, since we are looking at it from the point of view of the collector.

FÊTE. Do not omit the circumflex.

FEW. (i) *A few* is positive in import, and is opposed to *none*; *few* is negative, and is opposed to *many*. *A good few* is allowable colloquially. The expression is of fairly recent origin, and has arisen by analogy with *a good many*. *Quite a few* is illogical, but is accepted as an understatement for 'a fair number'.

(ii) Care is necessary when *one of the few* is followed by a relative clause. The verb of the relative clause should be plural, since it refers back to *few*, not to *one*: e.g. 'He is one of the few people in this country who *have* a knowledge of Japanese'. It must be admitted, however, that sometimes, despite grammar, the singular verb sounds more natural: *e.g.* 'He is one of the few men alive who *was* able to study the hoard of German official documents captured by the Allied armies'. In such cases, provided no ambiguity can result, it seems justifiable to disregard grammatical rules and use the singular.

FEW AND FAR BETWEEN. When Thomas Campbell declared, in his poem *The Pleasures of Hope*, that his hours of bliss had been 'like angels' visits, few and far between', he started on its career a phrase which has since degenerated into a pointless piece of jargon. The meaning is 'few in number, and far between them'. It is correctly used in the sentence 'This summer the fine days have been few and far between', and again in '. . . Huge tracts of wild moorland, where the villages are few and far between', but when we get to statements like 'Nowadays well qualified science teachers are few and far between' or 'There may still be some households where grace is said before each meal, but they are few and far between', it is a meaningless cliché. *Few* alone is all that is needed.

FEWER. (i) For the difference between *fewer* and *less*, see under *less*.
(ii) 'The number of people present was fewer than we expected' is correct if we are thinking of the people individually, but if we are thinking of a figure (e.g. 75 instead of 100), and not of individuals, then we must say 'The number was *smaller* than we expected'. But the plural *numbers*, in the sense of 'members of a group', takes *fewer*. 'Their numbers were fewer than we expected.'

FIANCÉ : FIANCÉE. (i) A woman's betrothed is her fiancé (masculine), a man's his fiancée (feminine).
(ii) The words are not equivalent in meaning to *sweetheart*. They should be used only if the persons are actually engaged to be married.

FINALISE. An ugly word, un-English, and quite unnecessary. Instead of 'The scheme has now been finalised' say 'The scheme has now been completed' or 'put into its final form'.

FIRST. (i) 'When we were first married', 'When we first came to live here', 'When the house was first built'. Accepted idiom, which goes back to at least the time of Chaucer, in the late fourteenth century. The objection (sometimes raised) that it implies that we have been married, that we have come to live here, or that the house has been built more than once, is merely pedantic, and may be disregarded.

(ii) *Travel first class* (no hyphens), but *a first-class ticket, first-class fare,* etc.

(iii) On *first* (adv.) and *firstly,* see the next entry.

FIRSTLY. If used at all, it should be only in an enumeration of the points of an argument, a list of reasons, etc., to be followed by *secondly, thirdly,* etc.; but even here *first* is to be preferred.

FISH : FISHES (Plural). *Fishes* when thought of individually, *fish* collectively. 'We'll go and look at the fishes in the aquarium.' 'There are more fish in the sea than ever came out of it.'

FLAUNT. A leading article in the *Evening News* (September 1960) spoke of 'flaunting the law', meaning 'openly defying the law'. But *flaunt* does not mean this. The word required is *flouting*. To *flaunt* means 'to display ostentatiously' (e.g. 'wealthy people flaunting their riches').

FLU. No sign of abbreviation is needed, but if one is used it should be the apostrophe before the *f,* not a full stop at the end of the word.

FOLK. (i) Do not use *folk* as a substitute for *people* : e.g. 'A large number of folk were present'. Say 'a large number of people'.

(ii) *Folk* is a collective noun, and there is no plural, though colloquially *the old folks* has come to be accepted when the reference is to one's own relatives : but a church, club or philanthropic organisation arranges a treat for the old folk (not the *old folks*). For the genitive the apostrophe should go before the *s* : *an old folk's outing.*

FOOT (Measurement). (i) The normal plural is, of course, *feet: foot* is colloquial, and even there its use is restricted to the simple number of feet, or feet and inches where the actual word *inches* is not expressed : *six foot, six foot four,* but *six feet, four inches.*

(ii) In compound adjectives the singular *foot* is always used : *a two-foot rule, a twelve-foot plank* (cf. *a five-pound note, a ten-penny piece*).

(iii) Used adverbially to modify an adjective, *feet* is the correct word if the adjective is employed predicatively. Attributively, the adjective and adverbial qualification usually combine to make a double compound, and *foot* is used: 'The path was eight feet wide', 'A house approached by a path eight feet wide', but 'an eight-foot-wide path'. (Cf. 'a building ten storeys high', but 'a ten-storey-high building.')

FORBEAR: FOREBEAR. *Forbear* is a verb = hold back from doing something. *Forebear* is a noun = ancestor (usually in the plural: *one's forebears*).

FORBID. Past tense, *forbade*, pronounced *forbad*. Forbid a person *to do* something, not *from doing* it.

FORBIDDING: FOREBODING. Sometimes confused: e.g. 'With its heavy iron gates, its walls surmounted by spiked railings, and a huge mastiff prowling in the courtyard, the house had a foreboding appearance'. *Forbidding* is the word required, i.e. an appearance which seemed to forbid or discourage any approach or entry. *Foreboding* = indicating or suggesting in advance: 'the heavy, black clouds, foreboding a storm', 'a hard face, foreboding cruelty of character'.

FOREGO: FORGO. The former means 'to go before'. Only the participles are in common use (*the foregoing facts, a foregone conclusion*). *Forgo* means 'to do without something to which one is entitled', e.g. *forgo one's holiday*. Be careful over the spelling of the participles and the compound tenses: there is no *e* ('I am forgoing my holiday this year', 'He has forgone his holiday'). The past tense is *forwent*, but it is rarely used.

FOREVER: FOR EVER. The one-word spelling is to be discouraged: always use *for ever*. 'Bad luck cannot last for ever', 'She is for ever complaining', 'When it is done once it is done for ever'.

> Men may come, and men may go,
> But I go on for ever.

The expression *for ever and ever* obviously demands two words: *forever and ever* would be impossible, since the preposition governs both words *ever*.

Charles Stuart Calverley, a clever writer of parody and humorous verse, satirised very effectively the growing habit of writing *forever*, as one word.

> Forever: 'tis a single word!
> Our rude forefathers deemed it two.
> Can you imagine so absurd
>   A view?
>
> .   .   .   .   .
>
> And nevermore must printers do
> As men did long ago; but run
> 'For' into 'ever', bidding two
>   Be one.

FRANKENSTEIN.   Not a monster, but its maker, whom it ultimately turned upon and attacked (in Mary Shelley's novel of
that name).   Speak of *Frankenstein's monster*, not *a Frankenstein*.

FREE.   There are certain expressions in which *free* is always
followed by *of*, as *free of charge*, *free of cost*, *free of tax*, *free of
duty*.   The sense is 'exempt from', or 'not incurring'.   Apart
from these, *from* is more usual, though there is a tendency to
use *of* when we think of a state or condition resulting from
absence or removal of the thing in question: 'Most of the
roads are now free of snow', 'His ambition was to hand on the
property to his son free of debt'.   On the other hand, *from* is
the appropriate preposition when the thing in question is thought
of as an assailant: 'No-one can expect to live a life entirely free
from troubles', 'For the last month I have never been free from
pain'.   To keep a wound free *of* infection means to keep it
uninfected;   to keep it free *from* infection means to prevent
infection from getting into it.

FRIGHTENED.   Should not be followed by *of* or by an infinitive.
The legitimate constructions are (i) 'She was frightened by a
dog' (passive voice), (ii) 'The child was obviously frightened'
(past participle used adjectivally).
    The following are commonly heard, but are incorrect.   In
each case *afraid* should be substituted for *frightened*.   (i) 'She
is frightened of dogs', (ii) 'I am frightened of waking the baby',
(iii) 'He was frightened to cross the road'.

FRUITION.   The couplet:
                    Grant now a full fruition
                    To every seed of truth
(from a late nineteenth-century hymn) illustrates a very common
misuse of the word—so common that perhaps we must now
accept it as what Fowler called 'a sturdy indefensible'.   But
even if we feel it pedantic to cavil at its misuse by others, we
can still refrain from misusing it ourselves.   The word is not
derived from the English noun *fruit*; but from the Latin verb
fruor (= I enjoy), and 'to come to fruition' means 'to come to
the point of enjoyment'.

-FUL.   Words ending in *-ful*, like *cupful*, *spoonful*, *handful*, have
the plural *cupfuls*, *spoonfuls*, *handfuls*, not *cupsful* or *cups-full*,
etc.   *Two cupfuls of milk* is a measure (probably only one cup is
used, twice over); *two cups full of milk* means two separate
cups, each one full.

The sense will determine whether we write *-ful* or *full* (sing.), *-fuls* or *-s full* (plur.). 'He dropped *a bottle full* of lemonade' (it was the bottle he dropped); but 'He drank *a bottleful* of lemonade' (he did not drink the bottle).

FULL STOP. (i) It is assumed that anyone consulting this book will be competent in the use of the full stop at the end of a sentence. On the misuse of the comma where a full stop is required, see under COMMA.

(ii) Note that when a sentence ends with a question mark or an exclamation mark, these take the place of the full stop.

(iii) On the place of the full stop in conjunction with inverted commas, see under INVERTED COMMAS.

(iv) On the use of the full stop to denote abbreviations, see under ABBREVIATIONS.

FURNISH. 'We shall be pleased to furnish you any information you may require.' Unidiomatic. The verb *to furnish* does not take an indirect object. We furnish a person *with* something. But in any case *furnish* is the wrong verb here. Use *supply you with*, *send you* or *give you*.

FURTHER. See FARTHER.

G

GAOL: JAIL. The second spelling is to be preferred. The past tense and past participle of the verb are spelt *jailed* (one *l*).

GAP. 'The gap between imports and exports was cut further last month.' 'The trade gap has again fallen.' Both sentences, taken from B.B.C. news bulletins, should warn us of the care needed in using this word metaphorically. A gap does not fall, and if we cut a gap we make it bigger, not smaller.

GENDER. 'Being myself of the feminine gender, I suppose I should be favourably disposed towards any proposal which would place women on an equal footing with men.'—From a women's magazine. Incorrect. *Gender* is a grammatical term: only words have gender; human beings and other animals have sex. Substitute *the female sex* (not *the feminine sex*—see under *female: feminine*). Of course, the simpler way would be to say 'being myself a woman'.

GENITIVE CASE. (i) *The Use and Place of the Apostrophe.* (See under APOSTROPHE.)

(ii) *Genitive Case v. the 'of . . .' Adjunct.* Generally speaking, the genitive is used mainly of human beings and living creatures, and the *of . . .* adjunct of non-animate things. We do not normally say 'the house's owner', but 'the owner of the house'. There are, however, accepted genitive uses with non-animate things, as *a ship's compass, a stone's throw, a pin's head, the earth's surface, the sun's rays.* And of course, the *of . . .* adjunct is also used of human beings and animals: e.g. *the death of Nelson* as well as *Nelson's death*, or *the head of a man* as well as *a man's head*. As to which of these two constructions we should use in a particular context, instinct is a pretty safe guide. We tend to place first the word on which the notional emphasis falls. The death of Nelson is an event in history; Nelson's death is something that happened to Nelson. The head of a man is a particular kind of head; a man's head is part of a man.

(iii) *The Post-Genitive.* The name given to constructions like *a friend of my father's, a poem of Tennyson's*, with which we may also include the parallel use of the possessive pronouns, exemplified in *a relative of yours, a colleague of mine*, etc. The difference between *John's friend* or *my friend* on the one hand and *a friend of John's* or *a friend of mine* on the other, is roughly that between the definite and the indefinite article. To use *my friend* presupposes either that it will convey to the person to whom the words are addressed the identity of a specific person (as Mr Jones, Miss Smith, the person whom I have with me, the person to whom I have just referred, etc.) or alternatively that I have only one friend so that even if he/she is not known personally to my interlocutor it is quite obvious who is meant, as it would be if I said *my husband, my wife, my fiancée, my secretary*, etc. *A friend of mine*, on the other hand, is not definite and specific in this way; it means 'someone (unspecified) with whom I am friendly'.

Do not use *my friend, your friend*, therefore, unless the person to whom you are speaking will be able to identify the person so described; if such identification is not possible, use *a friend of mine, a friend of yours*. Having once, however, introduced a friend of mine, we may thereafter refer to him as *my friend*, as it is now clear who is meant — the person who has just been mentioned: e.g. '*A friend of mine* once left his hat and coat in the cloak room of a restaurant where he was having lunch. When he went to get them out the attendant handed him an umbrella with them. *My friend* protested that he had never left an umbrella . . . etc.'

As an apparent exception to the above rule we may speak of *my son, my daughter, my brother, my sister*, even though we have more than one, and even though the person to whom we are speaking does not know any of them; but the exception is only apparent, for the words *son, daughter, brother* and *sister* do denote a very precise relationship in a way that *friend* does not.

Finally, it is sometimes objected that we should not say *that wife of yours, that husband of hers, that red nose of Jim's*, since the idiom means 'that wife from amongst your several wives'. It is very doubtful whether this is the explanation of the idiom, but in any case the singular construction has been well established since the late fourteenth century, and whether it is logical or not has long been accepted.

GENT (for *Gentleman*). A vulgarism.

GENTLEMAN. 'A gentleman who looked like a commercial traveller got into the carriage.' Substitute *man*. Use the courtesy word *gentleman* only (a) for direct address, as 'Ladies and gentlemen', 'Gentlemen, you may now smoke', (b) when referring to a person in his presence: 'This gentleman wishes to see the manager'. (*Gentleman* may, however, be used of a third person who is not actually present, by a servant speaking to his master and vice versa.)

GERUND. (See -ING.)

GET. 'I should have liked to come, but I couldn't get.' Commonly heard in certain parts of the country, but not idiomatic. Say *I couldn't get there.* (See also GOT.)

GIPSY. Use this spelling in preference to *gypsy*.

GLADIOLI. Do not speak of *a gladioli*. *Gladioli* is plural; the singular is *gladiolus*.

GNAW. The past participle is *gnawed*, not *gnawn*.

GO PLACES. An Americanism, not recognised as idiomatic in the English of Great Britain. Do not use it.

GOD. (i) A capital when it means the one supreme God (Jehovah), a small letter when the reference is to a pagan god, and when the word is prefixed to the name of such a god, e.g. *the god Neptune*. *Goddess* always has a small *g*.
   (ii) A small letter for *godfather*, *godson*, *godparents*, etc. Also for *godfearing*, *godforsaken*, *godless*, *godliness*, *a godsend*.

GOLD (Adjective): GOLDEN. *Gold* when the meaning is 'made of gold' (*a gold watch*, *a gold ring*, *gold coins*). *Golden* was formerly used in this sense also, but it is now archaic, though it is preserved in a few traditional phrases, like 'the goose that lays the golden eggs'.
   In modern usage *golden* is restricted to (i) colour: *golden hair*, *the golden corn*, *the golden tints of autumn*, (ii) figurative use: *a golden opportunity*, *the golden age*, *golden opinions*, *a golden wedding*.

GOODBYE. Many dictionaries, and *R.C.R.*, hyphenate the word, but it is commonly written as one, and this spelling is recommended.

GOT. The indiscriminate banning of *have got* (in place of *have*) is absurd and pedantic. It has its place in spoken English, and is often useful for purposes of emphasis. 'We've got to do it' is more forceful than 'We have to do it', and 'I've got a present for you' is more natural than 'I have a present for you'. On the other hand, 'How many brothers and sisters have you?' is to be preferred to 'How many brothers and sisters have you got?'. The use or non-use of *got* may well be left to the good taste and linguistic sense of the individual.

GOTTEN. Quite common in American English as the past participle of *get*, but in British usage confined to the one phrase *ill-gotten gains/wealth*. Apart from this, use *got*.

GUESS. *I guess*, in the sense of *I should think*, though used by Chaucer, is now recognised only in American English.

H

HABITUAL. Though the *h* is sounded, *an* is usually used as the indefinite article (*an habitual action*).

HALF. (i) A singular verb for amount or quantity, a plural one for number : 'Half of the land is cultivated', 'Half of the apples are bad'.

(ii) Half a dozen, half an hour, half a pound, etc. (no hyphens), *but* a half-dozen, a half-hour, a half-pound (hyphenated). [cf. old currency: half a crown, a half-crown (12½p.).]

(iii) 'The bottle was half empty' (and similarly for other adjectives), but 'a half-empty bottle'.

(iv) 'I half expected this would happen', 'We half promised to go' (no hyphen); but if the two words form a compound expressing a single notion, then a hyphen must be used : e.g. *to half-baptise a child, to half-sole shoes*.

(v) 'The centaur was half man, half beast' (no hyphens).

(vi) No hyphen in *halfway, half past* (*six*), but hyphens for *half-day, half-holiday, half-hearted, half-pay, half-price, half-term, half-time, half-truth, half-wit, half-witted, half-yearly*.

(vii) *Cut in half.* Logically it should be *cut in halves*, and it is perhaps better to use this, but *in half* is accepted.

HALFPENNY. In standard usage the adjective from *twopence-halfpenny* is *twopenny-halfpenny* (*a twopenny-halfpenny stamp*); similarly *fourpenny-halfpenny, sixpenny-halfpenny*, etc. 'A twopence-halfpenny stamp' is regional usage.

HAND. On the misuse of *on the other hand*, see OTHER.

HANG. When death by hanging is meant, the past tense and past particle are *hanged* : in all other senses *hung*.

HAPPEN. If it has a personal subject *happen* must be followed either by an infinitive ('I happened to overhear what he said') or by *on* ('I happened on the very thing I wanted'). Sentences of the type *He happened an accident*, though heard in some parts of the country, are unidiomatic in Standard English.

HARDLY. (i) As an adverb of degree, *hardly* takes *when*, not *than* : 'He had hardly recovered from influenza, *when* he developed measles' (not *than he developed measles*). The alternatives are *no sooner . . . than — hardly . . . when*.

(ii) Speak of *hard-earned money, hard-won rights*, etc., not *hardly-earned* and *hardly-won*.

HAVE (Passive Voice). Except when *have* means 'obtain' ('It can be had for the asking') and, colloquially, 'deceive' ('You have been had over that bargain'), the passive voice is not generally used. 'A good time was had by all' is so obviously un-English that it should never be used outside facetious contexts.

HAVE/HAD as auxiliary verbs. See under PERFECT TENSES.

HAVE ONE DO SOMETHING. In the sense of 'get one to do something' ('I'll have the joiner mend this desk') American idiom, not British; but sentences like 'My wife would have me buy that television set' (with stress on *would*) and 'I won't have him criticise my work' are quite acceptable British idiom. In the former *have* means *insist on*, in the latter *allow to*.

In the passive voice, only the participle is expressed, not the infinitive auxiliary: ' I won't have it said that . . .' (not 'I won't have it be said').

HAVE/DO HAVE (in interrogative and negative sentences). An American will ask, 'Do you have any brothers or sisters ?', and receive the reply, 'I don't have any sisters, but I have two brothers'. Though this has recently begun to appear in the speech of some English people, it is not yet recognised as British usage.

The position may be summarised as follows :

(i) *Present Tense.* In British English, when *have* denotes possession or some notion closely akin to it, in interrogative and negative sentences the form with *do* is used for (a) what is general, recurrent or habitual, and (b) what is common to a whole class or species. When the reference is to one particular occasion (a strict present) the plain *have* or *haven't* must be used, without *do*. 'Have you indigestion?' (at this moment), 'Do you have indigestion ?' (generally, though not necessarily now). 'I haven't indigestion now' (at this moment, though I may still be subject to it), 'I don't have indigestion now' (a general statement applying to a long period of time, *now* being contrasted with *formerly*, when I used to have it). 'Does a dog have a keen sense of hearing ?' (*a dog* standing for the whole species), but 'Has your dog a keen sense of hearing ?' (one particular dog). Even when actually the whole species is meant we may say 'Has a dog, etc.?', thinking of each dog individually rather than of a typical one generically; but *do* (*does*) *have* cannot be used if the reference is clearly to a specific one or specific ones.

The same applies to *have* followed by the infinitive, to express obligation: 'When have you to be at the office?' (on a particular occasion), 'When do you have to be at the office?' (as a general rule). 'We haven't to go to school on Saturday' (this coming Saturday only), 'We don't have to go to school on Saturday' (the general rule).

(ii) *Past Tense.* The same principle applies to the past tense as to the present, but the position is rather more complicated, first because a distinction must be made between what we may call a 'real' past (like 'He had only thirty pence in his possession,' 'We had half an hour to spare') and a past tense used in indirect speech (often the conversion of a present, as 'He said he had half an hour to spare'), and secondly because, since a past event or situation is looked at from a point of time subsequent to it, as a present event or situation cannot be, it is possible to regard it either in isolation, or within the setting, and as part, of a larger past. So we may say 'Mr Jones called at the office this afternoon, but I hadn't time to see him' (the situation at a particular moment, when he called), or 'I didn't have time to see him' (during the whole period he was there). Cf. the distinction pointed out above between 'I haven't indigestion now' (at a particular moment) and 'I don't have indigestion now' (over a period of time up to the present moment). And similarly we may ask 'Had you an opportunity of calling on the Joneses while you were in Oxford?' (the opportunity thought of in isolation, as something that might arise at some particular point of time during the period) or 'Did you have an opportunity?' (the period thought of in its entirety, as containing many occasions each of which might have been an opportunity). If, however, any word in the sentence or context makes it clear that a specific moment or occasion is intended, and not a more extended period, then *did have* cannot be used. 'He called at three o'clock, but I hadn't time to see him then, so I asked him to come back in an hour's time.'

In indirect speech *had* (not *did have*) must be used if it presupposes *have* (not *do have*) in the direct form. The following, from a *Times* report of an inquiry into a railway accident, is therefore incorrect: 'The guard asked the chef for a large potato, to which to attach a message to throw out at the next signal box. The chef replied that he *didn't have* a potato.' The direct form would be 'I haven't a potato'; the indirect should therefore be 'he hadn't a potato'.

(iii) *Other Meanings of 'Have'.* As was stated at the beginning, the above remarks apply only when *have* denotes possession or some notion akin to it. When it means 'receive', 'suffer', 'indulge in', 'partake of', 'cause to be', etc., it follows the pattern of most other normal verbs. In the present tense it uses the continuous form for a specific occasion ('Are you having your dinner?', 'Is John having a bath?'), and *do have* for the general, habitual or recurrent ('When do you have dinner?', 'We don't have breakfast until nine o'clock on Sundays'). In the past tense *did have* may be used for both the general and the specific ('Did you have a bath this morning?', 'When I was a boy we didn't have lessons on Wednesday afternoons').

Note the difference between 'We hadn't anything to eat' (= we had no food in our possession) and 'We didn't have anything to eat' (= we did not partake of any food).

A fairly sound rule of thumb is as follows: if the meaning of *have* in a particular sentence could be conveyed colloquially by *have got*, then, for the negative or interrogative, use plain *have/have not*: *Do (not) have* is unidiomatic in such cases. E.g. Have you (got) any brothers or sisters? Have you (got) indigestion? I haven't (got) any money. The guard said he hadn't (got) a potato.

HAVER. A Scottish word meaning 'to talk nonsense', not, as many English people seem to think, 'to beat about the bush' or 'to hesitate'. Perhaps the incorrect use has been suggested by association with *hover* and *waver*.

HE OR SHE. Use *he* as common gender, unless it is really necessary that both sexes should be specified. Cf. *His or Her*.

HEADMASTER. Write as one word.

HELP. (i) *Help* followed by an infinitive without *to* (I helped him mend his bicycle', 'Help me lift this box'), once condemned as an Americanism, is now accepted in British English; but the *to* cannot always be omitted. We could scarcely say 'These tablets will help you sleep', or 'Writing out a poem will help you learn it'. It is never wrong to insert *to*; it can be omitted only when the 'helper' does some of the work, or shares in the activity jointly with the person that is helped. When we help a person mend his bicycle or lift a box we do some of the mending or lifting so that there is less for him to do; but the tablets do not do some of the sleeping, or writing out the poem some of the learning.

(ii) 'I could not help but laugh at what he said.' A confusion of two constructions: (a) 'I could not but laugh' (now somewhat archaic), and (b) 'I could not help laughing'. Use the latter.

(iii) 'I shan't stay longer than I can help.' Illogical, since it should be 'than I can't help', but no-one ever says this. The illogical is accepted idiom and may therefore be considered correct. Similarly with 'unless I can help it' ('I shan't stay until that late hour, unless I can help it'), though here the illogicality can be avoided by using *if I can help it*.

HERS. No apostrophe.

HIGH: HIGHLY. Where altitude or position is in question, the adverb is *high*: 'The eagle soared high into the sky'. 'By middle age he had risen high in his profession.' *Highly* means 'to a high degree'.

Generally, adjectives take *highly* (a highly desirable residence, a highly infectious disease, a highly controversial question); so do participles when the sense is that of degree or extent (a highly qualified person, a highly praised achievement, highly seasoned food). Note also *highly placed officials, highly paid workers*, but *a high-born person, high-sounding words* (i.e. a person born to a high social position and words that sound high), *a high-pitched voice, note, roof*, etc.

In compounds which are really 'group conversions' the pre-fixed word is *high*. Thus goods for which a high price is charged are 'high-priced goods', not *highly priced*, a chair with a high back is 'a high-backed chair', and shoes with high heels 'high-heeled shoes'. 'High-rated property' is property on which the rates are high; 'highly rated property' is property which is rated (i.e. esteemed) beyond most of its kind.

HIGH: TALL. See TALL.

HIS OR HER. Use *his* as common gender unless there is any real necessity to make the distinction: 'Each member has paid his subscription' — not 'his or her'. It is true, we could not say 'Every man and woman must play his part'. Here *his or her* can be justified, but even so, it is an awkward construction, and it would be better to recast the sentence to avoid it.

HISTORIC: HISTORICAL. *Historical* = concerned with history (a historical novel, a historical society, a historical account) or having an actual existence in history ('Many people doubt whether Robin Hood was a historical character'). *Historic* = having a long history attached to it ('Historic cities such as York and Chester', 'A fund for the preservation of historic buildings') or such as will go down in history (a historic document, a historic occasion, a historic trial).

HOARD : HORDE. An election address once prophesied 'hoards of government inspectors' if a certain party were returned to power. It was, perhaps, a printer's error, but it serves to illustrate the difference of meaning between two words that are sometimes carelessly confused. A *hoard* is a secret store or pile : *a horde* is, strictly, a large migratory tribe of savages, but in everyday English the word is more often used (always in a derogatory sense) of large crowds or numbers of any kind of persons (hordes of inspectors, trippers, ramblers, football fans, etc.). It should not be used of non-personal things, as 'hordes of official forms' or 'hordes of begging letters'.

HOME: AT HOME. *Stay home, keep a person home* are not accepted idiom. We go home, come home, arrive home, get home, and take, send or bring someone (or something) home ; but we stay *at* home, live at home, work at home, and keep a person, goods or money at home. *Home* is an adverb denoting destination, *at home* is an adverb phrase, in which the word *home* itself is a noun, and denotes locality. 'He is not at home' = he is not in the house. 'He is not yet home' = he has not yet arrived back from work, an outing, his holiday, etc.

HOPE. (i) As a verb, *hope* may be followed by an infinitive, either active or passive, referring back to the subject ('I hope to see him on Monday', 'She hoped to be given an opportunity of expressing her views'), but it cannot take an accusative + infinitive construction. We cannot say 'They hoped her to be selected for the post', or 'We all hope the scheme to succeed'. Amend to 'They hoped that she would be selected', or 'We all hope that the scheme will succeed.'

(ii) *Hope for* can be used in either the active or the passive voice ('We hope for an improvement', 'An improvement is hoped for', 'The reforms have not achieved all that was hoped for'), but *hope* can be used in the passive, only when the subject is the impersonal *it* with an infinitive or a noun clause in apposition : 'It is hoped that members will pay their subscriptions promptly', 'It was hoped that the reconstruction of the premises would be completed before Christmas', 'It is hoped to have the full details ready in time for the next meeting'. The following, however, are incorrect: 'The work is hoped to be finished this week', 'He is hoped to make a full recovery'.

There is an apparent exception in such a sentence as 'The economic situation has not improved to the extent that was hoped'. This is quite idiomatic, but it is an ellipsis of 'to the extent that it was hoped it would'. Actually, therefore, it is not an exception.

(iii) As a noun, *hope* may sometimes be followed by an infinitive in apposition, but the construction is better avoided. *Of* + the gerund is to be preferred: e.g. 'my hope of winning a scholarship to Oxford' rather than 'my hope to win a scholarship to Oxford'. There is no objection to 'It is my hope to win a scholarship to Oxford', but here the infinitive is in apposition to *it*, not to *hope*.

The plural *hopes* must always take a gerund, never an infinitive: 'The Labour Party's hopes of winning the next election' — not *to win the next election*. Even with the singular *hope*, only the gerund is possible when the word means 'chance', 'likelihood': 'He hasn't much hope of realising his ambition'. The infinitive can be used (if it is used at all), only when *hope* denotes desire or aspiration.

HOW. 'I shall never forget how that fellow cheated us.' 'He told me how his father had once been a wealthy man.' 'She reminded me how I had once said that one could be quite happy without money.' Sentences of this type are quite idiomatic English. Perhaps the best-known example from literature is that from the opening of Milton's sonnet on his blindness:

When I consider how my light is spent,
Ere half my days in this dark world and wide.

Very often *that* would be equally acceptable from a purely grammatical point of view, but *how* expresses a stronger element of feeling. It must not, of course, be confused with *how* which expresses method or means, and if there is any possibility that, in a particular sentence, it will be so confused, then it should be avoided. For instance, 'He told me how he had made over a thousand pounds in a few days' might mean simply that he told me that he *had* made that amount, or it might mean that he told me the way in which he had made it.

HOWEVER: HOW EVER. (i) Use one word when *ever* generalises ('However we do it, it will be a difficult job') or when it means *nevertheless* or *in spite of that* ('That, however, is another story'). If *ever* emphasises, then two words should be written

('How ever we are going to do it I do not know', 'How ever did you get your clothes in that mess?'). (See also under EVER.)

(ii) When *however* is used as a conjunctive or a disjunctive adverb, to contrast one statement with another, it needs a comma to separate it from the rest of the sentence, and two if it occurs parenthetically within the sentence: 'However, we need not discuss that now'. 'We need not discuss that now, however.' 'His friends, however, had other ideas.'

(iii) Disjunctive *however* means very much the same as *but*; the two, therefore, should not be used together, as they are in such a sentence as 'But that, however, can be left over till the next meeting'. Either *but* or *however* is redundant. (See BUT.) *However* may be correctly preceded by *but* when it is a generalising adverb of manner or degree: 'But however you do it, you will find it a difficult task'. 'But however hard he tried, he could not succeed.'

HUMANS. Do not use this word if it can possibly be replaced by *human beings*, *persons*, *people*, or *men*, as it usually can. It may occasionally be excusable, when a contrast with animals is implied, but even then it can often be avoided. Can one imagine Doctor Johnson saying that oats were eaten by horses in England and humans in Scotland?

HUMBLE BEE. The correct name is *bumble bee*.

HYPHEN. If there is any doubt whether a particular combination should be written as two words, one word, or with a hyphen, consult a dictionary. If one word is possible, that is to be preferred (e.g. *teaspoon* rather than *tea spoon* or *tea-spoon*, *today* and *tomorrow* rather than *to-day* and *to-morrow*). If the choice lies between two words and a hyphen, then choose the two words provided it does not violate sense or lead to ambiguity. In other words, dispense with the hyphen whenever possible. There are, however, certain cases where it must be used, or where it is advisable to use it; there are others where it should not be used. The following is intended as a guide.

(i) With prefixes, the hyphen is used chiefly in what we may call recent, temporary or nonce compounds (*ex-soldier*, *sub-let*, *non-intervention*, *anti-vivisectionist*). In long-established compounds the two elements have coalesced, but even with a few of these the hyphen is used if its absence would lead to an unnatural or unsightly duplication of letters: e.g. *co-operate*, *re-employ*, *mis-shapen*.

Re- may be hyphenated, even in compounds which are

normally written as one word, if it is used to denote repetition (e.g. *to assure and re-assure a person, to write and re-write a letter*). It should also be hyphenated, of course, when omission of the hyphen would lead to confusion with another word : e.g. *re-cover, re-form, re-act*, as against *recover, reform, react*.

A hyphen is also necessary when a prefix is attached to a noun or adjective which is spelt with a capital letter : *pro-German, anti-Catholic, non-Christian, un-English*.

(ii) When a hyphenated prefix requires a further prefix (e.g. the negative *un-* placed before *co-operative* or *co-ordinated*) how are we to write it ? Two hyphens are impossible, *unco-operative* looks like a Scottish expression for 'hard-working', and *un-cooperative* suggests a connexion with *cooper*. Use the diaeresis, and write *un-coöperative, un-coördinated*.

(iii) Where a phrase or expression consisting of two or more words is used as a compound adjective, the words must be joined by hyphens : *bread-and-butter considerations, a beggar-my-neighbour policy, a take-it-or-leave-it attitude*.

(iv) When an adverb modifies an adjective or participle, whether used attributively or predicatively, normally no hyphen is necessary (*a tastefully furnished house, a badly behaved child, an incredibly foolish act*), but with combinations like *well-known, well-designed, ill-behaved, wide-open*, where the first element might not at once be recognised as an adverb, a hyphen is necessary for the attributive function, but no hyphen is used when the pair are employed predicatively : *a well-known fact, a well-acted play, a well-designed house, an ill-behaved boy, a wide-open window*, but *This fact is well known, The play was well acted, The window was wide open*.

(v) Adjective-participle combinations like *hard-boiled, new-born, fresh-ground* are hyphenated both attributively and predicatively (though actually not many of them are used predicatively). An adjective or participle preceded by a noun (*blood-red, red-hot, ice-cold, poverty-stricken, stage-struck*) uses the hyphen both attributively and predicatively.

(vi) Compound adjectives made from an adjective followed by a noun with *-ed* added take the hyphen (*a good-sized house, a flat-footed person, a four-wheeled vehicle, a left-handed compliment*).

(vii) Compound cardinal numbers like *twenty-one, fifty-three*, etc. are hyphenated ; so are the corresponding ordinals (*one's twenty-first birthday*). With multiples there is no hyphenation of the cardinals (*two hundred, five thousand, three score and ten*), but the ordinals have a hyphen (*the two-hundredth anniversary*). Fractions are hyphenated when they denote a single amount (*two-thirds of a mile, three-quarters of a pound*), but there is no hyphen when a specified number of separate parts is intended.

(viii) As far as possible, avoid splitting words at the end of a line, but if splitting is necessary, then (a) place the hyphen at the end of the first line, not at the beginning of the second, and (b) see that the word is so split that the part of it on the first line is recognisable as a sense unit and does not mislead the reader : thus *wonder-ing*, not *won-dering* or *wond-ering*.

(ix) Avoid the unsightly and unnatural hyphens in *schoolboys and -girls, Englishmen and -women, grandfathers and -mothers, stepsons and -daughters*. Write *schoolboys and schoolgirls* (or *girls* with the hyphen omitted, if there could be no ambiguity), *English men and women, grandfathers and grandmothers, stepsons and stepdaughters*.

I

-ICS (as *Mathematics*, *Ethics*, etc.). (See SINGULAR OR PLURAL ?)

IDEA. *In my idea* is frequently heard in some parts of the country with the meaning 'in my opinion', or 'to my mind', but it is not accepted English.

I.E.: E.G. The two are sometimes confused, though a little thought would avoid the confusion. *I.e.* stands for the Latin *id est* (that is), and should be used only when what follows is an alternative rendering, by way of explanation, of what precedes. If only *examples*, and not a full explanation, are given, then *e.g.* (*exempli gratia* = for the sake of example, or for instance) should be used. The following is thus incorrect: 'professional people, i.e. doctors and solicitors'. There are other professional people besides doctors and solicitors; these two are only examples; *e.g.* should therefore have been used.

IF: WHETHER. There is no grammatical or idiomatic objection to using *if* to introduce an indirect question in the form of a noun clause, used as the object of a verb (e.g. 'Ask him if he would like to come to the theatre with us'), though it is only possible when the noun clause follows the verb on which it depends, never when the normal order is inverted and the noun clause precedes the verb to which it is the object. It is not, however, appropriate to all verbs, and even where it is appropriate it should be avoided if ambiguity might result from its use, as in such a sentence as 'Please let me know if you intend coming', which could be construed as meaning either that you are to let me know in any case, or that if you do not intend coming you need not let me know.

Whether is always safe, but where the two are possible the tendency seems to be to use *if* when the fact in question is something which the speaker desires, or when he hopes for a positive answer, *whether* when he merely wishes to satisfy himself one way or the other, or is prepared for either answer. 'Will you see if Mr Smith has arrived yet?' suggests 'I hope he has, because I wish to see him', or 'because he should have been here long ago'. 'Will you see whether Mr Smith has arrived yet?' suggests 'It is immaterial to me whether he has or not, so long as I know'.

IGNORAMUS. Plural = *ignoramuses*. To use *ignorami* is to write oneself down an ignoramus. *Ignoramus* is not a Latin singular noun, though to the uninitiated it may look like it. It is a plural verbal form (= we do not know) which has been made into a singular noun in English, and must therefore be given an English plural.

ILL : SICK. (i) When the reference is to health, *ill* is used only predicatively ('She is/has been/feels/looks ill'). We cannot speak of 'an ill person', though there is no objection to the compound 'an ill-looking person', but *ill* here is not really used in a non-predicative capacity, since it is predicative to the participle *looking*. An 'ill-looking person' is one who looks ill.

There is one exception to the above rule, and that is the compound *ill-health*. Apart from this, the attributive use always connotes condemnation, usually of a moral character (*ill deeds, ill repute, ill manners*), and the idea of physical illness is conveyed by *sick* (e.g. *a sick man, sick leave, sick pay*). In America *sick* is also used predicatively in this sense, but apart from the expression *to go sick* this is not the practice in British English, where it suggests nausea or vomiting. (Contrast 'I feel ill' with 'I feel sick'.) We do, however, say that a person is mentally sick.

(ii) 'That a scheme so illy contrived should end in failure was not surprising' (from a monthly magazine). Except in so far as some writers, like the one quoted above, use it under a misapprehension that they are being 'correct', *illy* does not exist as an English word. *Ill* is used as both adjective and adverb : 'You have been ill advised' (not *illy advised*).

ILLEGAL : ILLEGITIMATE : ILLICIT. *Illegal* = expressly forbidden by law. *Illegitimate* = not recognised by the law, or not having the sanction of law, as 'the illegitimate use of force'. *Illicit* does not, in itself, refer to law at all; it means 'not allowed'. The implied prohibition may certainly be, and often is, prohibition by the law, as when we speak of an illicit still, or illicit diamond-buying, but it may also be prohibition by rules or regulations of one sort or another : e.g. the illicit use of a dictionary in an examination. There is no law against it, but the rules of the examining body forbid it.

It may here be pointed out that *unlawful* overlaps to a large extent with *illegal*, but it applies over a wider field. *Illegal* refers only to the law of the land, and in many cases *unlawful* may be used more or less as a synonym of it. But while things that are illegal are unlawful, all things that are unlawful are not illegal. 'Unlawful purposes' are not necessarily purposes that are forbidden by law, but purposes which have as their object the circumventing of the law, or something which the law regards as wrong. A publican who serves alcoholic liquor to anyone under the permitted age is doing something illegal, since there is a law which expressly forbids it, but a solicitor who uses a client's money to invest on his own account is making an unlawful use of it. He is not violating any particular law which forbids such use, but a court of law would condemn his action as wrong. When we go beyond the law of the land, into the fields of moral or ecclesiastical law, then *illegal* cannot be used at all: it must be *unlawful*: e.g. unlawful rites and ceremonies, unlawful passions. It is *unlawful* for a Moslem to drink wine (his religion condemns it), but it is not illegal.

IMMUNE. Usually followed by *from* or *against*. There is no definite rule, but the tendency is perhaps to use *from* to denote a general condition, without reference to a specific situation, and *against* to denote a position when a specific situation arises. *The Learner's Dictionary of Current English*, by Hornby, Gatenby and Wakefield (intended primarily for foreign students of the language) gives 'immune from small pox' and 'immune against attack'. If we say that a person's position renders him immune *from* criticism, we mean that it prevents any criticism of him being expressed; if we say that his position renders him immune *against* criticism, we mean that criticism of him is made, but it is ineffective because he is protected by his position.

O.E.D. also gives *immune to* ('to render an animal immune to the action of the more virulent anthrax bacillus'), but this is less frequent.

The verb *immunise* always takes *against*: 'to immunise a person against diphtheria'.

IMPERIAL: IMPERIOUS. In the sixteenth and early seventeenth centuries the two words seem to have been almost interchangeable. Hamlet's 'imperious Caesar' refers to Caesar's position as Emperor, not to his character. Today *imperial* = pertaining to an empire or an emperor ('the imperial crown', 'imperial aspirations'): *imperious* = overbearing, domineering ('an imperious manner').

IMPERSONATE: PERSONATE. *Impersonate* = mimic, copy, pretend to be another person, usually for purposes of entertainment. *Personate* = claim to be another person with intent to deceive, for wrongful purposes. Under the laws governing parliamentary and municipal election in England and Wales, anyone *personating* another elector is liable to heavy penalties. *Impersonate* is sometimes mistakenly used where *personate* is needed.

IMPOSSIBLE. See POSSIBLE.

IMPRACTICABLE : IMPRACTICAL. The two are some-times confused — or rather the second is sometimes used for the first. A scheme, plan, idea, etc. which cannot possibly be carried out is *impracticable* (e.g. 'At one time it was thought impracticable for man to fly'). *Impractical* means (a) not much given to practical things, as 'He is a very impractical sort of person' (though for this, in British English at least, *unpractical* is more often used), (b) which could be done, but would require far too much time or trouble, as 'an impractical suggestion'. (See *Webster's Dictionary*.)

IMPROMPTU. See EXTEMPORE.

IN : AT. We usually speak of a person living *in* a country and *in* a large town, but *at* a village or a small town. Much, however, depends on the circumstances. A visitor to a village will ask an inhabitant how long he has lived *in* the village, while con-versely anyone who thinks of Birmingham and Manchester merely as places on the map, and not as large cities, may well say that a relative or friend of his lives *at* Birmingham or Man-chester.

For houses and places of residence. In for the kind of residence (in a cottage, a mansion, a bungalow, a flat, a hotel, a caravan) : *at* for a specific one (at The Hollies, at 53 Cambridge Terrace, at the Portland Hotel).

For places of work. For the kind of place, *in* (in a shop, an office, a bank, etc.). For a specific building or commercial concern, *at* (at the Public Library, at Selfridge's). For par-ticular departments of a business, *in* (in the Accounts Depart-ment of the Electricity Board).

IN AN AFTERNOON, IN A MORNING, ETC. 'Oh, the busy work Miss Matty and I had in chasing the sunbeams, as they fell *in an afternoon* right down on this carpet through the blind-less window.'—Mrs Gaskell, *Cranford*. A regional use charac-teristic of the northern parts of England, and still commonly heard there. (Mrs Gaskell spent her girlhood in Cheshire, and all her married life in Manchester.) The Standard English idiom, to express frequency, regularity or repetition, is '*of* an afternoon', '*of* a morning', etc., but 'in *the* afternoon', 'in *the* morning'.

IN-LAW.   Plural: *mothers-in-law*, *sisters-in-law*, etc., but 'to live with one's in-laws' (the stress falling on the *in*).

IN ORDER THAT.   Never followed by *can/could* or *will/would*. The usual verb is *may/might* ('They arrived early, in order that they might get a good seat.' 'We are sending our representative to see you, in order that you may discuss the position with him'), but *shall/should* is also possible, mainly in negative clauses which express something that it is desired to avoid ('They left by a side door, in order that no-one should see them'). The infinitive, of course, is also idiomatic: e.g. 'He decided to go himself, in order to find out the truth'.

IN SO FAR.   Three words, not one.   *Insofar* is sometimes seen, but it is not recognised as a legitimate spelling.

IN TO: INTO.   (See INTO.)

INCULCATE.   'Inculcate a person *with* something' is incorrect. We inculcate something *on* (or sometimes *in*) a person.

INDEX.   Plural: *indices* (scientific and mathematical signs), *indexes* (to books, documents, etc.).

INDIFFERENT.   (i) Normally followed by *to* ('indifferent to fame, money, worldly success', etc.), but *as to* seems permissible where processes, courses of action, developments, etc. are concerned: e.g. 'I am indifferent as to the result', 'She professed herself indifferent as to the outcome of the negotiations'.

(ii) *Indifferent* in the sense of 'impartial', as in Sir Philip Sidney's line, 'The indifferent judge between the high and low', is now archaic.   In modern English 'an indifferent judge' would suggest 'a mediocre judge'.   (Cf. 'Goods of indifferent quality', and the phrase 'good, bad and indifferent'.)

INDIVIDUAL (Noun).   The only correct use is to denote one member of a group as contrasted with the group as a whole (e.g. 'The interests of the individual must sometimes be subordinated to those of the community'.   Used merely in the sense of 'a person', without any suggestion of his being one unit in a greater whole, it is always derogatory or humorous.   ('He was not the kind of individual to get abashed at the sound of his own voice.'—Joseph Conrad, *The Brute*. '"Having a ride today, sir?", asked a cadaverous, blue-chinned individual, who might have been either a groom or a horse-dealer.'—Siegfried Sassoon, *Memoirs of a Fox-Hunting Man*.) Do not speak of 'a number of individuals' if you merely mean 'a number of persons'. Do not say 'The committee consists of the following individuals', but 'of the following persons', though it is, of course, quite correct to say 'Applications should be addressed to the committee, and not to individuals', since here there is a contrast between the committee as a body, and the individual people of whom it is constituted.

INDOOR : INDOORS. *Indoors* is the adverb (*to go indoors, stay indoors*, etc.), *indoor* the adjective (*indoor games*).

INFAMOUS : NOTORIOUS. *Notorious* means 'well known for something discreditable', and in this sense is the opposite of *famous* (a notorious pirate, a notorious liar, a district notorious for its fogs). *Infamous* means 'evil' or 'wicked', though not necessarily well known on that account. It merely expresses a moral judgement, and therefore is not really an antonym of *famous* : 'an infamous scoundrel', 'an infamous deed', 'a tyrant whose name has become infamous in history'. (Cf. the noun *infamy*.)

INFER : IMPLY. 'His words seemed to infer that he thought I knew the secret.' 'What do you infer by that remark?' Both incorrect. The word required is *imply*. *Imply* means 'suggest, without actually stating', *infer* means 'read a meaning into, draw a conclusion'. 'What do you *imply* by that remark?' (What do you mean to suggest by it?) 'What are we to *infer* from that remark?' (What conclusion are we to draw from it?)

INFERNO. 'A raging (or blazing) inferno', for a fierce fire, is a journalistic cliché. Do not use it.

INFLICT. Punishment, or a heavy task, is inflicted *on* a person; a person is not *inflicted with* them. The mistake perhaps arises by confusion with *afflicted*. Sometimes, however, the confusion works the other way, and *inflicted* is used instead of *afflicted*. A person is *afflicted* (not *inflicted*) with rheumatism, blindness, etc.

INFRINGE. '. . . the development of practices which would infringe on their [the managers'] traditional prerogatives'

(Gerhard W. Ditz, *British Coal Nationalized*). Not idiomatic. *Infringe* is a transitive verb: we infringe laws, rights, prerogatives, etc., not infringe on them. The misuse has perhaps arisen by confusion with *impinge upon*.

-ING (Verbal Ending). The parts of the verb ending in *-ing* are the present participle and the gerund. Here they will be treated together. The following are the chief points to observe.

(i) Be careful to avoid the error of the unrelated (or more often the misrelated) participial phrase: e.g. '*Standing at the top of the cliff*, the people below were scarcely visible'. A participle, together with the words dependent upon it, has the force of a compound adjective, and qualifies the first noun or pronoun that follows it, in this case *the people below*. But it obviously was not the people below who were standing at the top of the cliff, though that is what the sentence says. Possible methods of correction are:

(a) Alter the first part so that it is no longer a participial phrase: 'From the top of the cliff' or 'As we stood at the top of the cliff'. Both these are adverbial, and modify *were visible*.

(b) Retain the participial phrase, but follow it up with the word to which it really refers: 'Standing at the top of the cliff, we could scarcely see the people below'.

The error is particularly liable to occur with the impersonal subjects *it* and *there*.

Having heard the evidence, it should now be possible to arrive at a decision.

(*It* (which here stands for the infinitive construction *to arrive at a decision*) has not heard the evidence. Amend to 'We should now be able to arrive', etc.)

Not being stamp-collectors, there was nothing in the exhibition to interest us.

(Correction: either *As we were not stamp-collectors* (adverb clause), or . . . *we found nothing*, etc.)

(ii) The same error may arise with the elliptical clause ('While picking raspberries a wasp stung him') or with a phrase introduced by a preposition and a gerund ('On opening the door a cloud of smoke poured out of the room'). The wasp was not picking raspberries, nor did the cloud of smoke open the door.

Corrections: (a) 'While he was picking raspberries' (complete the clause) or 'While picking raspberries, he was stung by a wasp'. (b) 'On *his* opening the door', or 'On opening the door he was met by a cloud of smoke pouring out of the room'.

(iii) Certain absolute constructions based upon a present participle (some of them elliptical in character) are however, recognised as idiomatic. They modify or depend upon no other word in the sentence.

Considering its lack of training, our team did very well.

Speaking of novels, what was the title of the one you recommended to me the other day?

Seeing it is your birthday, you may stay up an hour later tonight.

Referring to, often used (or misused) at the opening of business letters, is not one of these : e.g. 'Referring to your letter of August 3rd, the goods have been dispatched today'. This falls into Class (i).

(iv) Should one write 'I object to my son being punished for so trivial an offence', or 'my son's being punished'? 'I disapprove of schoolgirls using cosmetics', or 'of schoolgirls' using cosmetics'? Theoretically the form with the apostrophe should be used, since it is not my son that I object to, but his being punished, and not schoolgirls that I disapprove of, but their using cosmetics. In practice, however, the apostrophe is often omitted. Our advice is as follows :

(a) For personal pronouns, always use the possessive form : 'Please excuse *my* coming late' (not *me*), 'I object to *his* being punished' (not *him*), 'There is not much likelihood of *their* coming now' (not *them*), 'Do you think there is any possibility of *its* raining?' (not *it*).

(b) For the demonstrative pronouns there is no genitive or possessive form, so we must say 'There is no likelihood of *that* happening'. (*Of that's happening* would be impossible.)

(c) For singular nouns use the genitive (apostrophe) form if possible ('Please excuse John's coming late' — not *John coming*) but do not hesitate to discard it in favour of the non-genitive for the sake of euphony ('We were discussing the possibility of the house being converted into flats' — *the house's* would sound awkward and unnatural) or, in speech, if the genitive might be mistaken for a plural and so lead to misunderstanding. We may write either 'He did not like the idea of his *daughter* going out to work' or 'He did not like the idea of his *daughter's* going out to work' (though the latter is to be preferred), but in speech it might be advisable to say *daughter*, since *daughter's* might be confused with the plural *daughters*.

(d) When we come to plural nouns we have two classes to consider. First, what we may call the 'normal' plurals, i.e. those that end in -s. Here the problem is merely one of the written form, since in pronunciation there is no difference between *dogs* and *dogs'*, *boys* and *boys'*, etc. Generally speaking, the apostrophe may be omitted ('The possibility of aeroplanes colliding in the air is very remote'), though it may be advisable to use one if it removes possible ambiguity, e.g. 'Many of the difficulties have been caused by employees' living a long distance from their place of work.' To omit the apostrophe might suggest that the employees themselves had caused the trouble (i.e. the gerund might be taken for a participle). Secondly there are the special classes of plurals — those ending in -en, those which are the same as the singular (sheep, deer, etc.), and those like people, police, clergy, which are always singular in form but denote a collectivity and take a plural verb. With most of these euphony forbids the use of the genitive; it would sound wrong to speak of 'the possibility of children's damaging the exhibits', 'the danger of sheep's wandering on the highway', 'the risk of people's taking infection'.

(v) The use of the active voice where we might expect the passive (e.g. 'In the kitchen dinner was preparing.'—Hardy, The Woodlanders) is not wrong, but it requires a good deal of discrimination, and only certain verbs lend themselves to it — mainly those denoting some process or activity which is in course of performance. Except for a few traditional uses, like 'The book is reprinting/binding', 'the tonnage of craft already building', 'the film now showing at the Odeon', it is best left to the practised writer.

(vi) 'Do you want this letter typing?', 'I want this work doing immediately', 'You need your face washing' are commonly heard, even in the speech of educated people, in parts of the Midlands and the North of England, but they are incorrect. Here is an example from a letter of Winifred Holtby, printed in Selected Letters of Winifred Holtby and Vera Brittain (1960): 'Unless you want anything explaining, I will not write again about this'. In all the foregoing sentences the present participles should be replaced by the past (typed, done, washed and explained). The present participle is always active, and therefore denotes what is done by the noun it qualifies, not what is, or is to be, done to it. The mistake may have arisen by confusion with 'Your face wants (needs) washing', 'This work needs doing immediately', 'Does this letter need typing?', 'Unless anything needs explaining'. These, of course, are correct, since the -ing words here are gerunds, not participles.

INGENIOUS: INGENUOUS. Ingenious = clever: ingenuous = natural, artless, free from deceit. Thomas Gray, in the Elegy Written in a Country Churchyard, speaks of 'the blushes of ingenuous shame'.

INQUIRE, INQUIRY. (See ENQUIRE.)

INSIDE (OF). *Of* follows the noun ('The inside of the house'). It may also be used when *inside* is a pseudo-preposition denoting place, though it is better omitted: 'He parked his car just inside (of) the gate'. It should always be omitted when the reference is to time ('I shall be back inside an hour').

INST. (Short for *Instant*.) Once quite a respectable legal term, now a piece of commercial jargon for 'the present month' (e.g. 'We beg to recognise the receipt of your letter of the 25th inst.'). Use the name of the month instead.

INTO : IN TO. (i) 'Entries for the competition should be sent into the Editor by June 30th.' This, from a daily newspaper, is typical of a frequent, though careless, mistake. *Into* is a preposition introducing an adverb phrase. A person goes *into* a room, a house, a shop, etc., a child falls *into* a pond, someone who is annoyed flies *into* a temper, and a conjurer changes a handkerchief *into* a loaf of bread. In all these, and in many more constructions like them, the single word is correct. But two words (*in to*) must be written (a) when *in* is an adverb attached to the verb and *to* is a preposition introducing the phrase ('Entries should be sent in to the Editor', 'We went in to dinner'), (b) when *to* is part of an infinitive ('They went in to look at the exhibition').

(ii) Frequently *in* and *into* are both acceptable; e.g. 'He put the papers in his brief-case' or 'He put the papers into his brief-case'. 'She poured the water in the basin' or 'She poured the water into the basin'. *Into* suggests the whole process of pouring the water from one receptacle to another, or of transferring the papers from one place to another; *in* suggests merely the resultant position.

INTRIGUE. The use of this verb in the sense of 'arouse interest or curiosity' is to be discouraged. Its only legitimate meaning is 'to plot' or 'to conspire'. The use to which we are here objecting is perhaps now less common than it was twenty or thirty years ago, but is still heard, especially in the conversation of women. It probably originated from the French *intriguer*, used of the action of a person at a fancy-dress ball or a carnival who accosts another and addresses him in a disguised voice, so as to puzzle him and arouse his curiosity.

INVERSION OF VERB AND SUBJECT. (i) Inversions like *said she, replied the captain* are quite normal when they follow direct speech, but, except in verse, where they have long been recognised, they should never be used to introduce it. Sentences like *Said Mr Smith, 'We are very proud of John's achievement'* are a recent invention of popular journalism which should not be copied.

(ii) Inversion of the type *Came the war*, to denote the next occurrence in a series of events, or in a narrative, is another neologism which should be avoided. Use inversions of this kind only after adverbs like *there, then, next*.

(iii) For singular or plural verbs with inverted constructions, see under As, CASE and THAN.

INVERTED COMMAS. A. *For Speech.* (i) Use inverted commas only for direct speech, not for what is sometimes called 'substitutionary speech', i.e. speech in which the direct *form* of statements and questions is retained, but the tenses of verbs and the persons of pronouns are changed as they would be in indirect speech: *He would be interested to hear my story, he said. Would I tell it to him?* His actual words would be 'I should be interested to hear your story. Will you tell it to me?'

(ii) Transcribed speech, set down with the names of the speakers at the beginning, in the manner of a play, is not to be regarded as direct speech, and requires no inverted commas. It is on a par with a letter which has been taken down from dictation by a stenographer and then typed out.

Mr Jackson: Can we be assured that we shall have a full report as soon as the facts are available?

The Secretary: I can certainly give that assurance.

Similarly the dialogue in a play has no inverted commas.

(iii) Direct speech which is spoken by a person to himself should be given inverted commas just as if it had been spoken to someone else, but no inverted commas should be used for a verbatim report of unspoken thoughts that pass through the mind: *I am a fool, he thought, to indulge myself in such hopes.*

(iv) Though normally, as stated above, indirect speech should not be given inverted commas, it is permissible to enclose an indirect statement or question (or part of it) in inverted commas if the writer wishes to draw attention to the words used, but this should be done very rarely, and the word *that* must never be included in the quotation marks.

In France, to hold a notebook in your hand and take down the words spoken is an invaluable method of learning nothing. A French statesman said that it 'shuts your mouth while it opens your eyes.'—F. J. Mansfield, *The Complete Journalist.*

(v) Do not use inverted commas for a direct question which

merely explains a previous noun but is not actually represented as being spoken :

The question is, what are we to do ?

What is troubling the committee is, where is the money to come from ?

The question everyone was asking was, why did he do it ?

B. *For Quotations.* For a detailed treatment, see under QUOTATIONS. The following points may be noticed here as the most important.

(i) Do not use inverted commas for brief quotations of a few words which have become part of the common stock of idioms : e.g. hoist with his own petard, an itching palm, trailing clouds of glory, a man more sinned against than sinning.

(ii) For a verse quotation, use no inverted commas if it is set out in metrical form, and stands on a line of its own : but, even for a complete line of verse, inverted commas are needed if it is included as a syntactic element in a sentence.

(a) Who does not know Gray's famous *Elegy Written in a Country Churchyard,* with its opening line,

The curfew tolls the knell of parting day,

perhaps the best-known line of poetry in the English language ?

(b) 'The curfew tolls the knell of parting day' is the opening line of Gray's *Elegy.*

(c) Inverted commas are also necessary for a passage set out metrically if it happens, in a particular case, to be also direct speech ; e.g. if someone is reciting it.

Sylvia faced the audience and began :

'The curfew tolls the knell of parting day,

The lowing herd wind slowly o'er the lea.'

(iii) If a quotation consists of more than one paragraph, the quotation marks are placed at the beginning of *each* paragraph, to show that we are still continuing the quotation, but only the last paragraph has them at the end also.

C. *Other Uses.* (i) Titles of literary works, names of newspapers, magazines, etc., may be placed in inverted commas or they may be underlined (to represent italics in print) : but both methods cannot be used together. For a more detailed treatment, see under TITLES. Note, however, the following points :

(a) Original titles (i.e. titles given by an author to his own work) have no inverted commas.

(b) Inverted commas should not be used for copied (or reproduced) titles when given as items in a list or a programme.

(ii) Inverted commas (or alternatively underlining) may be used for the names of ships, aeroplanes, railway engines, etc., but not, of course, for the names of classes or types. The word *the*, when used, should be given a small letter, and not included in the inverted commas (or not italicised, if italics are used instead).

The sinking of the 'Titanic' (not 'The Titanic').

The sinking of the *Titanic* (not *The Titanic*).

(iii) For the names of houses, inns or hotels inverted commas should *not* be used: The Laurels, 21 Belvedere Road (not 'The Laurels').

(iv) Inverted commas may also denote that a word is used in irony or sarcasm, in a sense which is not its generally accepted one, or that it is a slang or a dialect term. For this last purpose, however, they should be employed only if it is felt necessary to apologise for the use of such words. Where the slang or dialect word is natural in its setting, no inverted commas should be used.

D. *Double and Single Inverted Commas.* Generally, use double inverted commas, though single ones may be more appropriate for one word or for a brief phrase where double ones would give a 'heavy' appearance.

Where one set of inverted commas occurs inside another set, as, for example, a quotation within a passage of direct speech, use the double type for the outer set and the single for the contained set: e.g. "Do you know the origin of the expression 'There are wheels within wheels'?" she asked.

(*N.B.*—This is the general practice in writing, though some publishing houses favour the reverse order in print, especially in novels where there is a great deal of dialogue. If it is necessary to use inverted commas frequently, the single type are less obtrusive than the double and for this reason they have generally been used throughout the present book.)

E. *Other Punctuation Marks with Inverted Commas.* (i) A punctuation mark normally belongs to the group of words which precedes it; hence if a group of words is enclosed within inverted commas, the punctuation mark with which the group ends goes in along with it. Notice, for example, the position of the comma, full stop and question mark in the following sentences.

'If you don't mind,' she remarked, 'I should like that window closed.'

'Could you come on Tuesday?' he inquired.

(ii) If a sentence ends with a quotation or a title written in inverted commas, then the final punctuation mark goes inside the inverted commas only if it is part of the title or quotation; if it belongs to the sentence as a whole it must go outside.

She was reading a novel entitled 'Who Killed the Marquis?'

Who said 'Reading maketh a full man'?

(iii) If a sentence of direct speech is a question enclosed in double inverted commas, but ends with quoted words (in single inverted commas) which are not themselves a question, then the question mark must go between the single and the double quotation marks.

"Did he say, 'I refuse to do it'?" asked the magistrate.

(iv) A sentence does not have two punctuation marks at the end. If it finishes with a contained quotation or title which needs a question mark, no full stop follows if the sentence as a whole is a statement, and no further question mark if it is a question.

Have you ever read 'Who Killed the Marquis?'

(v) When a sentence of direct speech is broken for the insertion of *he said, she replied,* etc., the inserted words are treated as a parenthesis and are preceded and followed by a comma; but when a quotation is included in a sentence, and placed in inverted commas, no comma separates it from the rest of the sentence unless the normal syntax of the sentence requires one.

'The great unwashed' was a term used by Burke to describe the lower orders of England.

F. *Abuse or Misuse of Inverted Commas.* Some misuses of inverted commas have already been mentioned under various headings above. Two others, in a class by themselves, remain to be noticed.

(i) The placing of what a writer feels to be important or key words in inverted commas. We may, perhaps, regard with incredulous amusement the parent who wrote to his son's form-master:

Will you please excuse John's absence from 'school' on Friday? He was suffering from 'toothache' and it become so bad that my 'wife' had to take him to a 'dentist'.

But he is in no worse case than the correspondent of the *Inquirer* (February 3rd, 1951) who wrote to the Editor:

Sir,—It is now more than twenty-five years since I was 'converted' to 'Unitarianism'. I have since learned much of the strength and weakness of our 'movement'.

This wholly unjustifiable use of inverted commas inevitably suggests to the reader a certain innuendo which was far from the intention of the writer.

(ii) Inverted commas employed to draw attention to, and invite applause for, what is a very obvious and often a rather strained metaphor, but which the writer apparently considers a rather smart *tour de force*. The following comes from the *Star* (Sheffield) of August 2nd, 1952, and describes the Bank Holiday rush at the Sheffield railway stations.

Though the turn-out has been as big as last week's, with about 45,000 people leaving by train and coach, the railway 'officers' found few queues to discipline, and less unruly excitement in the 'ranks'. . . . 'Major battle' came this afternoon, when the 'reserve battalions' of week-enders and out-going holiday-makers clashed with the 'invading forces' of bronzed — in fact 'browned-off' — homecomers. . . . All available rolling-stock was brought into the 'front line'. . . . In only an hour 2,500 were 'evacuated' through Victoria and 3,000 through the Midland station.

In fairness it should be stated that the full report has not been quoted, so that the effect in the original was not quite so concentrated as it appears here; but it was bad enough. The labouring of the metaphor is in itself indefensible. To draw attention to it, and so force it upon the reader's notice, is to add insult to injury.

INVITE. The only legitimate use of this word is as a verb. As a noun, in the sense of *invitation*, it is a vulgarism.

-ISE, -IZE (Verbal Endings). Is it not about time we established a uniform spelling for verbs with these endings? At present it is a matter of etymology, with the result that the ordinary writer of English, who cannot be expected to know the derivation of every verb he uses, is puzzled by the system and has constantly to consult a dictionary. Since some words (e.g. *advise, advertise, exercise, improvise, compromise*) must be spelt *-ise*, there seems to be a good case for spelling them all in this way, at least in writing. Where printed matter is concerned it might well be left to the printer to settle the question in conformity with the rules of his house, or with those of the publishers for whom he is producing the work.

ISSUE WITH. Since it is so common in the services, the expression 'to issue people with things' has now become accepted in everyday English (e.g. 'All the students were issued with two notebooks each'). It is, however, better avoided. Notebooks are *issued to* students: students are *provided with* notebooks.

ITALICS. (i) Strictly speaking, since the word is an adjective (short for *italic type*) we should say that a word is printed in *italic* (cf. *roman*, *gothic*), but *italics* has become accepted.

(ii) In print italics are used for titles of literary and musical works, and for names of newspapers and periodicals (see under TITLES for details); for the proper names of ships, aeroplanes, etc.; for foreign words and expressions which have not been fully adopted into the English language; occasionally to emphasise a word or draw special attention to it (though this should be resorted to very rarely); and to denote a word as distinct from the thing the word stands for:

A book was lying on the table.

In the above sentence *book* and *table* are both nouns.

In longhand and typewritten material underlining is the equivalent of italics in print. *R.C.R.* gives long lists of foreign words and expressions that should and should not be printed in italics (i.e. underlined in writing). Those in commoner use that should not be italicised are as follows: aide-de-camp, aurora borealis, beau idéal, bizarre, bona fide, bric-à-brac, café, canard, chargé d'affaires, cliché, communiqué, confrère, contretemps, cortège, crêpe, cul-de-sac, débâcle, debris, début, débutant(e), dénouement, depot, detour, dilettante, dramatis personae, éclat, ennui, ensemble, entourage, entrée, fête, flair, hors-d'oeuvre, innuendo, levee, literati, matinée, mêlée, menu, milieu, motif, naïve, nuance, papier mâché, parvenu, passepartout, per annum, per cent, plebiscite, post-mortem (noun), précis, prima facie, protégé, régime, résumé, rôle, sang-froid, savant, seance, soirée, suède, terra firma, tête-à-tête, verbatim, versus, via, vice versa, volte-face.

Those in commoner use that should be italicised (underlined) are: *ad hoc, ad nauseam, a fortiori, amour propre, ancien régime, a priori, au revoir, bête noire, billet doux, bonhomie, bon mot, bourgeoisie, carte blanche, casus belli, chef d'œuvre, coup d'état, coup de grâce, démarche, de rigueur, déshabillé, double entente (entendre), élan, élite, en bloc, en masse, en route, esprit de corps, ex cathedra, ex officio, ex parte, fait accompli, habitué, hors de combat, in camera, laissez-faire, lèse-majesté, ménage, mise en scène, modus vivendi, multum in parvo, naïveté, née, nem. con., noblesse oblige, par excellence, pari passu, per capita, per se, pièce de résistance, post mortem (adverb), pro rata, pro tempore, raison d'être, rapprochement, sine die, sine qua non, sotto voce, tour de force, ultra vires, vis-à-vis.*

ITEMIZE. An ugly word which should be, and usually can be, avoided.

ITS: IT'S. There is no apostrophe in the possessive *its. It's* is short for *it is* or *it has.*

J

JACOBEAN : JACOBITE. *Jacobite* : a name given in the eighteenth century to supporters of the exiled descendants of King James II, particularly to those who regarded the Old and the Young Pretender as the lawful claimants to the throne of England. *Jacobean* = pertaining to the period of King James (usually James I). Speak of the Jacobite rebellion, a Jacobite plot, a Jacobite song, etc., but Jacobean furniture, a Jacobean style of architecture.

JARGON. Strictly speaking, jargon is the specialised vocabulary of a particular trade, professional, academic or other group which is introduced into everyday English, where it is out of place. It has come to be used also in the sense of the mechanical, unimaginative copying of clichés, circumlocutions, etc., in place of simpler and more direct language. Any writer who has a regard for style and sincerity of expression will avoid it. We may distinguish five main types of jargon :

(i) The substitution of a high-sounding or 'fancy' term for a very plain or ordinary word : operative (for workman), meat purveyor (for butcher), medical adviser (for doctor).

(ii) The pointless use of a conventional adjective : practical chimney sweep (What is a theoretical chimney sweep ?), a select dance (though anyone who cares to buy a ticket may attend), under active consideration (Is there such a thing as passive consideration ?), exclusive fashions (usually this means 'snobbishly expensive'), a grand concert.

(iii) The use as clichés of academic or technical expressions : the psychological moment, a vicious circle. (Incidentally, both of these are used in the wrong sense.)

(iv) Phrases from literature and elsewhere, used slavishly and often wrongly : the inner man (the stomach), an aching void (hunger), a movable feast (a meal which is not rigidly fixed to time). None of these is the correct meaning.

(v) Circumlocutions : the lower income brackets, to sustain injuries, partake of a meal, be made the recipient of a gift.

These are only a few examples. Others will be found at various places throughout this book.

JEWELLERY : JEWELRY. Both spellings are accepted, though the former is to be preferred.

K

KENT (Adjective): **KENTISH.** The usual adjective is *Kentish*: 'the Kentish dialect', 'a Kentish village', 'Kentish hops', 'Kentish cherries', 'Kentish fire' (slow, measured clapping). But we say the Kent County Council, the Kent Education Committee, the Kent County Cricket team (that which represents Kent), and possibly also the Kent coast and the Kent countryside, though for these last two *Kentish* is also possible, and is perhaps to be preferred. It is difficult to find any clear-cut system behind the use of one word or the other, but perhaps *Kent* is felt to suggest a closer attachment to, or identification with, the county than does *Kentish*.

KENTISHMAN: MAN OF KENT. A traditional distinction, a Kentishman being born west of the Medway, and a Man of Kent east of it; but in everyday English any native of Kent may be referred to as a Kentishman, and most of them would so refer to themselves, though the county association is known as the Association of Kentishmen and Men of Kent.

KIND. (i) The construction 'Those kind of people', 'These kind of chocolates', where we have a plural demonstrative adjective qualifying a singular noun (*kind*) is often heard in speech, and we should perhaps be tolerant of it as a colloquialism, but it is best excluded from written English. The alternatives are 'That kind of person', 'This kind of chocolates', and 'People of that kind', 'Chocolates of this kind'. Incidentally we may notice that 'This kind of chocolates' may refer to the make or brand, whereas 'Chocolates of this kind' refers to some characteristic or quality of them. (*N.B.* — The same observations apply to *Sort*.)

(ii) Fowler (*M.E.U.*) condemns 'What kind of trees are those?' as grammatically incorrect, contending that it should be 'What kind of tree are those?' But should it? If we can say 'We have only this kind of biscuits' and ask 'What kind of cigarettes do you smoke?' there seems no objection to 'What kind of trees are those?' The belief that since it is singular, *kind* must always be followed by a singular noun is not borne out by usage.

(iii) Some people also object to *what kind of a* + noun, contending that the article should not be used; but there is a difference. 'What kind of workman is he?' enquires about his trade or occupation. 'What kind of *a* workman is he?' inquires about his proficiency or capability. Similarly: 'What kind of doctor is he?' (a doctor of medicine, science, philosophy?): 'What kind of *a* doctor is he?' (what are his capabilities as a doctor?). 'What kind of holiday did you have?' (camping, touring, by the seaside?): 'What kind of *a* holiday did you have?' (how did you enjoy it?).

(iv) *All kind of things* is often heard in speech, but is not accepted idiom. Amend to 'all kinds of things'.

(v) 'She kind of giggled.' Accepted colloquially, but not to be used in literary English.

KINDLY. (i) What is the difference between *kind* and *kindly* as adjectives? *Kind* = characterised by kindness in itself (a kind thought, a kind deed, a very kind person, i.e. one from whom others experience kindness). *Kindly* = prompted by kindness, or indicative of kindness (a kindly smile, a kindly thought, a woman of a kindly nature).

(ii) As an adverb, *kindly* corresponds to the adjective *kind*; one who does a kind action acts kindly. The adjective *kindly* has no adverbial counterpart. We must say *in a kindly manner* or *in a kindly way*, not *kindlily*.

(iii) 'You are kindly requested to close the door behind you.' Incorrect. The request is not kind, though compliance with it would be. 'Kindly close the door behind you' or 'Please close the door behind you' would be shorter, just as courteous, and more grammatical. Why is it that those who draw up notices of this kind think that a circumlocutory manner is more polite than a simple and direct one? If 'No Smoking' is felt to be rather curt, 'Please do not smoke' is every whit as courteous as 'Patrons are earnestly requested to refrain from smoking', and only half the length.

KNIT. When the reference is to knitting garments, either on knitting needles or by a knitting machine, the past tense and the past participle are *knitted*. ('She knitted her husband's socks', 'She has knitted herself a cardigan', 'This garment is badly knitted'.) In all other senses both past tense and past participle are usually *knit*. ('He knit his brows', 'The ends of the rope were knit together', 'A play with a well-knit plot'.)

KNOT (Unit of speed). A knot is one nautical mile an hour. A ship therefore travels at so many knots, not so many knots an hour.

KORAN. There are other spellings, but this is the one recommended in English. Do not use inverted commas or italics.

L

LACK: ABSENCE. 'The poem [Wordsworth's *The Forsaken Indian Woman*] is the more affecting because of the lack of all false sentiment.'—From a student's essay. Incorrect. The word required is *absence*, not *lack*. *Lack* means absence or insufficiency of something necessary or desirable, as 'lack of time', 'lack of money', 'lack of food'. We may speak of a person's lack of manners, experience, intelligence, etc., but not of his lack of nervousness, affectation or self-consciousness.

LADEN. See LOADED.

LADY: WOMAN. For the mere indication of sex use *woman*: woman teacher, woman doctor, women students, women writers. Apart from its use to denote character or social rank, *lady* is a courtesy term, and should be employed only (i) for direct address, and then only in the plural, as *Ladies and Gentlemen* (*lady* used for this purpose is a vulgarism: the singular is *madam*), (ii) in the presence of the person concerned: 'Could you find this lady a seat, please?' 'If any lady owns this watch, will she please come forward and claim it?' A subordinate speaking to a superior, as a servant to her master or mistress, will probably refer to a visitor as a lady, not a woman — again as a matter of courtesy.

Charlady, *saleslady* and *forelady* are vulgar affectations, and *lady cat*, *lady dog* prudish euphemisms.

LAID. (i) A frequent mis-spelling is *layed*. There is no such word. Note, too, that *laid* is the past tense and the past participle of the verb *to lay* (transitive), not of *to lie* (intransitive). The latter has the past tense *lay* and the past participle *lain*. 'She laid down' is therefore incorrect. It should be 'She lay down'. (See under LAY: LIE.)

(ii) 'He was laid on the couch' (i.e. recumbent) is very common in certain parts of the country, even amongst normally well-spoken people, but Standard English does not admit this use of the past participle. Amend to 'He was lying on the couch'. 'He was laid' is correct only when the meaning is that someone placed him there.

(iii) 'Several of the hens have not laid for the last few days' is, of course, accepted idiom; so is 'Whole fields of wheat have been laid (i.e. flattened) by the wind'.

LAST. 'Last night', 'last Tuesday', 'last week', 'last month', 'last year', used adverbially, are idiomatic English, but not 'last century'. We must say 'in the last century' or 'during the last century'.

LATE. Used of a person who has relinquished an office or a position (the late Headmaster, the late Archbishop of Canterbury), *late* is not incorrect, but it is best avoided if it might suggest that the person is dead.

LATTER. (i) *The latter* should be used only for the last of two. If more than two things or persons are concerned, *the last*, or *the last mentioned* must be used, or the noun must be repeated; and *the latter* should never be used in the sense of 'the thing, or the person, just referred to' when it is the only one mentioned: e.g. 'About a quarter of a mile further on stood a large, old-fashioned house. The latter appeared to be uninhabited.' *Latter* is contrasted with *former*, and if there is no former there can be no latter. Even where two things or persons are concerned there is no point in using *the latter* if the sentence would be clear without it: e.g. 'We knocked at the door, which was opened by a rather aged butler. The latter asked us our business.' (One would hardly expect the door to make the enquiry.) 'Our attention was attracted by a small boy, accompanied by a woman who appeared to be his mother. The latter was about thirty years of age.' (There is no likelihood of our supposing it was the boy who was thirty years of age; and in any case, *she* would have been sufficient indication.)

(ii) *Latter* in the sense of 'the last few', or 'the part towards the end' is accepted in such expressions as 'the latter years of Queen Victoria's reign', 'in the latter part of his life' (i.e. in the last few years), 'the latter days of summer', 'at the latter end of the holidays' (just before the end). It is a survival of an older use which is found fairly frequently in the Authorised Version of the Bible.

'The second half of the nineteenth century' is to be preferred to 'the latter half of the nineteenth century', since *latter* is really only appropriate if a former has been mentioned, from which it is to be distinguished. 'The latter *part* of the nineteenth century', in the sense of the word given in the previous paragraph, is, of course, correct, but not 'the latter nineteenth century', for that would imply that there were two nineteenth centuries.

(iii) *Latterly* sometimes occurs as an adverb, but there is really no need for it. It conveys no more than is conveyed by *lately* or *recently*.

LAUDABLE: LAUDATORY. *Laudable* = deserving of praise (a laudable effort). *Laudatory* = bestowing praise (a very laudatory review of a book).

LAWFUL: LEGAL. There is a considerable area of usage where the two words overlap. Indeed, both *O.E.D.* and *C.O.D.* explain *legal* as meaning *lawful*, and vice versa. But there are differences, and one cannot always be replaced by the other.

Legal is always used when the sense is 'concerned with the law' or 'pertaining to the law': e.g. the legal profession, a legal point, a legal ruling, legal documents, legal proceedings. Anything which has to do with the application or administration of the law, that is to say, is denoted by *legal*.

But *legal* refers only to the law of the land. Where the moral or ecclesiastical law is concerned, *lawful* is the word: 'It is lawful for a Christian to bear arms'. 'When the wicked man turneth away from his wickedness and doeth that which is right and lawful', 'It was not considered lawful to work on the Sabbath'.

Lawful may, however, also be used when the law of the land is in question. There are the expressions 'one's lawful wife', 'to be engaged in one's lawful business', 'on all lawful occasions'. *Lawful* business and *lawful* occasions are obviously something quite different from *legal* business and *legal* occasions, while lawful purposes are not the same as legal purposes. We may say that certain forms of marriage which are recognised in some foreign countries are not legal in England, but we could scarcely say they are not lawful. *Lawful* means 'conforming with the law', or 'not violating or transgressing the law'. *Legal* means 'sanctioned by the law', 'conferred and enforceable by law', or 'expressly recognised by the law': e.g. one's legal rights, legal tender, the legal guardian of a child.

LAY: LIE. (i) *To lay* is transitive, i.e. it must have an object *to lie* is intransitive, i.e. it has no object. We advise a person to *lie down* (not to *lay down*), but we *lay down* our duties, *lay down* the law, *lay* a book on the table, *lay* a carpet, linoleum, etc., and a person who dies in battle *lays down* his life for his country.

(ii) *To lie* has the present participle *lying*, the past participle *lain*, and the past tense *lay*. (He is lying on the couch. He has lain on the couch. He lay on the couch.)

To lay has the present participle *laying*, and the past participle and past tense *laid*. (They are laying a cable under the river bed. They laid a cable under the river bed. They have laid a cable, etc.) Note the spelling: there is no word spelt *layed*.

(iii) On the regional *He was laid on the couch* (in the sense of 'was lying'), see under LAID. The same mistake occurs with *stand* ('He was stood at the door'), and *sit* ('She was sat by the fire').

(iv) 'The lie of the land', not 'the lay of the land'.

N.B.—The verb *to lie* in the sense of 'to tell a falsehood' is quite a separate word from that which is treated above. It has the present participle *lying*, and the past tense and past participle *lied*. Their use presents no difficulties.

LEAST. (i) 'Least said, soonest mended.' This is the accepted form of the proverb, though logically it should be 'Less said, sooner mended.'

(ii) *Leastwise* is obsolete, *leastways* colloquial, if not actually a vulgarism. Use *at least*.

LEAVE. (i) On *leave alone* and *leave go*, see under LET.

(ii) 'I'd as leave be dead as lead such a life as she does.' This is sometimes heard in speech and seen in writing, but it is wrong. The word required is not *leave* but *lief*, an old word connected with the verb *to love* (In *Morte d'Arthur* Tennyson has 'thou art lief and dear'). A satisfactory modern translation of 'I'd as lief' would be 'I would as soon', though actually it means 'I should love as much'.

LEG. (i) 'To give a person a leg up' and 'to leg a person over' (or 'leg him up') are accepted colloquialisms.

(ii) *Leg* in the sense of a stage of a journey, or a round of a sporting event, is a piece of journalese which is best avoided. The following example is quoted from a daily newspaper: 'The visit to the U.S. was his first leg of a trip round the world. The next leg will be Australia and India.' It is presumably taken from the idea of a stride, but what merits it has over *stage* it is difficult to see.

LESS. (i) Use *less* for quantity or amount (*less time, less money, less trouble, five pounds less*), but for number, if unqualified by a numeral word, use *fewer* (*fewer persons, fewer opportunities, fewer cars on the road*).

(ii) Some people would insist that even when preceded by a numeral *less* is incorrect for number, but this seems rather pedantic. *A few fewer, many fewer, several fewer* are obviously impossible. *We could do with a few more workers and a few less supervisors* is perfectly good English; *a few fewer* supervisors is not. Even with a definite number *less* is often to be preferred to *fewer*. It is quite natural to say 'Five more candidates entered this year than last, but three less passed', or 'Now that the children are away at school we have two less mouths to feed'; and the sentences can be defended on the ground that we are thinking of an unspecified number which is less by two or three, as the case may be, than another number, in the same way that we say that eighteen is two less than twenty (not *two fewer*).

(iii) Do not speak of *a less price* or *a less number*. Say *a lower price* and *a smaller number*. But 'The number was less than we expected' is correct, since here again we are comparing two numbers thought of as mathematical quantities.

LESSER. A double comparative form, used only attributively, in the sense of the less important, or the less serious, of two things : the lesser light, the lesser of two evils, the lesser novelists of the nineteenth century.

LEST. Followed by *should* ('They took their umbrellas lest it should rain') or by a subjunctive ('Lest we forget'), but not by *will* or *would*.

LET. (i) When used either in the sense of *allow* ('They would not let us go into the room) or with something of an imperative force in the first and third persons ('Let us pray', 'Let the evil-doer beware'), *let* is a transitive verb. If it has a double object, both object words must be in the accusative case.

Let *you and me* always strive to do our duty. (Not *you and I*.)

When the object pronoun is followed by a relative clause introduced by a nominative, there is a temptation to use a nominative for the object word also ; but it is incorrect.

Let *them* (or *those*) who make wars fight them. (Not *they who make wars*.)

(ii) 'Let those flowers alone', in the sense of 'do not interfere with', is accepted colloquially, but, except in a few traditional expressions like *let well alone*, it is better to use *leave*. On the other hand, we always say 'Let them be', never 'Leave them be'.

(iii) *Let alone* may be used in informal conversation in such sentences as 'I can scarcely afford to live in my present house, let alone in a more expensive one', but in more formal contexts *much less* should be used.

(iv) *Let go* and *leave go* are both accepted ('Don't let go until I tell you', or 'Don't leave go until I tell you'). 'He let go the rope' is, historically, the correct form, *go* being an infinitive and the whole sentence meaning 'He allowed the rope to go';

but, probably by analogy with *take hold of* (where *hold* is a noun, and therefore needs the preposition to link it to the noun that follows), the tendency is to say *let go of* and *leave go of*, and these may be considered idiomatic. The *of* is always necessary when a pronoun follows as the object : 'Don't let go of it'. Even when the object is a noun *of* is generally used after *leave go*.

LIABLE. (i) Since no-one is infallible, we are all *liable* to make mistakes, but a person who is not so careful as he should be is *apt* to make mistakes (not *liable to*). Similarly, 'apt to lose one's temper', 'apt to resent criticism', 'apt to make promises which are not fulfilled'. *Liable* really means 'bound by law'; when used of a person's character, actions or conduct, therefore, it can only be applied to characteristics which are a natural consequence of some inherent quality or of some infirmity, and for which the subject himself is not responsible.

(ii) Do not use *liable* for mere possibility or probability. 'We are liable to get fogs in November' is correct, 'We are liable to get a storm before the day is out' is not. *May have, are likely to*, or *shall probably* is required.

(iii) Perhaps insurance companies and motoring organisations are responsible for another mistake which seems to be creeping into the language — the use of *liable* and *liability* for *responsible* and *responsibility*. As used in the advice given to motorists involved in an accident — that they should say nothing which might be construed as admitting liability — the word may be defended on the grounds that it means not merely responsibility, but an obligation to pay for any damage ; but it cannot be defended if it means simply responsibility and nothing more : e.g. 'He admitted his liability for the mistake'.

LIBEL. Often used loosely in the sense of 'defamation of character', but in the strict sense libel is a defamatory statement appearing in writing or in print. It does not cover defamation by the spoken word, which is slander.

LIBERALITY : LIBERALISM. *Liberality* = generosity. *Liberalism* = a liberal outlook or policy in politics, religion, etc., or a broad, tolerant attitude of mind in matters of belief. The word should be written with a capital letter only if it refers to the Liberal Party and its doctrines. Thus write 'At the moment the future for Liberalism seems much brighter than it has done for many years' (i.e. for the Liberal Party and the principles for which it stands), but 'He always stood for liberalism in religion', 'In many countries a new spirit of liberalism is in the air.'

LICENCE: LICENSE. Like *practice* and *practise*, *prophecy* and *prophesy*, the spelling with the *c* is the noun, that with the *s* is the verb. (The key to them all is *advise* and *advice*, which no-one confuses.) *Licensed* is spelt with an *s*, not a *c*: e.g. 'Licensed to sell tobacco', 'a licensed hotel', 'I have licensed my car'. Since the adjective *unlicensed* is made up from the participle *licensed* with the negative prefix added, that too must be spelt with an *s* (e.g. 'unlicensed premises').

LIE. See *Lay*.

LIGHTED: LIT. (i) When *light* means 'come upon unex-pectedly', the past tense and past participle are usually *lighted*: 'I lighted upon just the thing I wanted'. 'I have just lighted upon the very house to suit you.' *Lit*, however, is also found.

(ii) When it has the more usual meaning of 'illuminate' or 'ignite', for the attributive function, if no adverb or other qualifying word is attached to it, *lighted* is always used (as *a lighted match*, *a lighted cigarette*), but when an adverb precedes, both *lighted* and *lit* are found. *Lit* is probably the more frequent, but sometimes the deciding factors are rhythm or euphony. Thus we should probably speak of a *badly lit street* and *a brightly lit room*, but *a brilliantly lighted shop window*.

The past tense and the past participle are, similarly, either *lighted* or *lit*, though *lit* is now the more usual.

(iii) When the sense is 'provide (a person) with light', the past tense and past participle are *lighted*: 'He lighted me down the steps with a torch'. 'We were lighted on our way by a full moon.'

(iv) *Floodlight* generally has the past tense *floodlit*. The past participle is usually *floodlit* when it forms part of a compound tense ('They have floodlit the Town Hall'. 'They suggested that the front of the cathedral should be floodlit'), but *flood-lighted* when it is felt to be a predicative adjective rather than a participle: 'The gardens will be floodlighted from 6.30 to 11 p.m.'

LIGHTENING: LIGHTNING. The spelling without the *e* is the noun (*a flash of lightning*, *a lightning conductor*), that with the *e* is the present participle and gerund of the verb *to lighten*, in whatever sense it is used: 'The driver was lightening the load on his beast'. 'A scheme for lightening the burden of taxation.' 'It has been thundering and lightening for the last half-hour.'

For the figurative use, when the sense is 'quick', 'rapid', the spelling is *lightning*, since the figure is taken from the rapidity of the lightning flash: 'to run like lightning', 'a lightning decision', 'a lightning war'.

LIKE (Verb). 'Which do you like best?' and 'Which do you like most?' are both acceptable. The former is probably the more usual when applied to things and people that we like on account of some quality they possess, so that we think of one as being better than another, the latter when the liking is more a matter of mere preference on our own part than an implied comparison between the qualities or characteristics of the things amongst which we have to choose: e.g. 'Which would you like most, to write a best-seller, to win a fortune on the football pools, or to rise to the top of your profession?'

LIKE (Pseudo-Preposition). (i) *Like you and me,* not *like you and I.* Though actually an adjective or an adverb, according to the context (it can have degrees of comparison, since we can say *more like you and me*), *like* is treated as a preposition, and pronouns that follow it must be in the accusative case.

(ii) 'Do it like I told you.' 'Please leave the room like you found it.' Both incorrect. *Like* cannot be used as a subordinating conjunction to introduce an adverb clause of manner or comparison. Use *as.*

(iii) 'I want a frock like Mary wears' is, however, correct, since it is an ellipsis of *like that which Mary wears.* The group of words introduced by *like,* that is to say, is not adverbial but adjectival. It is also permissible to use *like* instead of *as* when the words that follow it are felt to be descriptive of some characteristic or quality rather than to constitute a comparison of ways or methods: e.g. 'I can't sing like I used to'. (The reference is to the quality of the singing rather than the manner.) 'He writes just like his brother did when he was young.' (Descriptive of the style and appearance of the writing rather than the manner.)

(iv) *Like* for *as if* is a vulgarism: e.g. 'It looks like we are going to have a thunder storm'.

(v) Under the heading -ING, attention has been drawn to the error of the misrelated participle. A similar kind of mistake may occur with *like* and *unlike.* It is exemplified in the following quotation from an article on a new kind of anti-freeze for cars.

'A limited number of special compositions have appeared in the U.S. They are offered as permanent anti-freezes. . . . Unlike the corrosion inhibitors in ordinary anti-freeze, it is claimed that the special inhibitors in these products are not depleted during use.'

As it stands, the word-group 'unlike the corrosion inhibitors in ordinary anti-freeze' refers to *it*, which the writer of the article has apparently assumed denotes the new 'permanent' anti-freeze; but it does not. It is an anticipatory *it*, in apposition to the clause 'that the special inhibitors . . . during use'. The contrast is between the 'ordinary inhibitors' and the 'special inhibitors'. The sentence should therefore read, 'It is claimed that the special inhibitors in these products, unlike the corrosion inhibitors in ordinary anti-freeze, are not depleted during use'.

'Like his father, he was an agnostic' is correct. 'Like his father, he was said to be an agnostic' is also correct if it means that the father, as well as the son, was merely *said* to be an agnostic. If, on the other hand, the writer means that the father *was* an agnostic, and the son was said to be one also, then it is incorrect, and should be amended to 'either 'He was said to be an agnostic, like his father', or 'He was said to be (like his father) an agnostic'. The former is to be preferred.

(vi) 'The likes of us' is a vulgarism. If *like* must be used, use the singular (The like of us'), but better still, say 'people like us'. 'I have never seen the like of it' (but not *the likes*), is equally acceptable with 'I have never seen anything like it', though most people would probably use the latter. The plural *likes* is, of course, perfectly good English in the expression 'one's likes and dislikes'.

LIKELY. 'It will likely rain tomorrow.' 'Her train has likely been delayed by fog.' Not accepted English, either in Britain or in America. Use *probably* or *possibly*. There is no objection to *very likely*.

LIKES. (See LIKE (iv).)

LIMITED. The sense 'restricted' or 'not very great' is now accepted : *a person of limited means, rooms where space is limited.*

LIQUEFY. Note the spelling, with the medial *e*, not *i*.

LITERALLY. *Literally* is opposed to *figuratively*. It should never be used merely to give emphasis ('He literally ran down the road'), and above all it should not be attached to an expression which is obviously metaphorical. 'It literally rained cats and dogs' means that cats and dogs actually fell from the sky. Other examples : 'His eyes were literally glued to the television screen'. 'The tennis player literally wiped the court with her opponent.' 'The comedian's jokes literally brought the house down.' It is correctly used when it is employed to tell us that an expression which is generally understood metaphorically is, in this particular context, to be taken at its face value, and not metaphorically: 'I literally kicked the rude fellow out of the room'.

LOADED: LADEN. For the past tense and past participle of the verb, use *loaded*. *Laden* is an adjective meaning 'heavily burdened': *a ship laden with treasure, the smoke-laden atmosphere*. We may say that a tree is either *loaded* or *laden* with fruit. Fire-arms are *loaded*.

LOAN. *Loan* is a noun; the verb is *lend*. Do not say 'He has loaned me his typewriter', 'This book has been loaned to me by a friend'.

LOATHE: LOTH. The former is the verb, the latter the adjective. 'I loathe castor oil.' 'I was loth to do it.' (The adjective may also be spelt *loath*, but never with a final *e*.)

LOCAL. *The local* (a public house) and *the locals* (the inhabitants of a small town or village) are colloquialisms.

LOCATE. Really an unnecessary word, though if used at all it should only be in the sense of 'place', 'situate': 'It is important to locate new industries where labour will be easily available'. 'The greater part of Britain's coalfields are located in South Yorkshire, Durham and South Wales.' The use of the word as though it meant 'find' or 'discover' is to be deprecated: e.g. 'We have so far been unable to locate the fault'.

LOOK(S). (i) 'You can't judge a person by his *looks*' (i.e. his features, or his facial appearance: cf. *good looks*), but 'the *look* in one's face', 'the *look* in one's eye', etc.
    (ii) 'We are going to get a storm, by the *look* of it.' (Not 'by the *looks* of it'.) Similarly 'by the *look* of things', not 'by the *looks* of things'.
    (iii) Compounds like *good-looking, ill-looking, evil-looking, ugly-looking* must be written with a hyphen.

LORD MAYOR: LADY MAYORESS. (i) Be careful to avoid the solecism 'The Lord and Lady Mayoress'. Say 'The Lord Mayor and Lady Mayoress'.
    (ii) Plurals: Lord Mayors, Lady Mayoresses.
    (iii) The Lady Mayoress is the Lord Mayor's wife (or sometimes, if he is a widower, his daughter or other female relative). If a woman occupies the position of first citizen she is known

as the Lord Mayor, just as a man would be. Her husband has no official position.

(iv) The designation *The Right Honourable the Lord Mayor of . . .* is enjoyed by the Lord Mayors of London, York, Belfast and Dublin in the British Isles, and by those of Melbourne, Sydney, Adelaide, Brisbane, Hobart and Perth (Australia), *but not by any others*. In Scotland the Lord Provosts of Edinburgh and Glasgow are likewise entitled to the prefix *The Right Honourable*. In no case should it be placed before the personal name of the dignitary in question, as it pertains to the office, not to the person who for the time being holds it. The correct style is *The Right Honourable the Lord Mayor of X, Alderman A. B. Carter*, not *The Lord Mayor of X, The Rt. Hon. A. B. Carter*.

(Observations (ii) and (iii) apply also to *Mayor* and *Mayoress*.)

LOT(S). *A lot of* and *lots of* are treated as adjectives, equivalent in meaning to *many* or *much*, as the case may be. Any verb to which they are the grammatical subject, therefore, agrees in number, not with *lot* or *lots*, but with the noun or pronoun that follows *of*: 'A lot of money *has* been wasted'. 'A lot of people *have* been ill.' 'There *is* lots of time to spare.' 'There *are* lots of opportunities for young men in industry.'

LOUD: LOUDLY. The usual adverb when the reference is to volume of sound, is *loud*: 'Don't speak so loud', 'You played that note too loud', though we generally speak of a person snoring *loudly*, not *loud*.

Loudly is also the idiomatic word when the meaning is 'vociferously, clamantly, vehemently': e.g. 'He demanded loudly that he should be given what was due to him'.

LUXURIANT: LUXURIOUS. *Luxuriant* = growing abundantly or in profusion, and is usually applied to vegetation, foliage or hair. *Luxurious* = suggestive of costliness, extravagance, or over-indulgence: *luxurious furnishings, luxurious ways of living, a person with luxurious tastes*.

Recently *luxury* has also come to be used as an adjective, and has begun to displace *luxurious* in some of its applications. If it is used at all it had best be kept as an epithet descriptive of those things which may be considered luxuries in themselves (*luxury articles, luxury foods, luxury goods*), or which advertisers and publicists wish us to think of as such: e.g. *a luxury liner, a luxury hotel, luxury travel, luxury flats*. It can easily become a 'glamour' word, and for that reason is best avoided.

M

MAD. Margaret Nicholson (*American-English Usage*) states that the use of *mad* for *annoyed, cross* or *angry* is U.S. slang: but it is not confined to the United States, for it has long been used in that sense colloquially in Britain, and can be found so used in Shakespeare's plays: e.g. *The Merchant of Venice*, Act V, Sc. i.

> Now, in faith, Gratiano,
> You give your wife too unkind a cause of grief:
> An 'twere to me, I should be mad at it.

But the fact that Shakespeare used it does not make it acceptable as a literary term today.

MADAM. As a polite term of address for a lady, spelt without the final *e*. The abbreviated form (used only in speech, usually by a servant to her mistress) is spelt *Ma'am* and pronounced *Mam*, not *Mahm*, except for the rather disparaging *school marm*.

The French equivalent of the English *Mrs*, prefixed to a married lady's name, is spelt *Madame*, and is abbreviated to *Mme*. The plural is *Mesdames*, abbreviated to *Mmes*.

The French term *Madame* is also sometimes adopted by ladies in England, whether married or not, for professional purposes, especially by teachers of dancing, singing, music, elocution and acting.

MAJORITY. (i) *Majority* may be used only for number, not for amount or quantity. 'The majority of the eggs were bad' is correct; 'The majority of the butter was bad' is not. Similarly we cannot speak of 'the majority of the land', 'the majority of the time', 'the majority of one's wealth'. We must use *most*, or *the greater part*.

(ii) It is perhaps pedantic to object to the use of *majority* in the sense of *most*, or *almost all*. It is so used in the first of the examples given above, and there is no need to apologise for it. The use has become accepted, at least in conversational English, though it is as well to remember that *the majority* really means the greater as opposed to the smaller number. Fifty-one out of a hundred is a majority, but it is not most. When the word is given the more extended meaning it is to draw attention, by implication, to the minority to which the statement does not apply. If we are not concerned with the minority, *most* should be used. 'Most children like sweets' is a statement about children in general. 'The majority of children like sweets' reminds us that there may be some who do not. *The majority*, too, is collective, where *most* is distributive. 'Most Irish people are Catholics' thinks of those concerned individually. 'The majority of Irish people are Catholics' thinks of the individuals all together, as a group.

(iii) When *majority* means the numerical difference between the greater and the smaller figure, it is singular ('The candidate's majority was just over three thousand'). When it means the greater group thought of as a body, it is also singular ('The majority is always able to impose its will on the minority'). When it individualises within the group it is plural ('The majority of electors have already made up their minds which way they are going to vote').

MAKE-BELIEVE. So spelt, not *make-belief* ('It is all make-believe').

MAKE SHIFT. As a verb followed by its object, two words ('We must make shift with what we have'). As noun and as compound adjective, one word ('just a makeshift', 'a makeshift contrivance').

MANIKIN: MANNEQUIN. *Manikin* (only one *n*) = little man. *Mannequin* (double *n*) = a living model for the display of dresses, etc.

MANKIND. Singular number. Referred to by *it* and *its*, not *they* and *their*.

MANNER. (i) 'His manner of doing it' and 'The manner in which he did it' are both correct, but 'The manner how he did it' and 'The manner of how he did it' are not.

(ii) 'All manner of things' (where *manner* = kind) and 'by no manner of means' are both accepted English.

(iii) *Well-mannered* and *ill-mannered* are to be preferred to *good-mannered* and *bad-mannered*, though the latter pair can be defended on the ground that they are not participial compounds (there is no verb *to manner* from which a participle *mannered* could be derived), but 'block conversions' from *good manners* and *bad manners* (cf. *heavy-eyed*, *red-faced*).

MANUSCRIPT. The abbreviation is MS. (capitals, and only one stop) for the singular, and MSS. for the plural. In reading, the full word *manuscript* should always be pronounced, even though the abbreviated form is written or printed. It is not correct to say 'an emm-ess' or 'the emm-ess'. Consequently, write *a MS.*, not *an MS.* (See under ABBREVIATIONS.)

MASK : MASQUE. *Mask* = a covering or disguise for the face. *Masque* = the dramatic performance.

MASTERFUL : MASTERLY. 'He has done the work in a masterful fashion.' Incorrect. *Masterly* is required. *Masterful* means 'assertive, strong-willed, determined to be master'. *Masterly* means 'skilful, in the manner of one who is a master of his craft'. Thus 'a masterly piece of work', 'a masterly stroke', 'a masterly exposition of the subject', but 'a masterful child'.

MATHEMATICS. (i) 'Mathematics *is* an important subject.' 'His mathematics *are* weak.' 'Mathematics *was* never my strong point.' 'It comes to fifty-eight pounds, if my mathematics *are* correct.'

(ii) 'Mathematics master', 'Mathematics teacher', 'a mathematics lesson', etc. (no apostrophe). The simple noun is used attributively (cf. *history master*, *history teacher*).

MAUVE. Pronounced to rhyme with *cove.* The pronunciation with the same vowel as in *pause* is a regional one.

MAY. (i) On *may* and *can*, see under CAN.

(ii) Beware of using *may* as a past tense (e.g. 'We took our mackintoshes with us, as we thought it may rain'), a mistake which seems fairly frequent in certain parts of the country. *May* is used only as a present tense. Even when the reference is to the future it is not really a future possibility that is denoted, but a present possibility regarding the future (e.g. *It may rain tomorrow*). The past tense is *might*.

(iii) Whether we use *may* or *might* with a perfect infinitive (which itself, of course, denotes something in the past) depends on whether we think of the possibility as being a present or a past one. *He may have been injured* = in the absence of any information to the contrary the possibility still exists. *He might have been injured* = the possibility existed in the past, but exists no longer.

(iv) With a present infinitive, *might* shows a more remote possibility than *may*. 'I may be dead by this time next year' (a serious contemplation of the possibility). 'I might be dead by this time next year' (a possibility that cannot be ruled out, but not very likely).

(v) *May not*, in the sense of 'circumstances do not permit us to' ('We may not see into the future') is now archaic.

MAYBE. Written as one word and used as a synonym for *perhaps* ('Maybe I shall go, and maybe I shall not'), not recognised English idiom. Use *perhaps*. On the other hand *It may be* (two words) followed by a noun clause is quite good English. 'It may be that our letter never reached him.' The fact that Shakespeare uses *may be* (two words) for *perhaps*, does not make *maybe* (one word) good modern English.

ME. 'It's me' is recognised as idiomatic English, though *I* is generally used when followed by a relative clause introduced by *who*: 'Who's that? — It's me', but 'It is I who am to blame'.

On the use of *I* or *me* after *than*, and on *older than me, taller than me*, etc., see under THAN.

MEAN. To most British people, except perhaps the very young, who are well versed in Americanisms, to describe a person as *mean* implies that he is niggardly. In the U.S. it may also be a way of saying that he is surly, spiteful or vindictive. Perhaps it is an extension of the sense of the word in such expressions as 'a mean trick', 'to take a mean advantage of someone', both of which are perfectly good British English.

MEANS. 'His means (= monetary resources) *are* insufficient to keep him.' 'This means (= method) of transport *is* a very old one.' 'Several means (= methods) of transport *are* available to you.'

Shakespeare uses the singular *mean* for *method*, but this is now obsolete.

> No place will please me so, no mean of death,
> As here by Caesar, and by you cut off,
> The choice and master spirits of this age.
> *Julius Caesar*, Act III, Sc. i.

MEANTIME: MEANWHILE. Both are used as adverbs, though *meanwhile* is to be preferred. On the other hand, *in the meantime* is preferable to *in the meanwhile*, though the latter is not incorrect.

For *Greenwich Mean Time* write the two words separately (not *Meantime*).

MEDIAEVAL. *R.C.R.* recommends the spelling *medieval*, which consequently appears in all the publications of the Oxford

University Press, and is, of course, accepted, but the older spelling with *ae* is preferred by many people.

MEDICAL ADVISER. Usually just a piece of pompous jargon for *doctor*. Use the simpler word. (See JARGON.)

MEET. We *meet* a friend, *meet* our obligations or our debts, *meet* a deputation, and *meet* a person half way. We may also seek to *meet* someone's needs, demands or requirements, and we may modify a scheme in order to *meet* objections to it. We *meet with* an accident or a misfortune, our efforts *meet with* success, and we may ask, 'Does this suggestion *meet with* your approval?'

Meet is subjective, *meet with* objective. That is to say, the person or the thing that *meets* something or someone, is thought of merely as the agent of the meeting; the person or the thing that *meets with* something is thought of as being affected by the thing that is met, in much the same way that the object of a transitive verb is affected by the activity expressed in the verb. If a scheme meets *with* an objection, an objection is urged against it, or it encounters an objection; if it *meets* the objection, it is the objection that is affected and nullified. There is a similar distinction between *to meet with criticism* and *to meet criticism*, or *to meet with opposition* and *to meet opposition*.

Meet up with is heard very much amongst the younger generation nowadays, but it is a vulgarism, and should be avoided.

MELTED : MOLTEN. The past participle is always *melted*. *Molten* is used attributively, and then only of things which we normally think of as hard, solid substances: *molten metal*, *molten wax*, *molten candle grease*, but *melted snow*, *melted butter*.

MENACE. (Noun). The only legitimate meaning is that of 'threat', 'danger'. The recent use of the word as a synonym for *nuisance*, *annoyance* is a neologism which is not yet accepted.

MENTAL. 'He's mental' is a vulgarism. The only accepted meaning is 'pertaining to the mind': e.g. mental arithmetic, mental disturbances, to make a mental note.

MESSRS. In addresses use *Messrs* before the names of firms if they are also personal names, as *Messrs J. P. Brown & Co.*, *Messrs Freeman, Hardy & Willis, Ltd.*, but not otherwise. Do not write *Messrs The Excelsior Book Co., Ltd.*, or *Messrs The National Provincial Bank, Ltd.* A difficult point arises when a firm ha; pens to have a woman's name. For business use there is no corresponding word *Mesdames*. Should we, therefore, in the face of all logic, write *Messrs Susan Small & Co.*? In extenuation we can probably plead that *Messrs* is a merely formal prefix, which may be regarded as common gender; otherwise we had better write merely *Susan Small & Co.* (See also under Mr.)

METAPHORS.   (i) Beware of mixed metaphors.   Not many people are guilty of the more obvious kind, such as are given in so many textbooks of English composition, though the B.B.C. (March 1961) reported a Cabinet minister as saying that 'The dangerous hot-bed of war which has sprung up in Laos must be speedily extinguished'. The more common mistake is to slip from the metaphorical into the literal without realising it, so that targets are passed, raised, lowered, beaten, reached and achieved, gaps are made narrower by being cut, and a freer flow of goods is made possible by reducing bottlenecks. (See under Target, Gap, and Bottleneck.)

(ii) Avoid the temptation to 'stretch' a metaphor. It may seem clever to the writer, but to the reader it generally appears absurd. (For an example see Inverted Commas, F. (ii.).)

METER: METRE.   Meter = an instrument for measuring, as in *gas-meter* and in such combinations as *speedometer, hydrometer.* *Metre* = (i) the French unit of linear measurement, used in most continental countries, (ii) the 'measure' of verse.   The names of the various metres, according to the number of feet in the line, are, however, spelt *-meter* (hexameter, pentameter, tetrameter, etc.).

For the adjective, *metric* is used when the reference is to the metre as a unit of linear measurement (*the metric system*), *metrical* when it is to the metre of verse ('a metrical version of the Psalms').

METICULOUS.   Not a synonym for *careful, exact* or *precise*, though popular usage tends to make it so. It means over, or unnecessarily careful: 'He is most meticulous in everything he does'.

METRIC: METRICAL.   (See Meter.)

MEWS.   (A place where stables were once situated.)   Singular: 'The mews is just off Park Lane'.   When used as a common noun the word should, of course, be spelt with a small letter, but if it forms part of the name of a road or a street, as nowadays it often does in London, a capital must be used.

MIDSUMMER DAY. Note the spelling: not *Midsummer's*. But there is also *mid-summer's* (with a small letter and hyphenated). *Midsummer Day* is June 24th. A *mid-summer's day* means a day in mid-summer (i.e. the middle of summer). Cf. also 'We do not expect to get snow in mid-summer'.

MIGHT. (See MAY.)

MINIMUM: MINIMISE. (i) 'A minimum of business was transacted on the Sheffield Stock Exchange yesterday.'—*The Sheffield Telegraph*, December 23rd, 1960. Presumably what the writer meant was 'little business', but that is not what he has said. *Minimum* is a Latin superlative, meaning *least*. In English it is generally used to mean 'the smallest possible amount', which in this case would be none at all. However small the amount of business was, it was not a minimum if there might have been less. There are two respects in which a certain amount of latitude is allowable, but neither of them applies here. They are:

(a) *Minimum* may be used in the sense of 'the smallest amount possible *in the particular circumstances*': 'We will get the business cleared up with the minimum of delay'. 'The scheme of re-organisation has been so planned as to cause the minimum of dislocation in the factory.'

(b) It may also be used in the sense of 'the lowest permitted or agreed upon', as when we speak of a minimum wage, a minimum of two weeks' holiday a year, etc. The meaning here is that there may be more, but there must not be less.

The minimum temperature for a room is that below which the temperature should not be allowed to fall, but the maximum and minimum temperatures during the day, or over a period of time, as recorded by the thermometer, are the highest and the lowest that were actually reached.

(ii) 'The difficulties experienced by adults in learning a foreign language should not be minimised.'—From a well-known educational journal. But surely any teacher of any subject should seek to minimise for his pupils the difficulties of learning it, for *minimise* does not mean 'under-estimate' (the word that is required in the sentence just quoted), nor 'belittle' (as it is made to mean in such sentences as 'He always minimised the achievements of others, though he magnified his own'), nor merely 'reduce', but 'reduce to the smallest amount or number'.

And since it means this it is one of those absolute terms, like *unique* and *fundamental*, of which there cannot be degrees. A thing cannot be somewhat, partially, to some extent, or considerably minimised.

MINORITY. 'In only a minority of cases dealt with has prosecution been found necessary.'—From the report of a children's welfare organisation. Do not use the word in this way. *Minority* does not mean *few*, or *comparatively few* (i.e. few when compared with the total number of cases dealt with), but the smaller as contrasted with the larger number. Forty-nine out of a hundred is a minority. (See also MAJORITY.)

MINUS. Should be reserved for mathematical or statistical contexts. Except possibly in jocular conversation, or in writing of the lighter kind that is intended to be humorous, do not speak of 'a hat minus the brim', 'a bicycle minus the front wheel'.

MISTRUST. Not 'trust wrongly or mistakenly', but 'regard with misgiving or suspicion' ('I mistrusted his motives'). We usually *distrust* a person or his word (i.e. have no faith in them, or place no trust in them). *Mistrust* is rather more vague, suggesting an uneasy feeling that things are not what they appear, or what we should like them to be.

MOHAMMEDAN. This spelling is to be preferred to *Mahometan*, but it is better to use *Moslem* for the people, and *Islam* for the faith. To most Moslems the words *Mohammedan* and *Mohammedanism* are offensive, since they suggest worship of the Prophet, which their religion strictly forbids.

MOMENTARY : MOMENTOUS. *Momentary* = occurring in the space of a moment, as 'a momentary thought', 'a momentary suspicion'. *Momentous* = important on account of the consequences ('a momentous occasion', 'a momentous decision').

MONEYS (= sums of money). This spelling is to be preferred to *monies*.

MONOGRAM : MONOGRAPH. *Monogram* = a device consisting of two or more letters written together or intertwined. *Monograph* = a treatise written on one particular subject.

MORE. (i) *More than one*, followed by a singular noun as subject, takes a singular verb, despite the fact that 'more than one' is notionally plural ('More than one person has been concerned in this'): but *more* + plural noun + *than one* takes a plural verb ('More persons than one have been involved'). The number of the noun, that is to say, always determines the number of the verb.

(ii) Generally, the tendency to extend the use of *more* to adjectives which normally make their comparative in -*er* should be resisted (e.g. *more common* instead of *commoner*, *more silly* instead of *sillier*), but there may sometimes be justification for it if it emphasises the notion attaching to the positive degree: e.g. 'A more silly remark I cannot imagine'. It is often to be preferred also for compounds: 'a more common-looking person', 'a more badly-spoken person', 'a more healthy-looking child', rather than 'a commoner-looking person', 'a worse-spoken person', 'a healthier-looking child'.

(iii) The ordinary comparative, like *bigger*, *taller*, *longer*, is concerned with a comparison of the same quality or characteristic in two different things (the size of this compared with the size of that, etc.), but it is also possible to compare two different characteristics or qualities in the same thing. For this, *more*, not -*er*, is always used ('He is more lucky than clever' — not *luckier*. 'I was more sorry than angry at what happened' — not *sorrier*). The same is true when the comparison is concerned with the applicability or otherwise of the notion expressed by the adjective. 'He is no younger than I am' merely compares the ages of the two persons, without telling us whether either is really young or old. 'He is no more young than I am' means that it would be no more appropriate to call him young than it is to call me young. For the same two purposes, *more* can also be used before a noun. 'He is more a fool than a rogue.' 'He is no more a company director than I am' (said of someone who claims to be, or is generally thought to be, a company director).

MOST. (i) 'Most everyone has heard of *sake*, the famous Japanese wine.'—From an airline's guide to Tokyo.

An American illiteracy, as offensive to Americans with any degree of linguistic sensibility as it is to an English person. Use *almost*.

(ii) 'He told a most amusing story.' 'She was most rude to me.' This use of *most*, in the sense of *very*, is condemned by some grammarians, but it is very frequently heard, and may be accepted in colloquial English, though it is better excluded from writing.

MOSTLY. The normal adverb of degree is *most*: e.g. 'Of all the competitors she was the one who most deserved to win'. *Mostly* means 'for the most part, though not entirely': e.g. 'His stories were mostly about his travels in foreign parts'. 'The audience consisted mostly of women.' Occasionally the two may get confused, as in the sentence 'She is the person who is mostly to blame.' Since the sense is 'she more than any other', *most* is required.

MOWED: MOWN. *Mowed* is the normal past tense and past participle ('I have mowed the lawn'); *mown* is used only attributively, and usually in compounds, as *new-mown hay*.

MR, MRS. (i) Do not use a full stop. The shortened spelling is now regarded as the full one.

(ii) *Mr* must not be written before a name if *Esq.* is placed at the end. (See under ESQUIRE.)

(iii) Plural: *Messrs Smith and Jones, the Messrs Smith, the two Mr Smiths* (but never *the Messrs Smiths*): *Mesdames Smith and Jones, the Mesdames Smith, the two Mrs Smiths.* In spoken English *the two Mr* (*Mrs*) . . . is the usual form.

(iv) With foreign names use *Monsieur, Herr, Signor, Señor* (men) and *Madame, Frau, Signora, Señora* (married women) for persons from French, German, Italian and Spanish-speaking countries respectively and *Mr* and *Mrs* (or *Madame*) for others.

MS. (Plural MSS.). (See MANUSCRIPT.)

MUCH. (i) Generally participles are modified by *much* ('The privilege has been much abused', 'Her dress was much admired') and adjectives by *very* (*very good, very old, very clever*). Certain participles which have largely lost their verbal force and are felt to be adjectival, however, take *very*: 'I was very interested in his story', 'We are very worried about the position', 'I feel very concerned about him'. Conversely, participles used attributively to make a compound adjective with the modifying adverb, take *much*: 'a much abused privilege', 'a much travelled person', 'a much discussed question'.

(ii) 'I can't afford to pay that much for it.' Incorrect. Use *so much* or *so much as that*.

(iii) *It is much* used to express surprise ('It is much she consented to do it'), though at one time in general use, is now dialectal.

MUCH MORE: MUCH LESS. 'She scarcely deigned to look at us, much more speak to us.' Not *much more*, but *much less* (i.e. much less did she deign). *Much more* is correct, however, in 'I would help even an enemy if he were in distress, much more a friend' (i.e. much more would I help).

MUTUAL. If you can possibly avoid it, do not speak of people having *mutual friends*, *mutual interests*, etc. They have friends or interests in common. *Mutual* means 'acting in both directions in the same way, and at the same time': e.g. *mutual attraction*, *mutual regard*, *mutual distrust* (the attraction, regard, distrust, etc., which two people or two parties have for each other). Consequently (i) do not use the words *of each other* with *mutual* ('a mutual dislike of each other'), since they are redundant. (ii) do not speak of *a mutual agreement*, since there can be no agreement unless both parties accept it. But *an agreement for mutual assistance* is, of course, correct, since it is the assistance which is to be mutual.

What has been said of *mutual* applies also to the adverb *mutually*. Both adjective and adverb may be legitimately extended from their strict sense to cover cases where the idea of 'common' is combined with that of 'each other', as 'a scheme which should be to our mutual advantage' (i.e. A, by seeking an advantage for himself, also brings an advantage to B, and vice versa); but it cannot be used if this idea of the effect or action of two persons or things upon each other is absent, as it is used in the following sentence from Wilkie Collins's novel *The Moonstone* (chap. vii): 'Mr Franklin and I had both talked of foreign politics till we could talk no longer, and had then mutually fallen asleep in the heat of the sun'.

As for the difference between *mutual* and *reciprocal*, *reciprocal* takes the two things separately, whereas *mutual* takes them together. Consequently *reciprocal* may be used, as *mutual* cannot, of one only in its relation to the other. If two countries reach an agreement for a reciprocal reduction of tariffs, and A reduces her tariffs on goods imported from B, then B may be said to take reciprocal action when she follows suit by reducing her tariffs on goods from A. Fowler states (in *M.E.U.*), that though, for the reason just given, *mutual* cannot always replace *reciprocal*, *reciprocal* can always replace *mutual*. It is very doubtful, however, whether this is true. The fact is that *reciprocal* implies a two-way relationship in which each depends upon the other ; A's reduction of tariffs depends upon a similar reduction by B, and vice versa. *Mutual* may also imply this, but it need not do so. A's esteem for B does not depend upon B's esteem for A. Each is independent of the other.

MYTHICAL: MYTHOLOGICAL. *Mythical*=untrue, having no real existence. *Mythological*=pertaining to mythology.

N

NAÏVE. Though the French feminine form, in English used for both sexes.

NAMED. (i) 'He was named as John by his parents, but all his friends called him Jack.' Incorrect. Amend to 'He was named John'. *John*, or whatever name follows the verb, is a complement. But 'He has been named [i.e. mentioned by name] as the probable successor' is correct. So is the following, from Anthony Trollope's novel *The Warden* (chap. v):

'Was he [Mr Harding] to become a byword for oppression, to be named as an example of the greed of the English Church?'

(ii) 'He was named Edward, for his father.' 'She was christened Elizabeth Cleghorn, Elizabeth for her mother, and Cleghorn for James Cleghorn, a friend of her father's' (A. B. Hopkins, *Elizabeth Gaskell, Her Life and Work*, 1952). · An Americanism, not idiomatic in British English, where *after* is the word used. This particular sense of *after* (= in imitation of) is found also in such expressions as *after the style of, after the manner of* ('A poem in heroic couplets, after the manner of Pope'), and when we say that a child takes after its father.

NAMES. For the plurals of proper names, see PLURALS, and for the genitive form, see APOSTROPHE.

NAUGHT: NOUGHT. Use the spelling *nought* when the numerical cipher is meant, and *naught* for all other meanings. Thus *noughts and crosses*, but *set at naught, come to naught*, etc. This is consistent with the spelling of the adjective *naughty*, which originally meant 'good for nothing', but has since been weakened to a mild term of rebuke.

NEARBY. The adjectival use (*a nearby field, a nearby town*) has been gaining ground over the past ten or fifteen years, and we may have ultimately to accept it, but *neighbouring* is to be preferred. The only use at present fully accepted is the adverbial, consisting of two words (*a field near by*) though even here *nearby* will probably soon win the day.

NEARLY: ALMOST. (See ALMOST.)

NECESSARIES: NECESSITIES. The difference is one of degree. *Necessities* are things which cannot be dispensed with, or which one *must* have for a particular purpose, *necessaries* things which may not be indispensable but which we may consider necessary. The only necessities for a picnic are food and drink; the *necessaries* for a picnic, contained in a picnic basket, may include cups, plates, sandwich tin, vacuum flask, spoons, cutlery, etc. Of course, whether many of the things which we call necessities really are indispensable may be a matter of opinion, but in calling them necessities we imply that they are (e.g. 'In the modern home a television set is a necessity', 'Things that are the luxuries of one generation become the necessities of the next').

NEED. (i) 'He need not do it.' 'No-one need starve' (not *He needs not* and *No-one needs*). The same form is used for the past tense, but it is followed by the perfect infinitive: 'He need not have done it' (not *He needed not*).

(ii) 'If need be', not 'If needs be'. *Need* is here a noun, and the expression means 'if there be need'. A survival of the old genitive is found in 'He must needs go' (='of necessity'), though this is now an archaism.

(iii) On the difference between *need* and *want*, see under WANT.

NEITHER. (i) In Standard pronunciation the first syllable rhymes with *nigh*, not *knee*. The latter pronunciation is common in the northern parts of England and in Scotland, and is Standard American.

(ii) As an adjective or a pronoun, *neither* should be used only where two things or persons are concerned. Do not say 'neither of the three brothers'.

(iii) *Neither* takes each of the two separately, not together: consequently if each is singular it must take a singular verb ('Both Smith and Jones were invited, but neither *has* accepted' — not 'neither *have* accepted'). If each of the terms is plural, a plural verb is possible ('Both the Conservatives and the Liberals are to contest the constituency, but neither *have* yet announced who their candidate is to be'), though still the singular is more strictly correct, since *neither* means 'not this and not that (individual or group)'. The same principle applies to *neither of them*; the verb agrees with *neither* (which may be either singular or plural, according to the context), not with *them*.

(iv) As an adverb used for purposes of emphasis, *neither* goes with a positive verb, *either* with a negative: 'You don't believe his story?' 'Neither do I', or 'And I don't, either', but not 'I don't, neither'.

(v) On *neither . . . nor*, see under CORRELATIVES; but note also the following points:

(a) The correlation need not be restricted to two terms. Shakespeare (*Julius Caesar*) has 'I have neither wit, nor words, nor worth', and this is in accord with modern usage also.

(b) When one of the correlated terms consists of alternatives, great care is needed lest confusion arise between *or* and *nor*. E.g. 'He said he had neither father *nor* mother, *nor* any brothers *nor* sisters. The third *nor* is incorrect; it should be *or*: the correlated terms are 'father', 'mother', 'brothers or sisters'.

(c) In the same way confusion between the introductory adverb *neither* and the correlative *neither* may lead to the incorrect use of *nor*: 'I could not speak the language, *neither* had I friends *nor* acquaintances in the town'. *Neither* links the second statement to the first; it is not the first of a pair of correlatives. *Nor* should be amended to *or*.

NEXT DOOR. *He lives next door, the people next door* (two words), but *next-door neighbours* (hyphen).

NOBODY. (i) *Nobody* is singular; it takes a singular verb (*nobody is/was*) and is referred to by the singular personal pronoun and possessive adjective (*he, his*): 'Nobody likes his friends to take advantage of him' (not *their friends . . . of them*).

(ii) With tag questions referring back to *nobody*, the tag follows the usual rule, and is singular, when *nobody* individualises within a specified or understood group, as 'Nobody likes to lose money, does he?' (here the group is the entire human race), but plural when it denotes mere absence of anybody, as 'We kept ringing the bell, but nobody answered, did they?' 'Nobody has called while I have been out, have they?'

(*N.B.*—The above observations apply also to *no-one*.)

NO LONGER. The meaning 'not now', as contrasted with what was formerly the case, is quite idiomatic English: 'Mr Jones is no longer in our employ'. 'We no longer ascribe madness to possession by the devil.'

NOM DE PLUME. The expression is unknown in French. Use *pen-name* or *pseudonym*. The French expression is *nom de guerre*.

NONE. Singular when the reference is to amount or quantity ('None of the food *was* wasted'). When number is indicated, either singular or plural, according to the sense. 'Of his three sons none has any great ability.' 'None of the suggestions was acceptable.' (Singular, because *none* individualises, taking each one singly.) 'None of the letters have been opened yet.' 'A number of people are expected, but none have arrived yet.' (Plural, because *none* has the meaning 'not any').

NONE THE LESS. *Nevertheless* is one word, but *none the less* must be written as three.

NO ONE: NO-ONE. *R.C.R.* adopts the former spelling (two separate words), but the hyphened compound is to be preferred when the meaning is *nobody*. Two words must, however, be used when it means 'no individual one' ('This calls for a combined effort; no one of us can possibly do it on his own.') When in doubt, use the hyphen if in speech the stress would fall on *no* ('There was no-one in the room'), and two separate words if it would fall on *one*.

    No-one but ticket-holders was admitted (not *were admitted*). See under NOTHING BUT, and under NOBODY.

    The genitive of *no-one else* is *no-one else's*, not *no-one's else*.

NOR: OR. (See under NEITHER and CORRELATIVES.)

    Nor is sometimes used after a negative statement with the meaning '*and . . . not*' ('I cannot accede to your request now, nor can I make any promise for the future'). This justifies the use of *nor* in the following sentence quoted by Sir Ernest Gowers (*An A.B.C. of Plain Words*): 'He did not think that the Bill would be introduced this month, nor indeed before the recess.' *Or*, however, would be equally acceptable. If we use *or*, it links *before the recess* to *this month*, both adverbial expressions modifying *would be introduced*: if we use *nor*, it 'picks up' the first part of the sentence ('and he did not, indeed, think', etc.).

NO SOONER. Followed by *than*, not by *but* or *when*. ('We had no sooner set out than a thunderstorm broke.')

NOSTALGIA. The sense 'a wistful looking back to one's past life or to past times' is accepted. The literal meaning of the word is 'home-sickness'.

NOTHING BUT. Be careful when using *nothing but*, followed by a plural, as a subject. Remember that the actual subject is *nothing*, and that *nothing* is singular. It must therefore take a singular verb. 'Nothing but trees was to be seen' (not *were to be seen*).

NOT ONLY . . . BUT ALSO. To insist that *also* must never be omitted is pedantic. When two clauses are correlated it is legitimate to omit it if no misunderstanding can result and each clause has its own subject. 'He not only promised to fulfil the conditions, but he signed an undertaking to that effect.' 'Not only were the brakes defective, but the engine needed repair.'

For other points, see under CORRELATIVES.

NOTORIOUS. (See INFAMOUS.)

NOUNS AS ADJECTIVES. (i) In a booklet entitled *England Language Conditions* (originally given as a series of lectures) Lord Dunsany protests against the growing tendency to use nouns as adjectives. Unfortunately he spoils his case by over-stating it. It is quite legitimate to speak of the *Kent* or the *England* cricket team. There are plenty of Kentish and English teams (almost every village has one), but those that represent Kent and England respectively are another matter. Though we speak of a *wooden box*, we must say a *wood* fire, and a *machine* tool is something different from a *mechanical* tool, while the B.B.C. — quite properly — refers to its *Paris* studio, not its *Parisian* studio, and we drink *China*, not *Chinese* tea.

At the same time there is something in Lord Dunsany's pro-test. There is no justification (not even economy of space) for using a noun attributively merely to displace an existing ad-jective, as is done in the newspaper headline 'Australia Buys Italy Spectacles' (i.e. Italian), or for converting a genitive into a substantival adjective, as in *barber shop* and *teacher organisa-tions*. Anyone with a regard for style will avoid these mon-strosities.

(ii) Though not strictly adjectival, the use of nouns as epithets in such expressions as *headmaster John Summers, plumber Thomas Jenkins, accountant William Matthews*, is also to be deprecated. It is not accepted English usage, and had best be left to the kind of journalism which has given it currency.

NOUNS AS VERBS. The practice of using a noun as a verb is not a new one. For years people have *papered* rooms, *bottled* fruit, *bandaged* up a wound, and *oiled* a machine. There are many such verbs which have long been an accepted part of the English language, and we could not easily express ourselves without them. Others, like *to can vegetables, to censor letters, to button-hole a person, to concrete a yard* and *to initial a document* (the last two really examples of words which, starting as adjectives, have first become nouns and then verbs) have been introduced more recently. To these, too, there can be no objection. Generally speaking, the use of a noun as a verb may be justified if it expresses a meaning for which there is no existing word. *To service* (a car or a piece of machinery) is not the same as *to serve*, and *to power* (provide with a source of power) has a different meaning from *to empower*, while *to site* (in its correct sense of 'provide a site for') expresses a different idea from *situate*. All these serve a useful purpose. But there is no justification for using a noun as a verb when a well-established verb, or a brief formula, already exists. There may be a restricted use for *package, condition* and *contact*, but there is no excuse for *to audition* (give an audition to), *to bill* (charge to one's account), *to loan* (lend), *to message* (send a message to), *to signature* (sign), and *to suspicion* (suspect).

NUMBER. (i) *A number of* (= many) is plural in sense and takes a plural verb ('A number of people *were* left behind'). The same applies to *a large number of, a small number of*.

(ii) *The number of* (= a mathematical or numerical figure) is singular: 'The number of people who own cars *is* increasing every year'.

(iii) The plural *numbers* (= the total number of individuals that make up the membership of a group, body or institution) is a well-established idiom, but it is used only in relation to persons or animals, not to things. It of course takes a plural verb: 'Our numbers have increased considerably since the minimum age for membership was reduced to eighteen'.

(iv) On grammatical number in nouns, pronouns and verbs, see under SINGULAR OR PLURAL?

NUMBERS: METHOD OF WRITING. (i) Apart from mathematical or statistical matter, when they occur as part of a sentence numbers should normally be written as words, not as figures: thus *three hours, five miles, six years, twenty pounds*: but —

(a) If a long string of words would be involved, use figures. Thus *fifty thousand* will be written as words, as will *two million*, but *1,983* in figures.

(b) Figures should be used for dates (*1793, April 16th*) and for the numbers of houses (*65 Prince's Street*).

(ii) Write fractions as words (*two-thirds of the amount*). On the use or non-use of a hyphen in fractions and numbers involving more than one word, see HYPHEN.

(iii) For times of the clock, *half past two, twenty past five, seven o'clock,* or 2.30, 5.20, 7 p.m. (But not *two-thirty* or *twenty past 5.*)

For kings and queens *Henry VIII, George III,* is to be preferred to *Henry the Eighth, George the Third*: but never *Henry VIIIth, George IIIrd.*

(iv) *The twenty-third Psalm,* or *Psalm XXIII. The eighteenth century,* not *the XVIII century,* and certainly not *the XVIIIth century* or *c. 18.* (There is, of course, no objection to writing the last in notes intended merely for one's own use.)

O

O : OH. (i) *O* is used before a vocative case ('O Mary, go and call the cattle home', 'O listen, listen, ladies gay') and occasionally before a verb in the imperative mood, when the understood subject is felt to be invoked ('O talk not to me of a name great in story'). It is never followed by a comma or any other punctuation mark. In all other cases, use *Oh*. The writer of ordinary prose will find little occasion for *O*; it is confined almost entirely to poetry.

(ii) *Oh* is normally followed by a comma. An exclamation mark should be used only when the word is intended to be uttered in a sharp, exclamatory tone indicative of pain, surprise, etc. Use no stop at all in *Oh dear*, or when *Oh* expresses a wish or longing and is followed by *for*, *that* or an infinitive: 'Oh for the touch of a vanished hand', 'Oh that those lips had language', 'Oh to be in England'.

OBLIVIOUS. Followed by *of*, not *to*.

OBSERVANCE : OBSERVATION. *Observation* of the landscape, the building, the camp, etc. (i.e. something one sees): *observance* of the rules, regulations, the sabbath, religious rites (i.e. paying due regard or attention to).

OCCASION. The use of *occasion* as a verb has recently become a piece of official jargon ('We do not wish to occasion you any inconvenience'). There is no need for it. It can usually be replaced by *cause* or some other simple verb.

OCCUPANT : OCCUPIER. *Occupant*(*s*) of a railway carriage, a seat, a room, etc. (i.e. those who at the moment happen to occupy it). The *occupier* of a house or other premises (i.e. the person who lives or carries on business there).

OCCUPATION. When an official form asks for 'Occupation' the answer expected is *bank clerk*, *teacher*, *stockbroker*, *bricklayer*, etc. On a form, this will do, but not elsewhere, for none of these is an occupation, but a person. Do not write 'one of the most dangerous occupations is a miner', but 'that of a miner'.

Œ. Words like *œcumenical,* with the initial digraph, are now often spelt with a simple *e.* But the digraph must be retained in French words, like *coup d'œil, hors-d'œuvre.*

OF. (i) Normally, when constructions like *a crowd of people, a flock of sheep, a row of chairs, a bunch of grapes* are used as subjects, since the real subject word is the one that precedes *of,* it is with this that the verb must agree, not with the one that follows: e.g. 'A crowd of spectators was rapidly gathering', 'A bunch of delicious-looking grapes was hanging over the wall'. This is not, however, an invariable rule; we must be guided by the sense, and sometimes by the consideration that too strict adherence to what is formally correct may give rise to difficulties later in the sentence. In some cases the notion of the verb is felt to be applicable to the second rather than to the first noun, and in such cases it should agree with the second: e.g. 'A gang of youths were singing at the top of their voices'. 'A gang of youths was singing', though correct from a formal point of view, would hardly sound right; and it would be quite impossible to go on with the singular—'at the top of its voice'.

(ii) For the difference between the *of* adjunct and the genitive case (*the death of Nelson* and *Nelson's death*), see under GENITIVE CASE.

(iii) *Of a Saturday, of a morning, of an evening,* etc. are accepted usage to express frequency, repetition or regularity ('I always go to church of a Sunday evening'). (See also IN AN AFTERNOON.)

OFF. (i) *Off of* is a vulgarism.

(ii) 'He borrowed five pence off me.' Incorrect. Amend to *from me. Off* in such sentences may be a mistake for the older 'borrow something *of* someone', now archaic.

OFTEN. (i) It is incorrect to sound the *t.*

(ii) For the comparative, *more often* is to be preferred to *oftener* (e.g. 'more often than not', 'more often drunk than sober').

OLD ENGLISH. Should be applied only to the English of the Anglo-Saxon period (before about 1100). It is incorrect to call the English of Chaucer and his contemporaries Old English. It is known as *Middle English.*

OLDEN. Used only in *olden days* and *olden times,* and these expressions are best avoided in serious writing, since they are very vague and indefinite. To modern youth 'the olden days' are the days before television, jet aircraft and earth satellites.

-ON-. The *on* in such words as *none, tongue, constable, among, amongst, monk* is pronounced with the same sound as the prefix *un-*. The pronunciation like that of the preposition *on* is a regional one, not recognised by Standard English. One hears it frequently in the B.B.C. 'News of the North'.

One and *once* also have the same vowel as *won* and *un-*, not as *on*.

ONCE FOR ALL. Not 'once *and* for all'.

ONE (Generalising personal pronoun). (i) 'One should always make sure of his facts.' Amend to *one's facts*. If the reference is to the same person, *one* must be followed up by *one, one's, oneself*, not by *he, him, his, himself*, since *one* is general, where *he* is specific. Where this would lead to several repetitions of the same word, which would sound awkward, it is best to avoid *one* altogether. I am indebted to a friend for the following example (overheard in the streets of Rugby) of the tangled web we may weave for ourselves when we embark upon this use of *one*: 'One often does something he wishes we hadn't done, don't you?'

(ii) The affected, mock-modest use of *one* in place of *I* ('One can speak with some authority on this subject') is to be deprecated.

ONE WORD OR TWO? (i) For compounds like *table spoon* (or *tablespoon?*), *door mat* (or *doormat?*), consult a dictionary.

(ii) For *up on/upon, in to/into, all ready/already, a while/awhile*, see under the words concerned.

(iii) The mistake of writing *alright* instead of *all right*, and *onto* instead of *on to* is a very old one. Until recently illegitimate combinations of this kind have been confined to a few words which have become traditional stumbling-blocks, but over the past few years the reports of examiners for the G.C.E. have complained of a growing practice on the part of candidates of writing as one word expressions that should be two; and the experience of many teachers of English will bear out the complaint. The following are some examples: *alot (of), forever, incase, inbetween, infact, infront (of), inspite (of), innertube, thankyou*. All these should be written as two words.

ONESELF. Note the spelling — not *one's self* or *onesself*, though *one's self* does exist, as a rather specialised term in psychology, but it is not the reflexive pronoun.

ONLY. (i) Logically, *only* should be placed next to the word that it modifies; but we need not be too pernickety about this, provided no ambiguity or misunderstanding is likely to result. Thus all the following sentences would be condemned by the precisian, but to anyone else they sound perfectly natural, and no-one is likely to misunderstand them: they may therefore pass as good English. 'We only need another five pounds.' 'He only arrived this morning.' 'They have only been here a few weeks.' But the following might be misinterpreted, and should therefore be recast: 'Such abuses can only be checked by the force of public opinion'.

(ii) *Only too pleased* is acceptable in conversation, but *very pleased* is preferable in writing.

ONTO. Nowadays this appears so frequently as one word that the battle to keep it two, waged for several decades, seems already lost. Even Fowler gave his blessing to the union. Nevertheless, some people may still prefer to write 'The burglar climbed on to the roof', and if so they should not be discouraged. Two separate words *must* be written (a) when *on* has an independent meaning as an adverb and *to* as a preposition following it ('Keep right on to the end of the road', 'We decided to go on to Brighton') and (b) when *to* is part of an infinitive ('He went on to give an account of his experiences').

OPERATIVE. (i) Do not use *operatives* if it is possible to use *workers* (e.g. *building operatives* = building workers) or if a simple agent-noun would suffice (e.g. *printing operatives* = printers). Occasionally there may be some justification for the word, if it denotes those who actually operate a particular service (e.g. *transport operatives*) as distinguished from other workers who are employed on maintenance, etc., but usually it is just a piece of meaningless and high-sounding jargon.

(ii) Do not speak of the *operative* word in a sentence, or the *operative* clause in an Act or a document, if you merely mean the most important or the most significant.

OPPOSITE. She sat opposite the window. The bus stop is almost opposite the Town Hall (Preposition); 'Left' is opposite *to* 'right' (Adjective); 'Left' is *the* opposite *of* 'right' (Noun). It had just *the opposite* effect to that which was expected (Adjective).

OR. See under CORRELATIVES, and AGREEMENT OF VERB AND SUBJECT.

OSTLER. So spelt: not *hostler*.

OTHER. (i) 'One or other' (if more than two are concerned), 'one or *the* other' (if only two). 'Someone or other', 'some person or other', 'somewhere or other'.

(ii) 'We could do no other but agree to the proposal.' Incorrect. *Other* is followed by *than*, not by *but*, when it excludes any alternative. *But*, however, may be used if the intention is not to exclude but to limit: e.g. 'I have no other income [i.e. other than that already stated] *but* a few pounds which I receive as interest on Defence Bonds'. But even here *except* would be better.

(iii) 'York attracts more tourists than any cathedral town in Britain.' This implies that York is not a cathedral town in Britain. Insert *other* after *any*. The contrast is between York and the other cathedral towns.

(iv) *On the other hand* is sometimes misused for *on the contrary*: e.g. 'We do not regard the matter as a trivial one; on the other hand we are well aware of its gravity'. 'I informed him that General Forster was not like Lord Nithsdale, a man of a great estate, but *on the other hand* that his estates had all been sold up, so that he had nothing at all but what he would get at the death of his father.'—Walter Besant, *Dorothy Forster*, chap. xxxix. When the second statement contradicts or cancels out the suggestion contained in the first one, *on the contrary* is needed. *On the other hand* introduces a second statement in contrast to the first, but not irreconcilable with it: e.g. 'Food here is cheaper than in Britain: clothing, on the other hand, is dearer.'

OTHERWISE. (i) When *otherwise* means 'or else', it is not preceded by *or*. The alternatives are 'We shall have to hurry, *or else* we shall miss the train', and 'We shall have to hurry, *otherwise* we shall miss the train', but not *or otherwise*.

(ii) Fowler (*M.E.U.*) objects to the use of *otherwise* as an adjective (*meals, cooked or otherwise*) and as a noun (*the success or otherwise of the scheme*). While it is true that in such expressions *otherwise* can often be replaced by one word which is opposite in meaning to the one with which it is co-ordinated (*cooked or uncooked, success or failure*), and that sometimes it is merely tautological (*to report on the suitability or otherwise of the candidates*), it has become so firmly established that it seems that we shall have to accept it. And it does sometimes convey a meaning rather more comprehensive than a mere opposite would do: e.g. *all forms of government, communist or otherwise,* where *otherwise* suggests a variety of forms which the single word *non-communist* does not.

OUGHT.   (i) The negative is *ought not* (abbreviated in speech to *oughtn't*).   *Didn't ought*, *hadn't ought* and *shouldn't ought* are solecisms.   So is *did ought* as an emphatic form ('You did ought to be more careful').   Though now used as a present, *ought* is an old past tense of the verb *to owe*.   Like any other past tense form, therefore, it cannot take an auxiliary before it as though it were a participle or an infinitive.

(ii) There is no separate past form.   When the reference is to an obligation in the past, *ought* is followed by the perfect infinitive ('You ought to have done it'), though in subordinate clauses it may be followed by the ordinary (present) infinitive if the reference is to an obligation felt at the time to which the clause refers ('He knew that he ought to visit his brother, but he could not bring himself to do it').

(iii) Combinations like 'I ought, but cannot go' should be avoided.   Whereas *can* and *cannot* are followed by an infinitive without *to*, *ought* is followed by one with *to*.   Amend to 'I ought to go, but cannot'.

(iv) What is the difference between *ought to* and *should* when the latter is used to express obligation or duty?   Quite frequently they appear to be interchangeable, but there are some cases where they obviously are not.   We could not use *ought to* in place of *should* in the Victorian saying 'Children should be seen and not heard', and it would seem strange to use it in the pro-verb 'People who live in glass houses shouldn't throw stones'.   On the other hand, 'He ought to be ashamed of himself' could scarcely be changed to 'He should be ashamed of himself'.

Ought to is much stronger and more imperative than *should*, and the reason for this is probably that *should* merely expresses the speaker's view of the fact or situation, and therefore repre-sents a personal opinion, whereas *ought to* relates the obligation to what is thought of as some kind of law (moral, social or physical) which has its force and validity irrespective of any particular person's view or opinion.   'Though I say it as shouldn't' is a stock expression, used half humorously (as the unidiomatic *as* suggests), half apologetically, by a person who has said something he feels he should have left to others to say, since it amounts to praise of himself.   If someone complains of tiredness in the morning, we might say to him, 'You shouldn't stay up so late' (that is merely our own view of the matter), but if we feel that late hours are likely to undermine his health, we should then tell him, 'You oughtn't to stay up so late'.

And one other point. Since, as is pointed out above, *ought* is an old past tense of the verb *to owe*, it suggests a duty or obligation which we owe, and neglect of which constitutes a transgression of some rule or other. 'We ought to invite the Joneses' implies that failure to do so would be a transgression of the rules of hospitality or common courtesy. Consequently, *should* is generally used in instructing a person in what is expected of him according to accepted rules or practices (e.g. in books of etiquette) so as not to embarrass him by making him feel that his ignorance is almost a transgression or shortcoming.

To sum up, then; we generally use *ought to* when a person has transgressed, or we think he is likely to, and we are reprimanding or warning him: 'You oughtn't to speak to your aunt in that way'. 'You oughtn't to leave it too late before you start.' We use *should* for general advice, where there is no suggest of actual or possible transgression. We may, however, also use *should* as a 'toned down' substitute for *ought to*, in order to spare a person's feelings.

OVERALL. There is only one correct use of this word adjectivally, namely to describe a measurement between two extremities, as in 'the overall length of a ship'. It should not be used as a synonym of *total, complete, supreme*, etc., as it is in such expressions as *to give an overall picture, the overall profits of the company, in overall command*.

OVERFLOW. 'The River Medway has overflown its banks near Tonbridge' — a B.B.C. news bulletin. This would imply that the infinitive was *overfly*. *To overflow* has the past participle *overflowed*, not *overflown*.

P

PANACEA. Not 'an infallible cure', but a cure for all ills. Do not speak of 'a panacea for indigestion' (or for any other particular complaint). The word is nowadays most frequently used in a figurative sense, with reference to social, political or economic ills.

PANTS (= trousers). American, not British usage.

PARENTHESIS (Pl. parentheses). (i) Do not use frequent parentheses, and avoid the long parenthesis which makes it difficult for the reader to connect what precedes it with what follows.

(ii) Parentheses may be disjoined from the sentence in which they occur by commas, brackets or dashes. If commas are employed care must be taken to see that *two* are used, one at each end of the parenthetic words. A common fault of hasty or careless writers is to omit the second. (For examples, see under COMMA.) In no circumstances must a dash be used at the beginning of a parenthesis and a comma at the end, or vice versa. The following, from a denominational newspaper, is an example of a breach of this rule.

'I am also — like the Editor of *The Non-Subscribing Presbyterian*, offended by a certain narrow sectarianism to be found in our churches.'

(iii) Generally, if the parenthesis enters into the syntactic structure of the sentence (e.g. if it has the form of a non-defining or non-restrictive subordinate clause), commas should be used.

The house, which was built in 1763, was a rambling old place.

If it has the form of an independent sentence, complete in itself, or if, though a subordinate clause in form, it is felt to be an interpolation or aside disconnected grammatically from the rest of the sentence, brackets or dashes are the appropriate means of disjoining it.

As soon as we were out of the village (it wasn't our own village) Dixon gave the pony a flick with the whip.

If I were a millionaire (which I am not) . . .

A parenthesis beginning with the co-ordinating conjunction *for* should be enclosed between brackets or dashes, not commas.

(iv) There is little to choose between brackets and dashes,

though generally brackets are to be preferred. Dashes, however, may be more appropriate for a casual remark or observation which is thrown in in passing.

When I had scrambled up on to the pony's back again — a feat which I could only just accomplish without assistance — I felt what a poor figure I must be cutting.

(v) Note that an interpolated sentence included as a parenthesis in a larger sentence does *not* begin with a capital letter. (See example (ii), above). But a parenthetic sentence enclosed in brackets *between two other sentences* will have an initial capital in the usual way.

'Forty minutes later I had claimed my cup. (There was no ceremony of presentation.) Having crammed the ebony pedestal into my kitbag I came out into the paddock with the cup in my other hand.'—Siegfried Sassoon, *Memoirs of a Fox-Hunting Man.*

(vi) Whichever method of indicating a parenthesis is used, care must be taken to ensure that the disjunctive signs are correctly placed — that neither too little nor too much is included within them. The test is, to remove what purports to be the parenthesis. If the commas, dashes or brackets are correctly placed, the sentence that remains should run on consecutively and make complete sense. The following, quoted from a denominational weekly, shows the kind of mistake that may occur.

'The fact that a corresponding — or even worse sectarianism — is to be found within all the other denominations of the Christian Church, does not in any way excuse our own dogmatism and sectarianism.'

The second dash should have been placed after *worse.*

Care is especially necessary with words and phrases like *in fact, indeed,* which are often themselves used parenthetically, with a comma at each end, but in a particular sentence may only serve to introduce a parenthesis. The second comma is apt to get misplaced. The following example of misplacing is taken from the report of a well-known company.

'Purchase tax uncertainties make forward planning extremely difficult, in fact, impossible for manufacturers and traders alike.'

The second comma should have been placed after *impossible.*

(vii) On the use of other punctuation marks in conjunction with parentheses in brackets, see under BRACKETS.

PARTAKE.   'Over fifty schoolchildren will partake in the operetta.' Incorrect. Partake *of* a meal; *take part in* a dramatic performance, a concert, etc.

PARTIALLY. 'The letter was written partially in French and partially in English.' Incorrect. The word required is *partly*. *Partially* is an adverb of degree, and is opposed to *fully*: 'The meat was only partially cooked'. *Partly* = as regards one part.

PARTICIPLES. (i) The participles may be used (a) adjectivally, in an attributive capacity (a *crying* child, a *broken* window); (b) predicatively, as in the sentences 'The money is still *owing*', 'They found the tramp *sleeping* by the roadside', 'We noticed that his coat was *torn*' (this use is much commoner with the past participle than with the present); and (c) to make the compound tenses of verbs: 'It *is raining*', 'The sun *is shining*', 'Many houses *were damaged* in the gale', 'The cat *has eaten* the fish'.

(ii) Before the past participle of certain intransitive verbs, like *go, come, arrive, fall, rise*, expressive of motion or change of state or position, the auxiliary *to be* is permissible where we should normally expect *have*: e.g. He is gone to London. The post is come. How are the mighty fallen! The sun is risen.

These differ from the perfect tense with *have* in that they denote, not an activity or an occurrence, but a resultant situation.

(iii) The type of sentence with an introductory participial construction followed by a tense of the verb *to be* (a kind of inversion of the continuous tense forms) is, of course, quite normal: e.g. 'Standing in the doorway was a stout, dark-haired woman', 'Tied round the box was a piece of blue ribbon'. Its effect is to diminish the importance of the grammatical subject by directing attention first of all to the doorway or the box, then to the fact that there was something there, and finally by identifying or describing the person or thing in question. It probably reproduces the process by which the writer himself arrived at his appreciation of the facts; and it enables the reader to visualise the situation. But recently an unwarrantable extension of this practice has appeared in certain types of magazines which specialise in trivial gossip: 'Coming to this country next spring is the well-known American hostess Mrs . . .' 'Just arrived from South Africa is Miss . . .' To anyone with an ear for style they will sound wrong: they enable us to visualise nothing, and, far from wishing to diminish the importance of the grammatical subject (the names of the respective ladies), the writer's intention is to draw attention to it. A safe rule is, do not use this construction unless it would be idiomatic to put *there* before the finite verb ('Tied round the box (there) was a piece of blue ribbon.')

(iv) 'He was *sat* on the seat', 'She was *stood* by the window' (with an active meaning) are regional usage, against which examiners for the Northern Joint Board's General Certificate of Education are constantly protesting, though to little effect. In Standard English they could only mean that the person in question was placed there by someone else. Amend to *was sitting, was standing*. (See also LAID.)

(v) On the misrelated participle, exemplified in the sentence 'Looking from the upper window the scene was very impressive', see under -ING.

PASSED: PAST. Use *passed* when the word is a verb ('She passed her examination', 'Nearly five years have passed since then', 'Having passed the age of sixty-five, he decided to retire'): when it is any other part of speech, use *past*.

Notice the difference between 'With all his examinations passed, he could enjoy a care-free holiday' (i.e. now that he had passed them all), and 'With all his examinations past', etc. (now that they were all behind him, though possibly not all passed).

PASSIVE VOICE. Avoid the use of a double passive, as in 'Adjustments that are proposed to be made', 'The measures that were attempted to be taken', 'Alterations that were suggested to be made'. Amend to (i) Adjustments that it is proposed to make, *or* Adjustments that are proposed; (ii) The measures that were attempted; (iii) Alterations that it was suggested should be made.

On passive verbs followed by the substitute verb *do*, see under Do.

PENINSULA(R). *Peninsula* is the noun (*the Iberian peninsula*), *peninsular* the adjective (*the Peninsular War*).

PER. (i) 'We are sending the goods per parcel post.' A piece of commercial jargon. Use *by*.

(ii) Expressions like twenty-five pence per hour' 'thirty pence per person', 'six pence per ounce', 'forty miles per hour' should be left to business and commercial usage, where they have their place. In normal English use *a* or *an*. 'A bob a job' is crisper and more effective than 'one shilling [5p.] per job'.

(iii) Even in commercial English do not write *per year*, but *per annum*. *Per month* and *per day* are accepted commercialese, though strictly they should be *per mensem* and *per diem*. On *per capita*, see below.

PER CAPITA. A phrase that is often misunderstood, and consequently misused. It does not mean 'per head' (which would be *per caput*), but 'according to heads'. The Latin for *head* is *caput; capita* is the plural. 'A *per capita* payment' or 'a payment *per capita*' is correct (i.e. a payment according to the number of people, a stipulated amount being allowed for each person). 'A payment of twenty pence *per capita*', 'An allowance of four ounces of butter *per capita*' are wrong, and should be amended to 'twenty pence a head', 'four ounces of butter for each person' (or, in official English, 'per head' and 'per person').

PER CENT : PERCENTAGE. (i) *Per cent,* though actually an abbreviation of *per centum,* is no longer thought of as such, and requires no full stop. It should never be written as one word. But *percentage* is always one word.

(ii) It may be convenient to express an awkward fraction as a percentage (e.g. '17% of the cars exported go to the United States'), and for statistical purposes it is often necessary to express all proportions as percentages — 33⅓%, 50%, 100% — but in any ordinary context speak of *a third, a half, all,* etc. : 'A third of the candidates failed' (not 33⅓%); 'Half of the food was wasted' (not *fifty per cent of the food*); 'All the members signed the petition' (not *a hundred per cent of the members*); 'There was a full attendance' (not *a hundred per cent attendance*).

(iii) Do not say *a percentage* when you mean a few, a small number, or a small quantity : e.g. 'At every election there is a percentage of spoiled ballot papers'; 'Only a percentage of workers obeyed the call to strike'; 'We must always allow for a percentage of waste'. We might ask, 'What percentage ?' Ninety-nine out of every hundred is a percentage, just as much as one out of every hundred.

PERFECT (Adjective). (i) *Perfect,* being an absolute term, cannot normally be modified by *more* or *most.* We cannot say that one thing is more perfect than another, or that it is the most perfect of its kind : but 'We could not have had a more perfect day for the garden party' is allowable. Here the comparative denotes a nearer approach to the idea expressed by the absolute (cf. 'a fuller account of the incident', 'a more direct route').

(ii) *A perfect genius, a perfect fool, a perfect nuisance* are accepted colloquialisms, but should not appear in literary English. The same applies to *perfectly* in such expressions as *perfectly absurd, perfectly ridiculous.*

PERFECT TENSE. (i) The perfect tense represents a past activity, occurrence or situation as being in some way connected with the present. 'We have lived here eight years' (and we are still living here); 'There have been many strikes since the war' (from the war up to the present time); 'I have misplaced my pen' (the present position). IT MUST NOT BE ACCOMPANIED BY ANY ADVERB OR ADVERBIAL EXPRESSION WHICH DENOTES PAST TIME. We cannot say 'I have seen him last Wednesday', 'We have been there several years ago'. With such adverbial qualifications a past tense, not a perfect, must be used ('I saw him last Wednesday', 'We were there several years ago').

(ii) Take care to avoid the error of the double perfect. This may occur in two forms.

(a) The duplication of auxiliaries to make a non-existent tense form, as in the constructions 'If I had have known'. 'Had I have known', 'I wish you had have seen him' (or more often in the conversational form 'If I'd have known', 'I wish you'd have seen him'). These should be corrected to 'If I had known' (or 'If I'd known'), 'Had I known' and 'I wish you had seen him' (or 'I wish you'd seen him'). The perfect tense has the auxiliary *have* (*I have known, you have seen*), and the pluperfect, or past perfect, *had* (*I had known, you had seen*), but there is no tense form with the combined auxiliaries *had have*. The error is more frequent in negative sentences than in positive, possibly because the interposed *not* makes it less obvious: e.g. 'I should never have believed it if I hadn't have seen it with my own eyes'. 'He would have walked straight into the trap if you hadn't have warned him of it in time.'

(b) A perfect tense form, followed by a perfect infinitive: e.g. 'I should have liked to have stayed another week'. Only one of the verbs should be in the perfect: either 'I should have liked to stay' or 'I should like to have stayed'. Which is correct in any particular case depends on the notion to be expressed. If the desire is a past one, then *I should have liked* is the correct form, but if it is present, then *I should like*.

I should have liked (*then*) to stay another week.

I should like (*now*) to have known Shakespeare.

We must beware, however, of supposing that the use of the perfect infinitive after a perfect tense form is always wrong. Sometimes it is justifiable: e.g.

'He would have given the world to have been a little braver at the time.'—R. L. Stevenson, *The Body-Snatcher*.

'I should have liked to have been able to comply with his request.'

In the first sentence Stevenson is describing his character's feeling about a situation to which he is looking back, so that two different periods of past time are denoted, one earlier than the other. In the second, the circumstances which would have enabled the speaker to comply are thought of as existing not only when, but before, the request was made.

(iii) Akin to the mistaken use of a double perfect, is the combination of a past tense with a perfect infinitive: e.g. 'I intended to have called on you yesterday'. Amend to 'I intended to call on you yesterday'. Again, however, not all such combinations are illegitimate ones. The sentence 'He seemed to have lost his way' is correct, since here the infinitive refers to something that had occurred prior to the time denoted by the finite verb *seemed*. And similarly 'I hoped to have finished the work by now' is correct, since *to have finished* refers to a time prior to that denoted by *now*.

(iv) After the past tense of *hope, think, expect, fear*, the perfect of the conditional is used to express something that is not fulfilled: 'I hoped that you would have helped me' (implying 'but you will not'). 'I thought you would have known that' (implying 'but you do not'). With a negative verb in the main clause, the same construction is used to express something that *is* fulfilled when it was hoped, thought, expected, etc., that it would not be: 'We did not expect that you would have refused us a meal' (implying 'but you have').

The use of the plain conditional (*you would help me* etc.) in such circumstances is not excluded, but it does not in itself suggest either fulfilment or non-fulfilment.

PERMEATE. A transitive verb. Water *permeates* the soil, not *permeates through* it.

PERMISSIBLE: PERMISSIVE. *Permissible* = permitted, not prohibited. 'It is permissible to end a sentence with a preposition if it sounds more natural to do so.' *Permissive* = permitting, but not compelling. A permissive clause in an Act of Parliament is a clause which permits people or organisations to do certain things if they wish, but does not make it obligatory for them to do so. For example, the original Public Libraries Act *permitted* local authorities to levy up to a penny rate to provide Free Libraries, but it did not say that they *must* levy such a rate or provide libraries. The powers granted them were permissive.

PERMIT: PERMIT OF. 'Our parents would not permit of our going.' 'The law permits of children leaving school when they have attained the age of fifteen.' Both incorrect. Permit + the infinitive is required. *Permit of* means 'leave room for': e.g. 'The facts permit of only one interpretation'. 'His conduct permits of no excuse.' 'The situation permits of no delay.' (See also ALLOW.)

PERSON: PERSONAGE: PERSONALITY. *Person* means merely a man or woman; it suggests no particular characteristics. *Personage* = an important person. (Do not speak of 'that personage with the red nose and the very loud voice'.) *Personality* = someone of a distinctive character, or someone who is well known: e.g. 'He is quite a personality in the district'. 'A number of local personalities were present.'

The difference between *persons* and *people* is that *people* denotes merely human beings, whereas *persons* denotes human beings with characters, feelings, etc. Thus we say that some people are quite different persons amongst their friends from what they are in their business relations. But *persons* is also used as a formal word where in ordinary English we should use *people*. A recipe in a cookery book will tell us that a dish will provide enough for four persons, and a notice in a bus will announce that only six persons are allowed to stand when all the seats are full. In normal English we should say *people*.

PERSONA GRATA. 'He is *persona grata* in that quarter' (not *a persona grata*). The meaning of the expression is 'an acceptable person', or 'a person who is regarded favourably'. The opposite notion is expressed by *persona non grata*.

PERSONAL(LY). Hard things have been said about *personal* and *personally*, some of them rather pedantic. Both words are sometimes misused, and sometimes used pointlessly, but there are also certain common uses that should be accepted, at least in conversational English. In *a personal friend of mine* the word is pointless, and should be omitted, but *my personal opinion* seems allowable if it means that the opinion is not given in an official capacity, or that it does not commit any body or organisation with which one is connected. *Personally I should advise you to do so and so* implies that as a civil servant, an officer of the local authority, or an official of some other body, I might give different advice, in accordance with the policy of my committee. If the words are not used to make a distinction of this kind they are a mere cliché.

Again, 'The manager is dealing with the matter personally' is justifiable, since he might have delegated it to a subordinate; so are 'I have a personal interest in the matter', 'He has no personal ends to serve', but the word is not only redundant, but also pointless in such sentences as 'Personally I don't care for haggis', 'Personally I prefer a country holiday to one by the sea'.

PERSONATE. (See IMPERSONATE.)

PERSPICUOUS : PERSPICACIOUS. *Perspicuous* = clear, easily understood. Noun : *perspicuity*. *Perspicacious* = having the ability to see or understand clearly. Noun : *perspicacity*. A person is perspicacious ; his manner of expressing himself in speech or writing is perspicuous.

PICK : CHOOSE. There is a growing tendency for *pick* to usurp the place of *choose*. G.C.E. candidates, for instance, writing on *The Merchant of Venice* frequently say that Portia's suitors had to *pick* one of three caskets, and that Bassanio *picked* the lead casket. *Choose* is clearly the word required here ; and it is not merely that *choose* is more formal or more dignified than *pick*.
   Choose suggests careful thought and deliberation, and the weighing of one thing against another ; *pick* suggests merely selection, sometimes in a rather perfunctory manner. We pick a winner and pick a cricket team, but choose the material for a dress or a suit, choose a birthday or a wedding present, choose a name for a child, choose a site for a camp, and choose one of several things that are offered us.

PITIABLE : PITIFUL. *Pitiable* suggests degradation or wretchedness (*a pitiable plight, a pitiable attempt*). *Pitiful* = expressing or evoking pity (*a pitiful cry, a pitiful story*).

PLAIN SAILING. This spelling is the accepted one. *Plane sailing*, though historically correct, is now pedantic.

PLEASED. When *pleased* expresses approval or satisfaction it is followed by *with* (pleased with a person, pleased with my new house, pleased with his work). *Pleased with*, that is to say, expresses one's attitude towards the thing or the person in question. When *pleased* denotes a feeling of pleasure caused by something, it is followed by *about* ('pleased about your success', 'pleased about John's scholarship'). *At* is used before a gerund ('pleased at seeing so many people present', 'pleased at finding him so well'). *Pleased over* is a solecism.

PLEBS. A singular noun, meaning the common people collectively. Never speak of *a pleb* : there is no such word.

PLURAL OR SINGULAR? For cases where there may be doubt whether a singular verb, noun or possessive adjective should be used (e.g. 'Some people write with their left hand — or their left hands ?'), see SINGULAR OR PLURAL ?

PLURAL FORMS. A list of the plurals of words about which there may be some doubt is given in an appendix. The following points, however, may be noted here.

(i) *Words ending in -y.* If the *-y* is preceded by a consonant the *-y* is changed to an *i* and *-es* is added (*lorry, lorries; Tory, Tories; penny, pennies*); but if the *y* is preceded by a vowel symbol an *s* is added to the singular form (*monkey, monkeys*).

(ii) *Words ending in -o.* There is no consistent rule, but generally words in common use add *-es*, those in less common use merely *s*. (*Potatoes, tomatoes, negroes,* but *contraltos, solos, ratios.*)

All abbreviated words ending in *-o* merely add *s*; *photos, pianos, stereos.*

(iii) *Compound nouns.* In compounds consisting of a noun and qualifying words, it is the noun proper that takes the plural inflexion (*courts martial, prime ministers, jacks-in-office*). Compounds in which none of the words is a noun add the plural termination to the whole group (*go-betweens, try-outs, fly-pasts*). Compounds where the basic noun, even in the singular form, is already a plural (e.g. *a lazy-bones*) do not add a further plural inflexion (*all those lazy-bones*).

(iv) *Proper Names.* These do not follow the rules for common nouns. If they are English names they add *s* to the singular : *the Joneses, the Davises, the Merrys, the two Henrys, the Churchmans.* If they are foreign names, in English they also generally add *-s*, irrespective of what would be the plural form in their own language : *the two Brutuses, the Borgias, the Lavals, the Hauptmanns.* But notice the special cases of *the Gracchi* (where the Latin plural is used), and of French names ending in an *-s* which is not pronounced (e.g. *Dumas*). The written form is the same for the plural as for the singular (*the two Dumas*).

(v) *Unusual Plurals.* For plurals of single letters, of numbers written as numerals, and of words which are not normally nouns and therefore do not normally have a plural form, the apostrophe *s* is used : 'Mind your p's and q's'. 'The 20's of the present century.' 'The temperature was up in the 70's.' 'How's, why's and wherefore's.' (See also under APOSTROPHE.)

(vi) *Plurals of Initials.* J.P.s, M.P.s, B.A.s, M.A.s (persons), *but* B.A.'s, M.A.'s (degrees). Note also *MSS.* (manuscripts), *pp.* (pages), *ll.* (lines). (See also under ABBREVIATIONS.)

PLUS. Best confined to its mathematical use or to two things which are to be taken together to make a single amount or combination : e.g. 'the accusative plus the infinitive', 'the weight of the contents plus that of the container'. The word should not be used simply as a substitute for *and, with* or *together with* : e.g. 'We are

sending you the machine plus a book of instructions'. 'An elderly
lady plus two dogs and a servant arrived.' 'On one evening
each week a new supply of books, plus a librarian, is sent.' (From
a report on library services to prisons.) But to give the price of
an article as *£15 plus Value Added Tax* is, of course, correct.

POETESS. The word has come to have a depreciative connotation. Use *poet*, irrespective of sex. If it is necessary to indicate
sex, speak of *women poets*.

POINT OF VIEW. Often wrongly used for *view* or *views*. 'A
history of the Reformation from the Roman Catholic point of
view' is correct: 'Mr Johnson will now give us his point of
view on the matter' is not. Mr Johnson gives his *views*. A
point of view is the spot (metaphorically) on which one stands
to look at something: what one sees from that point is a *view*.

POLITICS. When *politics* is thought of as a science, or as a field
of activity, it is singular: 'Politics is the art of government'.
'Politics has no attraction for me as a career.' When it means
political beliefs or doctrines, or political developments, it is
plural: 'A person's politics are his own affair'. 'American
politics are not easily understood by the average Englishman.'

PORE: POUR. *Pore* over a book or document, *pour out* the tea.

POSSESS: POSSESSION. *To be possessed of* is active, and
means 'to have' or 'to possess': e.g. 'He is possessed of intelli-
gence/great wealth'. The sense 'dominated by' (e.g. *possessed
of the devil*) is archaic, though there is a survival of it, without
the preposition, in the phrase *like one possessed* (i.e. out of his
mind), and in such sentences as 'What on earth possessed you
to do that?' The passive sense is now usually expressed by *by*:
'He was suddenly possessed by a desire to rush from the room'.
    In possession of is active (= *possess*): 'My solicitor is now in
possession of the documents'. *In the possession of* is passive
(= *possessed by*): 'The documents are in the possession of my
solicitor'. But not 'My solicitor is now *in the possession* of the
documents', which would mean that the documents possess the
solicitor, not vice versa.

POSSESSIVE ADJECTIVES AND PRONOUNS. (i) Avoid
such combinations as 'my and your opinion', 'his and her
responsibility', 'your and our interests'. They are not ungrammatical, but they are awkward and offend against euphony.
But much worse than these are 'mine and your opinion', 'yours
and her efforts'. *Mine* and *yours*, being pronouns and not

adjectives, cannot qualify a noun, and, moreover, they can have no definite meaning until the noun for which they stand has been mentioned. Write 'your opinion and mine', 'his responsibility and hers', 'our interests and yours', 'her efforts and yours'.

(ii) A possessive adjective placed before a noun cannot be 'carried over' and understood before a subsequent *self*; nor can the first element of a reflexive pronoun be detached from -*self* and understood as a possessive adjective before another noun: e.g. 'Kind regards to your mother and self', 'in the interests of myself and family'. Say 'your mother and yourself', 'myself and my family'.

(The first element of *myself* and *thyself* is not really a possessive at all, but a corruption of *me* and *thee* (i.e. an accusative). The original accusative still remains in *himself*, *themselves*, *oneself* (note the spelling — not *one's-self*) and *herself*, though most people probably take this last as the possessive *her*. *Ourselves* and *yourselves* are certainly possessive in form, but they were later formations by analogy with *myself* and *thyself*, after the corruption had taken place.)

POSSIBLE.   *To be possible* (or *impossible*) can be followed by an infinitive, either active or passive, only when the subject of the finite verb is an introductory *it*, with the infinitive in apposition: e.g. 'It is possible to be drowned in a few inches of water', 'It was impossible to hear what he said'. With any other subject the infinitive is not permissible. We cannot say 'They are possible to be late', 'Roses are not possible to grow in this soil', 'His speech was impossible to be heard'. Amend to 'It is possible that they will be late', 'It is not possible to grow roses in this soil', 'It was impossible to hear his speech'. Even with *it* the construction is unidiomatic if the pronoun stands for something other than, and is the subject or object of, the infinitive, as in the sentences 'I hope it [e.g. the building of a wall] is possible to be done before Christmas', 'It [e.g. a watch] is so badly damaged that it is impossible to repair'.

Usage, however, does permit 'a result not possible to foresee', 'a question impossible to answer', as ellipses of 'which it was not possible to foresee', 'which it is impossible to answer'. In such cases the noun which precedes *possible* or *impossible* must be the object of the infinitive. We cannot say 'a situation possible to arise', where the noun is the subject of the infinitive.

POST- (Prefix).   *Postgraduate* and *postscript* are written as one word, but in most other words in which it occurs the prefix is hyphenated: *post-war*, *post-operational*.

POST MORTEM. Two words when used adverbially (an examination *post mortem*), but hyphenated when an adjective or a noun : *a post-mortem examination, to conduct a post-mortem.*

POTENT : POTENTIAL. *Potent* = strong, powerful (*a potent influence for good*). *Potential* = that could be, but is not yet (*a potential influence for good, a potential source of wealth*).

p.p. (or *per pro.* = *per procurationem*). Does not mean 'on behalf of', but 'by delegation to'. Hence it is the substitute's name that appears after the *p.p.* or *per pro.*, and the name of the person for whom he is signing before it, not vice versa. It is a very common mistake for John Smith, who is signing on behalf of William Jones, to write 'John Smith, p.p. William Jones'. He should write 'William Jones, p.p. John Smith'.

PRACTICABLE : PRACTICAL. The two words are sometimes confused. *Practicable* means 'such as can be carried out'. *Practical* means either (i) carried out in practice, as *a practical joke, the practical application of one's knowledge*, or (ii) suited, or adapted, to the prevailing circumstances, as *a practical suggestion*, i.e. one which has regard to an existing situation and is made in the light of it. A practicable suggestion (one which could be carried out) might not, in certain circumstances, be a practical one. (See also IMPRACTICABLE.)
Practically, in the sense of *almost*, is permissible, but the adjective *practical* cannot be used in the same way. We may say 'The match is practically over', but not 'This is the practical end of the match', 'He is practically an imbecile', but not 'a practical imbecile'.
Practical before the names of trades or occupations is usually a meaningless piece of jargon : *practical tailor, practical upholsterer, practical chimney sweep.*

PRACTICE : PRACTISE. The difference of spelling has nothing to do with the kind of practice, whether medical, legal or otherwise ; it is purely grammatical, and depends on the part of speech. The noun is spelt with a *c*, the verb with an *s*. (The Americans, however, use the *c* for both.)
Note the two adjectival uses : *a practice match* (a match played for practice), but *a practised speaker* (the participle used adjectivally).

PREFACE (Verb). 'He prefaced his remarks *with* a reference to the recent death of the chairman', but 'He prefaced his remarks *by* referring to the recent death of the chairman'. *With* before a noun, *by* before a gerund.

By, however, is used after a passive voice, even though a noun follows : 'His speech was prefaced by a reference to . . .'

PREFER. (i) *Prefer* is normally followed by *to*, not *than*: 'I prefer coffee to tea', 'She preferred sewing to knitting', 'We prefer going by car to travelling by train'. The difficulty arises when infinitives are involved. We cannot say 'She preferred to sew to to knit'. In such cases we use *rather than*, but never *than* alone.

Occasionally (more often in literary than in spoken style) *rather* is brought forward and placed before the first infinitive, and *than* is left before the second : 'He preferred rather to take the whole blame himself than to allow it to fall on the innocent'.

(ii) Even with nouns *rather than* is permissible in a situation where a choice specifically for that occasion is involved. Thus 'I prefer port to sherry' expresses a general preference. But if the question is 'What shall we have to drink ? . . . Port ? . . . Sherry ?', the reply might be, 'I should prefer port rather than sherry'. Perhaps there is a vague feeling that the infinitive *to have* is understood before each of the alternatives. But 'I should prefer port *to* sherry' is also correct.

(iii) On the various verbal forms and other constructions that are possible after *rather than*, see under RATHER.

(iv) 'Which do you prefer most ?' Incorrect. Literally, *prefer* means 'place before the other(s)'. It is therefore an absolute term, and cannot be modified by *more* or *most*.

PREFERABLE. One thing is preferable *to* another. *More preferable* and *most preferable* are solecisms. (See PREFER (iv).)

PREJUDICE. A prejudice in favour of or against ; prejudiced in favour of or against ; without prejudice to.

PREPOSITION. (i) There is no rule forbidding the use of a preposition at the end of a sentence. Sometimes it is the only possible place for it : e.g. 'Where has this bus come from ?', 'Who is that letter for ?', 'My little girl has no one to play with'. A writer must use his discretion and sense of style. Sometimes the preposition is best placed before the word it governs, sometimes at the end of the sentence or clause.

(ii) In English all prepositions govern the accusative case. 'For us who can remember the England of pre-war days this book will have a special appeal' (not *for we*). 'To us English the pace of American life seems very hectic' (not *to we English*).

If the preposition governs a combination of two co-ordinated pronouns, both must be in the accusative : 'Most of the work will fall upon you and me' (not *upon you and I*). 'Between you and me' (not *you and I*).

For special problems concerning *who* and *whom* with a preposition, see under WHO.

(iii) Be on guard against the intrusive, or duplicated preposition, usually the result of using a preposition before the word it governs, and at the end of the sentence as well : e.g. 'The car in which they came in', 'the instrument with which he did it with'. The same error may sometimes be the result of confusing to constructions, as 'The price for which we paid for it', a confusion of 'the price we paid for it' and 'the price for which we bought it'.

PRESCRIBE : PROSCRIBE. A doctor *prescribes* treatment or medicine, and an examining body *prescribes* certain books to be studied : a government *proscribes* (i.e. places outside the protection of the law) persons and practices it regards as undesirable.

PRETENCE : PRETENSION. *Pretence* = make-believe ('She made a pretence to faint'). *Pretension* = claim ('I make no pretension to scholarship.' 'His pretensions are quite without foundation.') *Pretence* is sometimes used where *pretension* is the correct word.

The Old and the Young Pretender were so called, not because they pretended that they were the rightful Kings of England, but because they claimed that they were. To speak of a person as the pretender to a throne is not to imply that his claim is false.

PREVENT. The idiomatic constructions are (i) 'prevent my doing it' and (ii) 'prevent me from doing it', but not 'prevent me doing it'. For constructions like 'prevent people being cheated', which is accepted English, see under -ING. The literal sense of 'go before (in order to guide)', as in 'Prevent us, O Lord, in all our doings', is now obsolete.

PREVENTATIVE : PREVENTIVE. There is no difference of meaning. The latter is to be preferred, whether as noun or adjective, though the former is sometimes used, more especially as the noun.

PREVIOUS(LY). The idiomatic constructions are *the previous day*, *the day previous*, *two days previous to Christmas*, *two days previously* (adv.), *previous to going* (not *previously*).

Sometimes *before* or *earlier* is preferable.

PRINCIPAL : PRINCIPLE. Whatever the part of speech, if the sense is *chief* the spelling is *principal* (the principal reason ; the principal of a college ; the principals in a choir, orchestra or cast of a play : 'principal' as opposed to 'interest'). *Principle* = a fundamental law governing one's conduct, natural phenomena, the functioning of a piece of mechanism, etc. (do a thing on principle ; against one's principles ; a person without principles ; the principle of gravitation ; an invention that works on the same principle as the old-fashioned water wheel). It is scarcely credible, but nevertheless true, that a few years ago an Education Committee in the north of England advertised a course at one of its technical colleges on 'Principals of Mining'.

PROCEED : PROCESS (Verb). Proceed = go forward, or continue on one's way. *Process* (with stress on the second syllable) = walk in procession. The verbal use with the stress on the first syllable (*to process foods, materials*, etc.) is a recent coinage by conversion of the noun.

PROGRAMME. So spelt in British English. The American spelling *program* should not be copied.

PROHIBIT. Prohibit a person *from doing* (not *to do*) something. 'Prohibit his doing it' is also sometimes heard, and seen in print, but it is better avoided.

Prohibit can also, of course, take a noun as its object : e.g. 'An order prohibiting the movement of cattle', 'An Act which prohibits unofficial strikes'. In the same way it may take a gerund provided the gerund is used in a general sense ('to prohibit the parking of cars in specified areas').

PROMPT(LY). The idiomatic constructions are (a) we shall start promptly, (b) we shall start promptly at 7.30, (c) we shall start at 7.30 prompt.

PROPORTION. (i) Strictly speaking, *proportion* means the relation of a part to the whole in one case, as compared with a similar relation in another case. Thus if a person with an income of £500 a year saves fifty pounds of it, and another person, with an income of £1000, saves a hundred pounds, they both save the same proportion of their income. If the latter saves £120 as against the former's £50, then he saves a greater proportion. But popular usage has extended the term to mean the part in relation to the whole, or the total, without any implication of a comparison with other cases: e.g. 'Only a small proportion of the candidates failed to complete the paper'. 'What proportion of the members are manual workers?' 'There was a high proportion of women amongst the audience.' This extension we may accept (though the last example is very vague, since we do not know what proportion was expected); but we should not go any further. Two misuses in particular we should avoid:

(a) The use of *a proportion* in the sense of *a few*, *a part*, *a number* or *an amount*: 'At every election a proportion of ballot papers are spoiled'. 'A proportion of the money raised will be retained to meet expenses.' 'We always expect a proportion of the goods to remain unsold.' Even allowing for the extended use of the word noted above, one might ask, what proportion? (See also the comment on PERCENTAGE.)

(b) The use of *the greater proportion* when all that is meant is 'the greater part', 'the greater number', or even 'most'. E.g. 'The greater proportion of the audience consisted of school-children.' 'The greater proportion of the land is still uncultivated.' 'A magazine, the greater proportion of whose readers are women.' Since *proportion* expresses, not merely number or amount, but a relationship, *the greater proportion* implies a comparison between two such relationships. We may correctly ask which of two persons spends the greater proportion of his income on food and clothing, or in which of two districts there is a greater proportion of manual workers, since we are then comparing proportion with proportion, not part with part or number with number.

(ii) The correct preposition to follow proportion is *to*, not *with*: 'in proportion *to*/out of all proportion *to* the work involved'.

In proportion as may be used to introduce a clause, but the construction is not very frequent: 'In proportion as the sales increase the profits will rise': i.e. a ten per cent increase in sales will mean a ten per cent increase in profits.

(iii) *Proportion* may be used as a verb, provided there is the sense of varying the amount in order to keep the same relation between two things in all cases concerned (e.g. 'to proportion the payment to the work done' or 'to proportion the tax to the value of the goods'), but it should not be used merely in the sense of *share*, or *share equally*: (e.g. 'to proportion the food out amongst the members of the party').

PROPORTIONAL: PROPORTIONATE. *Proportional* is usually used attributively (*a proportional amount, proportional representation*), *proportionate* predicatively (a share of the profits proportionate to the money invested, a reward proportionate to the effort).

PROTAGONIST. 'He was a staunch protagonist of all good causes.' Incorrect. *Protagonist* does not mean 'a fighter for' (as though it were the opposite of *antagonist*); it means 'one who plays a leading part'. The protagonists of a movement are the prominent figures in it. The word comes from Greek, and means, literally, the actor who takes the leading part in a play.

Another mistake sometimes made is to use the word as though it meant the earliest advocate of, or fighter for, a cause, a meaning perhaps suggested by a mistaken analogy with *prototype*: e.g. 'Mrs Pankhurst was one of the leading protagonists of women's suffrage'.

PROVERBIAL. 'We were up with the proverbial lark.' *The proverbial so and so* has become a cliché. Do not use it. Of course, there is no objection to such expressions as *proverbial wisdom* (the wisdom expressed in proverbs), *proverbial expressions* (expressions which have become proverbs).

PROVIDING THAT. (Conditional.) Much used, but incorrect. The correct form is *provided that* ('You may keep the book a further week provided that no one else requires it'). *That* may be omitted.

PROX. A piece of commercialese for 'next month'. Name the month.

PSYCHOLOGICAL MOMENT. 'He put his suggestion to the board at the psychological moment.' This use of the term (= the moment when their minds were disposed to receive it favourably), though strictly speaking incorrect, has become so common that it may now be accepted. It is illegitimate, however, to extend it to situations where mental receptivity, or effect on the mind, is not involved: e.g. 'The rain came at the psychological moment for the crops'.

PUMICE: POMACE. *Pumice* = the solidified lava used as an abrasive. *Pomace* = apple pulp that is left after cider-making.

PUNDIT: PANDIT. Two different forms of the same word. *Pundit* is used as the common noun (= a learned person, one who is supposed to be an authority on some subject), *Pandit* as a Hindu title, before a personal name, as *Pandit Nehru*.

PURGE. 'Six Pound a Week Typist Purged', 'Purged Alderman appeals to Minister of Health' (newspaper headlines). Anyone who uses this piece of modern political jargon should remember that literally the word means 'to rid of impurities'. It is therefore the party or organisation that is purged, not the persons who are expelled from it.

PURPORT (i) Noun. The purport of a letter or document is its apparent meaning or signification. The word does not suggest either that the apparent meaning is true or that it is not.

(ii) Verb. (a) Can be used only in the active voice. 'The letter purports to be a copy of one received by him on June 11th' (not *is purported to be*).

(b) *Purport* cannot have a personal subject unless the word itself is followed by *to be* with a complement. We cannot say 'They purported to have confidential information'; but 'They purported to be messengers from the king', is accepted usage.

(c) As the verbal use is confined to the active voice, only the present participle, never the past (which is passive), can be used adjectivally to qualify a noun preceding it: *a letter purporting* (not *purported*) *to come from his father*.

PURPOSE. Note the constructions *on purpose* (not *of purpose*), but *of set purpose, to some/no/little purpose, with the purpose of* + gerund, *not to the purpose* (irrelevant).

PURPOSELY: PURPOSEFULLY: PURPOSIVELY. *Purposely* = intentionally. *Purposefully* = in a determined manner, as if animated by a strong purpose ('They set about the task purposefully and without delay'). *Purposively* = in such a manner as to achieve an end or purpose. ('Studies which are purposively directed.')

Q

QUERY. Do not use this verb as a synonym for *ask* ('"Can we rely upon your help?" he queried'). Its only legitimate meaning is *to question* in the sense of 'to cast doubt upon': e.g. 'I am inclined to query the accuracy of that statement'.

QUESTION MARK. (i) The question mark is used for direct questions (including rhetorical questions), but not for indirect. It is incorrect to write 'I asked him whether he could direct me to the station?'. (See, however, point (v) below for exceptional cases.)

Though a direct question is normally characterised by the inverted verb-subject order ('Have you seen my purse?'), the statement order of subject-verb is possible ('You've not seen her since last Thursday?'). A question mark is still required.

(ii) Requests that start with *will you* . . .? are direct questions in form, and therefore normally require the question mark, but there seems a good case for omitting it when the request is followed in the same sentence by a statement so that the original question has been left far behind and the sentence has lost much of its interrogative force by the time the end is reached: e.g. 'Will you please complete the enclosed form and return it to us, when we will examine the matter further and let you know whether we think it is possible to take any further action.' (*M.E.U.*, however, insists, rather pedantically, that the question mark should be used even here.)

(iii) Since some exclamations have the same word-order as questions, care must be taken to distinguish the two. Contrast 'How exciting were those old melodramas!' and 'How exciting were those old melodramas?' Special care is needed with elliptical sentences, where the verb is omitted. The test is to ask ourselves what the form of the sentence would be if the verb were expressed. 'What nonsense, to talk like that!' is an exclamation, since it is short for 'What nonsense it is'. But 'What wonder that young men will not enter the profession?' is a rhetorical question, since it is an ellipsis of 'What wonder is it?'.

(iv) Sentences of the type 'Who should be there but Squire Faggus', 'What should he do but tell the secret to the first person he met!', expressive of surprise or annoyance, are not really questions, and do not require a question mark. A full stop is often sufficient; otherwise, if very strong feeling is indicated, an exclamation mark should be used.

(v) It has been pointed out above (Section i) that an indirect question does not take a question mark. One may nevertheless be used after such constructions as *I wonder whether* . . . if the whole sentence has the force of a request. It would clearly be incorrect to use a question mark after 'I wonder whether it will snow this Christmas', but one would be permissible after 'I wonder whether you could lend me fifty pence?', 'I wonder whether I might borrow your dictionary?', as these are felt to be equivalent in meaning to 'Could you lend me . . . ?', 'Might I borrow . . . ?' (That is to say, an answer is expected.) Similarly with *I suppose* followed by an indirect statement: 'I suppose Jane knows we are expecting her to tea?', as contrasted with 'I suppose we shall have to do the work ourselves'.

(vi) A subsidiary use of the question mark is to query the appropriateness of a word, or to suggest that it is used ironically: e.g. 'I am just enjoying (?) a few days' holiday'. This may be pardonable occasionally, but it should not be resorted to frequently. There is a certain cheapness about it. Fowler's comment is apt: 'It is a sure sign of the 'prentice hand'.

QUICKER (Adverb). (i) The normal comparative is *more quickly*, but when we are thinking of length of time rather than speed the tendency is to use *quicker*: 'As we get older the years seem to pass more quickly' (the speed of their passing), but 'The train will get you there quicker than the bus' (i.e. in a shorter time).

(ii) *Quicker*, used in this sense, differs from *sooner* in that *sooner* refers merely to a point of time, *quicker* to length of time. If train and bus arrive at the same time one will not get us there any *sooner* than the other, but it may get us there *quicker*.

(iii) Sometimes, even where speed is concerned, *quicker* is to be preferred to *more quickly* for euphonic reasons: e.g. 'I cannot walk any quicker than that'. 'Any more quickly than that' would sound awkward and cumbersome.

QUIT. (i) Past tense = *quitted*, past participle = *quit*.

(ii) *Quit* in the sense of 'give up', 'leave off' is an Americanism, which is not accepted in British English.

(iii) *To be quits* (even) is an accepted colloquialism.

QUITE. Some grammarians object to the use of *quite* before a noun ('Quite a crowd gathered', 'Quite an argument ensued') and before adjectives denoting an idea which can have no upward limit, or which is not absolute ('It's quite warm today', 'We had quite an enjoyable holiday'). But it can be defended on the ground that it means 'sufficient to justify the use of the word in question'.

Quite, used instead of *yes*, to express a mild form of agreement, is a genteelism that should be avoided.

QUIZ. *Quiz* was once a verb, meaning 'to make a person look foolish', or 'to pull one's leg'; then it meant to pry into the affairs of others, or to question a person in order to get from him information without his realising it. Recently the wireless and television have made it into a noun and given it a new meaning — a series of questions put to a person or a panel of persons in order to test their knowledge. We shall probably have to accept this extension of the word, but the journalistic use of it as a synonym for 'questionnaire' cannot be too strongly deprecated (e.g. 'Trade Unions to Get Quiz on Unofficial Strikes').

QUOTATION. (i) Quote only if there is a point in doing so. Quotation for quotation's sake, or merely to display one's knowledge or erudition, is a literary sin.

(ii) Quote correctly. If you are not sure of a quotation, verify it; and be particularly careful about well-known quotations, for sometimes the well-known form is an incorrect form. Coleridge did not write

　　　　Water, water everywhere,
　　　　And not a drop to drink,

but 'Nor any drop to drink', and Milton did not speak, in *Lycidas*, of 'fresh *fields* and pastures new', but 'fresh *woods* and pastures new'. C. P. Scott's famous dictum was not 'Comment is free, *news* is sacred' (the form in which it is frequently quoted), but '*fact* is sacred'. Lord Acton did not say 'All power corrupts', but 'Power *tends* to corrupt', which is a rather different thing. Shakespeare, according to Ben Jonson, had *small* (not *little*) Latin and less Greek, and Napoleon's boast was that 'the word *impossible* is not in my vocabulary'. To substitute 'in the dictionary', as is often done, misses the point and makes the statement not only false but absurd. James Thomson wrote 'Britannia, rule the waves' (either an exhortation or a wish), not 'Britannia *rules* the waves'; Macbeth determined to make assurance *double* (not *doubly*) sure, and dared Macduff to *lay on*, not to *lead* on, while his wife urged him to screw his courage to the sticking *place*, not the *sticking-point*. Kipling wrote 'The female of the species is more *deadly* than the male', not 'more dangerous', and Pope that 'a little *learning* is a dangerous thing (not *a little knowledge*).

The best way to verify a quotation is, of course, to turn to the work from which it comes. Failing that, there are various dictionaries of quotations. The best-known are Bartlett's *Familiar Quotations* and *The Oxford Dictionary of Quotations*. *The Penguin Dictionary of Quotations*, though not so comprehensive, includes quotations from recent works which are not found in the others. Some rather more obscure quotations, which have become clichés, will be found in Eric Partridge's *Dictionary of Clichés*. For the Bible, Shakespeare and some of the major poets, concordances exist.

(iii) If an author or source is given, see that the ascription is correct. Even writers who should have known better have been guilty of fathering a quotation on to someone who was not responsible for it.

(iv) Quote honestly. Do not use a quotation to prove something that its author never intended it to, or give its meaning a 'twist' to make it suit your own purpose. (How often have the words 'God's in his heaven, all's right with the world' been unfairly used to prove that Browning suffered from a smug religious optimism !) And remember that the meaning of a quotation may be changed or misrepresented if it is taken apart from its context. Thomas Gray did not declare that 'ignorance is bliss', but that

> Where ignorance is bliss
> 'Tis folly to be wise

— a very different idea. 'One touch of nature makes the whole world kin' is constantly misapplied. It does not mean that some simple natural act awakens a kindly and friendly response in the breasts of all. Shakespeare (*Troilus and Cressida*, Act III, Sc. iii) goes on to specify the 'touch of nature' — 'That all with one consent praise new-born gawds'. In other words, the whole of humanity has a common failing or weakness — the tendency to 'fall for' anything new and attractive-looking, no matter how specious it may be. It is a cynical evaluation of human nature, not the opposite. When John Knox wrote his *First Blast Against the Monstrous Regiment of Women* (1558) he was not anticipating the W.R.A.C. By *regiment* he meant 'rule' or 'government'. The unitarian fiend of Wesley's oft-quoted verse was the Moslem, not unitarian Christians (though Wesley had no great liking for those, either); when Cowper, in a well-known hymn, spoke of an 'aching void' he was not thinking of an empty stomach, but of an emptiness left in his life by the death of friends, while 'the inner man' of the Prayer Book service for the visitation of the sick does not refer to the intestines and the digestive organs, but the heart and mind, or the soul. The phrase *the patience of Job* means 'the suffering, or the afflictions, of Job' (Job was not especially notable for patience in the present-day sense of the word): 'a custom more honoured in the breach than in the observance' (a quotation from *Hamlet*) is not a custom which is more often neglected than observed (though that is the sense in which we often hear it applied), but a custom which it would be more honourable to break than to keep. Hamlet uses the words in reference to the traditional heavy drinking that takes place at Danish state banquets, a custom which disgusts him. 'Conspicuous by their absence' is not the same thing as 'conspicuously absent', though nowadays it is generally applied in that sense, an error for which perhaps Lord John Russell was responsible when he used the words half humorously and half sarcastically, in 1859, in a speech against Lord Derby's Reform Bill. They are actually a translation (though a bad one) from the Latin of Tacitus, who, in the third book of his *Annals* tells how the Roman patricians Brutus and Cassius became *conspicuus* (to use the Latin word) because their images were absent, by official command, from the funeral of Junia, the wife of Cassius and sister of Brutus. Two points should be noted: first, it was not the absence of the *persons* that rendered them *conspicuus* (to repeat the Latin word), but the absence of their images, which many people felt to be an unjustifiable slight; and secondly, the Latin adjective *conspicuus* is not the equivalent of the modern English *conspicuous* in the sense of 'clearly noticeable'. It means *illustrious*. To say that 'women members were conspicuous by their absence', when all we mean is that none were present, or that the kidney which is supposed to be in the steak and kidney pie is 'conspicuous by its absence' when we merely mean that there is none, or very little, is to use a meaningless and rather absurd cliché. And is it not time we ceased quoting 'The play's the thing' as though it meant that the play is all that really matters? It is another incomplete quotation (again from *Hamlet*). The full form is

'The play's the thing
Wherein I'll catch the conscience of the king'.

(v) Do not use inverted commas for brief quotations of a few words which have become part of the common stock of the English language, *a man's a man*, *for a' that*; *the first shall be last*.

'The departure for home of the Persian Prime Minister, trailing clouds of glory after a triumphant three-day progress. . . .'—The *Observer*, November 25th, 1951.

The words *trailing clouds of glory* come from Wordsworth's 'Immortality' ode, but to place them in quotation marks would be to offer an affront to the knowledgeable reader (who could be trusted to recognise them without that aid) and merely to puzzle the ignorant.

(vi) No quotation marks are needed when what is actually a quotation is presented as an original observation and then referred to its author. *The paths of glory lead but to the grave, Gray tells us. Fools rush in where angels fear to tread, as the poet Pope reminds us.*

(vii) A verse quotation consisting of a complete line should not be incorporated in the text, but set on a line of its own. If it consists of more than one line it must be set out in the correct metrical form. IT MUST NOT BE QUOTED AS THOUGH IT WERE PROSE.

No inverted commas are required.

(viii) If words are omitted from a quotation, indicate the omission by a hiatus (a series of dots).

(ix) On minor points concerning the use of inverted commas for quotations, see under INVERTED COMMAS.

QUOTATION MARKS.   (See INVERTED COMMAS.)

R

RACE. 'The British are a humane race.' The British are not a race. Substitute *nation* or *people*. A race is a group of people, usually consisting of several nations, all of whom possess certain physical characteristics in common. Thus the British, Germans, Dutch and Scandinavians all belong to the same race. It is, of course, correct to speak of a race of giants, a race of dwarfs, or a race of pygmies.

RACK AND RUIN. So spelt — not *wrack*.

RAISE: RISE. (i) *Raise* is transitive (i.e. it must have an object), *rise* intransitive. We raise prices, raise money, etc., but prices *rise*.

(ii) *Principal parts*: raise, raised, raised: rise, rose, risen.

(iii) A person whose wages are raised gets a *rise*, not a *raise*. *Raise* is not used as a noun, except in a few place names, like *Dunmail Raise*.

(iv) *Raised*, in the sense of *brought up* ('In Kentucky, where I was raised', 'Raised in a small Lancashire mill town, he went to London at the age of eighteen') is tolerated in America as a colloquialism, but many well-spoken Americans object to it. In British English it is a vulgarism.

RAPT. (See WRAPPED.)

RAREBIT. (See WELSH RAREBIT.)

RARELY. (i) 'It is very rarely that opportunity knocks twice.' Since *it* is here a pronoun anticipating the noun clause 'that . . . twice', we might expect the predicative adjective *rare*, but the adverb *rarely* is idiomatic in such sentences. There are the parallel cases of *seldom* and *not often* (both adverbial), which are similarly used. *Rare* is necessary, however, when *for* + an infinitive follows instead of a noun clause: e.g. 'It is very rare for a dog to live for twenty years'.

(ii) 'It is very interesting to note that the lack of "communication", which invariably indicates a lack of ability to think clearly in the realm of the intangible, appears much less rarely in candidates for positions where an Arts rather than a technological education is the required background'.—From a letter in the *Financial Times*, October 15th, 1960.

Here the word *rarely*, itself something of a negative, coupled with other negatives or semi-negatives like *less* and *lack*, has landed the writer in a state of mental confusion, with the result that, without realising it, he has said the opposite of what he intended. *Less rarely* means *more frequently*, yet the whole purport of his letter is that the lack is found *less* frequently amongst those who have had an education in the Arts. If it is less frequent (or rarer), then it appears *more rarely*, not less rarely. The ability is less rare, the lack of it more rare. Perhaps the writer has muddled two different ways of saying the same thing: 'the lack appears much less' and 'the lack appears more rarely'.

(iii) 'Rarely, if ever', 'rarely or never', but not 'rarely or ever'.

RATHER. (i) *Rather a foolish person* and *a rather foolish person* are both acceptable: in the first *rather* modifies the entire idea expressed by *a foolish person*, in the second only the adjective *foolish*. With expressions like *a long way*, *a long time*, which are almost compounds expressive of a single notion, *rather* must precede the article: *rather a long time*, not *a rather long time*. Note the difference between 'We have come rather a long way' (= distance) and 'We came a rather long way' (= route).

(ii) *Would rather* and *had rather* are both idiomatic. Generally, when *rather* is followed by an infinitive without *to*, whose subject is the same as that of the auxiliary, *would* is used, the two being felt to make up a compound tense: 'I would rather have tea than coffee'. 'We would rather go today than wait till tomorrow.' When *rather* is followed by a clause the tendency is to use *had*: 'I had rather you did it'. 'We had rather the matter were not made public.' *Would*, however, is also possible in these cases. In spoken English, of course, the two are usually indistinguishable, since both are abbreviated to *I'd*, *we'd*, etc.

Would is always used in questions: e.g. 'Would you rather I did it?' (not 'Had you rather?').

(iii) The following are the idiomatic verbal constructions that may follow *rather than*.

(a) When the two alternatives have the same subject and the verb is a compound tense, only the non-finite part is used, the auxiliary being understood from the earlier part of the sentence: 'He should be rewarded rather than punished'. 'These measures will aggravate rather than relieve the situation.' 'He was bolting his food rather than eating it.'

(b) If the verb which precedes *rather* is a simple tense form, however, a corresponding simple tense form must be used after it: 'He made a mistake rather than acted dishonestly'. 'His action aggravated rather than relieved the situation.'

(c) If *rather than* comes at the beginning of the sentence, the constructions given in the last two paragraphs are impossible : instead the gerund is used. 'Rather than being punished, he should be rewarded', 'Rather than relieving the situation, his action aggravated it.'

(d) If the alternative expressed by *rather than* represents the cause of the fact expressed in the first clause, or an inevitable or probable consequence had that fact not been fulfilled, then if the subject of the two clauses is the same, *rather than* is followed by a plain infinitive (without *to*) irrespective of the verbal form that precedes it : 'He suffered death rather than betray the secret'. 'He sold the vegetables at half price rather than allow them to go bad.' Actually this is an ellipsis of 'rather than he would betray/allow, etc.

The same form is used even when *rather than* comes first : 'Rather than allow the vegetables to go bad, he sold them at half price'.

(e) If the subject of the second clause is different from that of the first, then the ellipsis is not possible ; the full tense form must be used. 'She chose to go out to work rather than allow her son's education to suffer' (the same type as the previous one), but 'She chose to go out to work rather than (that) her son should be deprived of his education.' Again, the same form is used if *rather than* comes at the beginning of the sentence : 'Rather than that should happen, I would give up my job'.

(iv) On *rather than* with *prefer* (prefer one thing rather than another), see under PREFER.

(v) The case of pronouns after *rather than* may sometimes give trouble. The following illustrate the possibilities. 'I blame you rather than him' (object of *blame*). 'You are to blame rather than he' (*he* because it is short for *than he is*). 'It is for you, rather than him, to make the decision' (governed by the preposition *for*). 'It was you, rather than he, that caused the trouble' (short for *rather than it was he*, hence nominative, as the complement of *was*).

RE. Use no full stop. It is not an abbreviation of *regarding*, or *referring to*, as many people appear to think, but the ablative case of the Latin *res*, and therefore a complete word. The full phrase is *in re*, a legal term meaning 'in the matter of'. In print it is italicised.

Apart from its use in legal documents, *re* should be confined to formal headings of official or business letters : *re John Smith, deceased, re The Fisher Charity*. Do not use it in a sentence (e.g. 'I am writing to you re the repairs recently carried out at

15 Blackstone Road'. 'Re your letter of July 27th, we write to say . . .'). Use *about, regarding,* or *with reference to.*

REACTION. Should be used of a person only when it is meant to express a sudden, almost automatic response (e.g. the reaction of Claudius to the play that Hamlet caused to be acted before him to test his guilt). As a synonym for *opinion, feeling, view, impression,* it is a piece of jargon. Do not say 'Listen to this letter, and tell me your reaction', but 'Tell me your opinion of it' or 'Tell me what you think of it'.

REASON. (i) 'The reason for the delay is because we have had difficulty in obtaining materials.' *The reason . . . is because* is always incorrect. Amend to *The reason is that . . .* Alternatively we may retain *because* and re-word the first part of the sentence: *The delay has arisen because . . .*

(ii) Similarly incorrect are *the reason is because of, the reason is due to.* 'The *delay* is due to our having difficulties in obtaining materials.' The *reason* for the delay is not due to that; that *is* the reason.

(iii) 'Because you hadn't a ticket is no reason why you should be refused admission.' Again incorrect. Amend to 'The fact that you hadn't a ticket' or 'You shouldn't have been refused admission merely because you hadn't a ticket'.

RECEIPT. Do not speak of a *receipt* for making jam, cakes, etc. The correct word is *recipe* (though *receipt* was used in this sense in older English).

RECOURSE. (See RESORT.)

REDOLENT. Followed by *of,* not *with.*

REFERENCE. A written document testifying to a person's character, abilities, suitability for a post, etc., should not be called a reference, but a *testimonial.* Employers who ask applicants for a post for 'references' often mean this, but they are using the word incorrectly. 'Give two references' should mean 'Give the names of two persons to whom we may refer for information about you'.

REFLEXIVE PRONOUNS. (See -SELF.)

REFRAIN. 'The writer has refrained from the temptation to condemn merely on moral grounds.' Incorrect. *Resisted* should have been used. *Refrain from* can be followed only by (i) a gerund in the active voice (*refrain from doing something*),

(ii) a noun with an active sense (*refrain from theft, from crime,* etc.). It cannot take a noun, like *temptation,* which is passive in sense. We refrain from doing something which we are tempted to do ; we resist the temptation to do it.

REGARD. The constructions are (i) to have regard to (no -*s*), (ii) with regard to (no -*s*), (iii) as regards (verb), (iv) to have regard for, (v) give one's regards to (= pay one's respects), (vi) with kind regards (the formal ending of a letter to a friend or acquaintance).

Have regard to = take into consideration : 'In planning the syllabus we must have regard to the needs of those students who are taking the commercial course'.

Have regard for = show consideration for : 'He has no regard for other people'.

With regard to = concerning : 'With regard to the point you have just raised, I will have the matter investigated'.

Without regard to = without considering or taking into account : 'He always does what he thinks right, without regard to the consequences'.

The use of *regardless* as an adverb ('He spends money regardless') is a colloquialism bordering on slang.

REGISTER OFFICE. The correct term for the office where births, deaths and marriages are registered, and where civil marriages take place. The latest edition of *C.O.D.* gives qualified approval to *registry office,* but though this is often heard it is generally considered incorrect.

REHABILITATE. This word is fast becoming a piece of official jargon for *repair* or *restore.* ('A grant of £500 was made towards the rehabilitation of the church at Dover' — From a Free Church weekly.) It should not be used in this sense. Its strict meaning is, to restore a person (or a group of persons) to a position of respectability or usefulness : e.g. the rehabilitation of a person discharged from prison, the rehabilitation of disabled persons, the rehabilitation of 'disgraced' members of the Communist party, etc. It may legitimately be extended to an organisation or an institution (e.g. the rehabilitation of a club or a dance hall which has fallen into disrepute), but not to a building which has fallen into disrepair or suffered material damage.

RELATION : RELATIONSHIP. The difference of usage between these two words is easier to illustrate than to explain. The dictionaries are not very helpful, and Fowler (*M.E.U.*) avoids the difficulty by condemning *relationship* in all its uses other than those where family connexion is denoted. But it is useless, and indefensible, to condemn what has long been established.

Perhaps we may say that *relationship* expresses the general, abstract idea of one thing or one person being related to another, whereas *relation* suggests a more definite or specific connexion. We say 'He is a relation of mine' (i.e. a person who is related to me) and ask 'What relation is he to you?' (i.e. cousin, uncle, brother-in-law?). But we cannot ask 'What is his relation to you?' Here we must use *relationship* (i.e. the way he is related).

When we come to things or facts that are related, *relation* suggests a definite line of connexion: e.g. 'Doctors think there is a relation between smoking and lung cancer'. 'That has no relation to the matter under discussion.' *Relationship*, on the other hand, expresses the general idea, or the state or fact, of one thing being related to another: e.g. 'Such words as *ratio* and *proportion* connote a relationship'.

'The firm is proud of the good relationship that has always existed between management and employees.' Incorrect. Substitute *good relations*.

RELATION: RELATIVE: RELEVANT. (i) For persons to whom one is related both *relation* and *relative* may be used There is little to choose between them, and it is very largely a matter of personal preference, but the tendency is perhaps to keep *relation* for one to whom we are closely related, and *relative* for those with whom the connexion is more distant. In official language *relative* is used to cover both (e.g. *dependent relatives*). Sometimes rhythm may be the deciding factor. We speak of *rich* (or *poor*) *relations*, but *elderly relatives*.

(ii) *Relative* (adj.). (a) As related one to another. The relative weights of two objects means the weight of one in relation to that of the other. (b) Relating specifically to one thing and to no other: 'We have sold for you 1000 shares in the XY Manufacturing Company. Will you please let us have the relative certificate?' (i.e. the certificate which relates to these shares).

Relevant = having a bearing on the matter in question: e.g. the relevant information, the relevant facts, the relevant documents, the relevant parts of the letter.

RELATIVELY. *Relatively* should not be used as a synonym for *rather* or *fairly*. A *relatively* short distance is not a fairly short distance, but one that is short as compared with, or in relation to, another. A person who has to make a daily journey of ten miles to his work may not think it a short one, but it may be *relatively* short if most of his colleagues have to come twenty-five or thirty miles. (See also COMPARATIVELY.)

RENDITION. 'Miss Betty Jenkinson's rendition of several seventeenth-century songs was loudly applauded.' 'The supreme duty of the translator must be to seek as exact a rendition as possible'—From a letter in the *Observer*. This use of the word is to be deprecated. Substitute *rendering*.

REPLACE. Care is needed with prepositions. When *replace* is active it has for its object the name of the thing that is replaced, and is followed by *with* ('We are replacing all the old typewriters with new ones'). When the verb is passive, with the thing that is replaced as its subject, *by* is used ('All the old typewriters have been replaced by new ones'). But in a passive sentence where it is necessary to use *by* to denote an agent, *with* must be used before the name of the thing that is substituted ('All the old typewriters have been replaced by the management with new ones'). (See also SUBSTITUTE.)

REQUIRE. (i) When used in the active voice, *require* cannot be followed by an infinitive which has as its subject the subject of *require* itself: e.g. 'You require to have a University degree for a post of that kind'. The correct alternatives are (a) 'You require a University degree', (b) 'You need to have a University degree'. It is perfectly idiomatic, however, if the infinitive has a subject of its own: 'We require you to have a University degree', 'The law requires all parents to send their children to school until the age of fifteen'. This, changed into the passive voice, gives 'You are required to have a University degree'; 'All parents are required by law to send their children to school until the age of fifteen', which is also correct.

(ii) The passive voice of *require* cannot be followed by a passive infinitive: e.g. 'The money is required to be paid by Saturday next'. The two acceptable constructions are (a) 'We require the money to be paid' (active voice of *require* + passive infinitive), (b) 'You are required to pay the money' (Passive voice of *require* + active infinitive).

RESIGN. One *resigns* a position, *resigns from* an organisation, and is *resigned to* one's fate or to a situation which one accepts because there is no escape from it.

RESORT : RECOURSE. The idiomatic constructions are (i) *resor to compulsion*, (ii) *have recourse to compulsion*, but not *have resort to.* We do something *as a last resort,* not *as a last recourse.*

RESPECTIVE(LY). The legitimate uses are (1) to express an exact correspondence or relationship between the individual members or items of two series or sequences : 'John and James went to Harrow and Rugby respectively' (i.e. John went to Harrow, James went to Rugby), (2) in a distributive sense, as 'Three Directors of Education explained how the problem was being dealt with in their respective areas' (i.e. A in his area, B in his area, and C in his).

The following exemplify some incorrect uses :

(i) 'The meeting was addressed by Smith, Jones and Brown respectively.' (Here the intended meaning is presumably 'in that order'; but that is not the meaning of *respectively.*)

(ii) 'The members took their respective seats.' (Here *respective* adds nothing to the meaning of the sentence.)

(iii) 'Each of the delegates gave his respective views.' (When *each* is used, *respective* is merely tautological.)

(iv) 'We all have a right to our respective opinions.' (*Respective* is here wrongly used as a synonym for *own.*)

(v) '*Vanity Fair, The History of Henry Esmond,* and *Bleak House* were written by Thackeray and Dickens respectively.' (Of course, what the author of the sentence meant was that the first two were written by Thackeray and the third by Dickens; but to express this notion *respectively* will not do. The reader will, no doubt, guess that two of the works must have been written by one of the novelists, but how can he tell which two, and which novelist ? — unless he knows already, in which case the information is superfluous.)

(vi) 'He was a Fellow of the Royal Historical Society and of the Royal Society of Literature respectively.' (Here *respectively* seems to be used in the sense of *both.*)

(vii) 'We have interviewed the four applicants respectively.' (It is difficult to know quite what *respectively* means here. *In turn ? Individually ? All four applicants ?*)

REVEREND : REVERENT : REVERED. (i) *Reverend* = worthy of reverence; *reverent* = showing reverence. *Revered* = accorded great reverence : e.g. 'a much revered man'.

(ii) *Reverend* (often abbreviated to *Rev.*) is prefixed to the name of a clergyman or minister; but it should *never* be prefixed to the surname alone : *the Rev. J. G. Elton, the Rev. John Elton, the Rev. Mr Elton, the Rev. Dr Elton,* etc., but NOT *the Rev. Elton.*

(iii) In introducing a minister or clergyman, either to a friend or to a public gathering, introduce him as *The Reverend So-and-so*, but thereafter refer to him as *Mr* or *Dr*, as the case may be.

(iv) Certain purists insist that the only 'Reverend Doctor' is a Doctor of Divinity, and that clergymen who hold other doctorates should be described as *Dr the Reverend*; but this seems unnecessarily pedantic.

(v) Since *reverend* is an adjective, strictly speaking there is no plural form of it; but *the Reverends J. C. Smith and S. L. Brown* is frequently seen in print, and may be regarded as accepted usage.

(vi) *A reverend* (as a synonym for a clergyman) is a vulgarism.

RID. Past tense and past participle both *rid*: 'The Pied Piper rid the town of rats'. 'He has at last rid himself of those undesirable companions.'

RIGHT: RIGHTLY: RIGHTS. (i) For the adverb, *rightly* must always be used when it modifies a whole sentence or expresses an opinion on the fact stated in the sentence.

They rightly refused the offer.

He declined to answer the question, and rightly so.

Quite rightly, she referred the complaint to the manager.

When it is merely the verb of the sentence that is modified, *rightly* again is necessary if the adverb precedes the verb ('She had not been rightly informed'). When the adverb follows the verb *rightly* and *right* are often equally acceptable (e.g. 'If I remember right' and 'If I remember rightly'), but when the meaning is 'in such a way as to produce a right result', only *right* is possible: 'I seem unable to do it right'. 'This machine won't work right.' 'You haven't added the figures up right.' 'I can never spell that word right.'

(ii) *Right* in the sense of *very* is archaic, though it is still heard in regional speech: e.g. 'He was a right clever person'. 'It's right warm today.'

(iii) *Right now* and *right away* (= immediately) are Americanms, not recognised in British English.

(iv) *Set a thing to rights* is accepted colloquially, but *by rights* incorrect, though frequently heard in speech. The correct form is *by right*: 'By right, the house should have belonged to his brother' — not *by rights*.

RIGHT HONOURABLE (Abbrev. *Rt. Hon.*). Used of members of the Privy Council (which includes Cabinet Ministers and ex-Cabinet Ministers), peers and peeresses, the children of those peers above the rank of Viscount, and certain Lord Mayors; but it is incorrect to prefix it to the office of all Lord Mayors. (See under LORD MAYOR.)

RIME: RHYME. The *rhyme* in poetry. A nursery *rhyme*. Coleridge called his well-known poem *The Rime of the Ancient Mariner*, and when the full title is quoted the word must be so spelt, but otherwise use *rhyme* for a poem. The verb *to rhyme* is spelt in the same way. *Rime* = hoar frost.

RISE: ARISE. (i) A person *rises* from his chair or his bed, *rises* at 7.30, *rises* in the world, *rises* to the occasion, etc. The sun, the temperature, the barometer and prices all *rise*, while an aeroplane *rises* into the sky. *Rise*, that is to say, is the word that is used when the meaning is 'getting, going or coming up'.

Arise = 'come into being'. A quarrel, an argument, a difficulty, a doubt, a question, a storm, an awkward situation *arises*. 'A wind arose' (suddenly blew up), but 'The wind rose to gale force' (increased in velocity or intensity).

(ii) In older English *arise* was often used where today we should use *rise* or *rise up*: e.g. 'My lady sweet, arise'. 'Let God arise.' 'I will arise and go to my father.' But except in verse this is now archaic.

(iii) *Rising twenty-one* (i.e. approaching) is still heard, but is rather old-fashioned.

(iv) On *rise* and *raise*, see RAISE.

RISQUÉ. Not *risky*, in the sense of 'fraught with danger', but 'verging on impropriety'.

ROAD. (i) When the word is part of the proper name of a thoroughfare, write it with a capital (Euston Road, Westbourne Road, etc.). Some newspapers have recently adopted the practice of printing *Westbourne-road*, but this should not be copied. A small letter is, of course, needed when *road* is not part of the name, as *the London road* (the road leading to London).

(ii) We may speak either of 'a shop in Edgware Road', 'a flat in Bayswater Road' or '. . . in *the* Edgware Road', '. . . in *the* Bayswater Road', etc. The use of the article in this way is quite common in London and the south of England, but is practically unknown in the Midlands and the North. (It is never used before *Street*, except for *the High Street*. We cannot speak of *the Oxford Street, the Bond Street*.)

ROUSE: AROUSE. *Rouse* means, primarily, 'wake one from sleep'. ('He gave instructions that he was to be roused at six o'clock.') From this literal sense it is applied figuratively to awakening any power, quality or attribute that is thought of as being dormant: *rouse one's anger, spirits, energies; rouse one to action.*

Arouse = 'give rise to; bring into being; cause to arise': *arouse criticism, comment, fears, suspicion, interest, opposition, resentment,* etc.

Rouse may be used both transitively and intransitively; *arouse* transitively only.

RULE THE ROOST. Now the accepted form, though originally *rule the roast.*

RURAL: RUSTIC. *Rural* is the uncoloured term, and is contrasted with *urban: a rural life, a rural scene, rural areas. Rustic* suggests a certain quaintness, simplicity or crudity (*rustic characters, rustic speech*).

S

SABBATH. Spelt with a small *s*. Use the word only when the religious character of the day is to be stressed: *sabbath observance, sabbath breakers, working on the sabbath*. For all other purposes use *Sunday*. The word was originally, of course, applied to the Jewish holy day, which is Saturday.

SACCHARIN: SACCHARINE. The spelling without the *e* is the name of the substance (*flavoured with saccharin*: *saccharin tablets*), that with the *e* an adjective meaning *sweet*.

SAID. (i) Pronounced *sed*. The pronunciation with the diphthong as in *say* is a regional one.

(ii) The adjectival use of *said* in expressions like 'the said Henry Jackson' is accepted in the language of legal documents, but elsewhere it is out of place, except as a humorous device.

(iii) In prose the inverted formula *said Mrs Jones* should be used only within or after a passage of direct speech, never before it. Popular journalism has recently started using sentences like *Said the Headmaster, 'We are very proud of Tony's achievement'*. This should not be copied. In verse, however, it is accepted.

SAKE. (i) Normally there is no plural: 'for everyone's sake', 'for the children's sake', 'for Tom and Mary's sake', 'for our sake' (not *sakes*); but 'for all our sakes', 'for all their sakes' is allowable, though 'for the sake of us all' and 'for the sake of them all' is to be preferred.

(ii) *Sake* is usually preceded by a genitive: 'for God's sake', for heaven's sake', etc., but 'for goodness sake' (with no apostrophe *s*) has become traditional, and we say 'for conscience' sake' (note the apostrophe in the written form) for reasons of euphony. 'For Tom and Mary's sake' when the two persons are thought of together (e.g. as man and wife, or as brother and sister), but 'for Tom's and Mary's sake' when they are thought of separately.

SALTPETRE. Note the spelling: not *-er*.

SALUBRIOUS: SALUTARY. Salubrious = conducive to physical health (*a salubrious spot, not a very salubrious atmosphere*): *salutary* = beneficial morally (*a salutary lesson, a salutary experience*).

SAME. (i) 'Please complete the enclosed form and return same without delay.' A piece of commercial jargon, which should be avoided. Use *it* (or *them* if plural). *The same*, meaning 'that which has just been mentioned', is found in the Prayer Book and the Authorised Version of the Bible, but is now archaic.

(ii) Some grammarians condemn *the same that* and contend that we should always say *the same as*: but there is room for both. *As* must always be used when resemblance is in question ('She has the same fair hair and blue eyes as her mother had.' 'This coffee is the same as we had at Mrs Dawson's'), but *that* is permissible when identity is indicated: 'He was wearing the same coat and hat that he had on when we met him five years ago'.

(iii) 'He speaks with a slight lisp, same as his brother.' 'Why don't you walk to work of a morning, same as I do?' A vulgarism. Amend to *the same as*, or *like*.

SAT. 'She was sat by the fire reading a book.' Very common, even amongst well-spoken people, in certain districts, but not accepted as correct in Standard English, where *she was sat* can only be a passive voice meaning that she was placed there by another person. Amend to *was sitting* or *was seated*. The same applies to 'He was stood at the door' (see under STOOD) and 'He was laid on the couch', neither of which is accepted as idiomatic (except, of course, as a passive voice).

SATIRE: SATYR. *Satire* is the literary form, *satyr* the mythological creature, half man and half goat.

SAYS. Pronounced *sez*. The pronunciation like *say*, but with a sibilant added, is a regional one. With a certain class of writer it seems to have become an established convention to write *says* as *sez* when they wish to indicate uneducated speech, but as this is the pronunciation given to the word by educated people the practice seems pointless, at least so far as the third person is concerned. With the first person there may be a point, for while *he says* is normal English, and there is a recognised pronunciation for it, *I says* is not. The question therefore arises, what pronunciation is represented by *says* here? The same as in *He says*, or the same as *I say*, with the *s* sound added? The spelling *sez* indicates that it is the former.

SCARCELY. (i) *Scarce* as an adverb is now archaic (e.g. 'He ate scarce a crumb'). Use *scarcely*.

(ii) *Scarcely* is followed by *when*, not *than*: 'We had scarcely set out *when* it began to pour with rain'.

(iii) 'He escaped without scarcely a scratch.' Incorrect, since *without scarcely* is a double negative. The alternatives are 'without a scratch' and 'with scarcely a scratch'.

SCARIFY. 'The road to it [the house], particularly the last part, is scarifying, but it's well worth it when you get there.'— Noël Coward, *Pomp and Circumstance*. *Scarifying* is, presumably, used here in the sense of 'scaring', 'frightening' or 'terrifying', a very common misuse of it. *To scarify* has no connexion whatever with scaring; it means 'to lacerate' or 'to tear ruthlessly'. *Scarifying criticism* of a work of literature or of a person's conduct is criticism which, figuratively, tears it to pieces.

SCEPTIC: SEPTIC. A *sceptic* (pronounced *sk-*) is one who is inclined to disbelief: *septic* is an adjective meaning 'affected by sepsis, or poisoning of the blood'. The latter is sometimes mis-spelt *sceptic*, though it is very rare that the two words are confused in pronunciation.

SCHEDULE. In British English pronounced with *sh-* at the beginning. The pronunciation *sk-* is American.
  Behind schedule may be a useful phrase to denote failure to keep up to the time-table for the various stages of a process or an operation, but it should never be allowed to become a cliché for *late*. A building project may rightly be said to be 'behind schedule' if, at the end of six months, it has only reached the stage it was planned to reach in five months; and to the railway staff, who see each station at which a train is timed to stop merely as a stage in its entire progress from one end of its journey to the other, the train is 'running behind schedule'; but to anyone who is waiting for it at his local station it is merely late.

SCOT-FREE. So spelt: not *scott*. A *scot* was the name of an old tax, so that 'to get off scot-free' originally meant to get off without having to pay the tax.

SCOTCH: SCOTTISH: SCOTS. The Scots (or Scotch?) themselves are less particular than the English in the matter of these three words. The following recommendations are based upon what seems to be present-day practice in England.
  (i) For the noun denoting the people use *Scots*, not *Scotch*: and similarly *Scotsman*, not *Scotchman*. The famous express train is often incorrectly referred to as *The Flying Scotchman*.

(ii) For the adjective, use *Scottish* when the thing to be described is part of, situated in, native or indigenous to, or otherwise closely associated with Scotland : *the Scottish universities, the Scottish Highlands, the Scottish herring industry, a Scottish accent.*

Scotch is used when the adjective is thought of as denoting a *kind* rather than the place of origin : a Scotch terrier, Scotch whisky, Scotch plaid, Scotch tweed, Scotch eggs, Scotch pancakes, Scotch mist.

SCUTCHEON. *The blot on the scutcheon* is a traditional expression : in all other contexts use *escutcheon*. *Scutcheon* needs no apostrophe, though Browning gave it one.

SECUNDUM NATURAM. A Latin phrase meaning 'according to nature', or 'naturally', not, as is often supposed, 'second nature'.

SEEM. 'He can't seem to understand.' 'She won't seem to try.' Both incorrect. Amend to (a) 'He seems unable to understand' or 'He doesn't seem able to understand', (b) 'She seems unwilling to try' or 'It seems that she won't try'. *Can't* and *won't* should apply to the infinitives, whereas in the sentences as first given they are made to apply to *seem.*

SELDOM. *Seldom* is an adverb. We may say 'I seldom go to London', but not 'My visits to London are seldom', for here we are treating the word as a predicative adjective. It can be used predicatively (and then as an adverb) only in the following types of construction.

(i) After *It is* (*was*), and followed by a noun clause in apposition to the anticipatory pronoun *it* : 'It is seldom that we get such an opportunity as this'.

(ii) In a relative clause that refers back to the whole notion expressed in a preceding adverb clause of time : 'When she lost her temper, which was seldom, . . .' 'Whenever I take a day off from work, which is seldom, . . .'

(iii) In a parenthetic clause referring back to the entire notion expressed in a preceding adverb clause of time : 'Whenever he went to chapel (and that was seldom) . . .'

It is not altogether impossible in relative clauses referring back to a conditional clause introduced by *if ever* ('If ever I have a stroke of good luck, which is seldom, . . .'), but 'as I seldom do' or 'which I seldom do' is to be preferred.

Note the phrases *seldom if ever* and *seldom or never* (but not *seldom or ever*).

-SELF, -SELVES. (i) The pronouns ending in -*self* and -*selves* may be either reflexive or emphasising. The forms are *myself*, *yourself*, *himself*, *herself*, *itself*, *oneself*, *ourselves*, *yourselves*, *themselves*. Note the spelling *oneself* (not *one's self*). *One's self* does exist, but it is not the personal pronoun. It means 'one's essential personality'.

(ii) The form *ourself*, instead of *ourselves*, is permissible when the reference is to an editorial *we*, though *ourselves* is to be preferred. Shakespeare uses *ourself* several times to refer to a royal *we*.

(iii) *Hisself* and *theirselves* are illiteracies, but *their* is accepted in such sentences as 'They have only their two selves to please'. 'How's yourself?' is a vulgarism.

(iv) A -*self* pronoun cannot be used alone as the subject of a verb. 'The manager himself is attending to the matter' is correct, as here *himself* stands in apposition to *manager*, but not 'Himself is attending to the matter', 'Myself heard him say it', etc. In certain cases, however, the subject may be omitted if it is understood from a previous clause : 'He is always urging others to take risks, but never takes them himself'.

The remarks in the foregoing paragraph apply to normal modern English prose. In Ireland *himself* is sometimes used colloquially as an emphatic subject, to denote a person of some importance, often the master of the house ('Himself will see you in a moment'), while Shakespeare has 'Thyself shalt see the Act' (*The Merchant of Venice*), and FitzGerald 'Myself when young did eagerly frequent Doctor and Saint, and heard great argument' (*Omar Khayyám*). But these are special cases. Reflexive or emphasising pronouns also occur several times as subjects in the various volumes of Sir Osbert Sitwell's autobiography. This, however, is a characteristic of the style of this particular writer.

(v) Avoid the pointless or unnecessary use of the emphasising pronoun. There is a point in using it in 'I saw it myself', but not in 'I think myself that we ought to reconsider the matter'.

There are one or two expressions in which the -*self* pronoun (in this case a reflexive) can be either used or omitted : e.g. 'He knows how to behave (himself)'. 'She wouldn't trouble (herself) to do it.' 'He will worry (himself) about trivialities.' The use of the reflexive pronoun makes it more vivid and personal, and perhaps rather more forceful.

(vi) In some cases the -*self* pronoun competes with the simple personal pronoun : e.g. 'This tax will fall very heavily on people like you' or 'on people like yourself'. Both are correct ; the difference is one of viewpoint. *You* represents the second person as he is seen by the speaker, *yourself* as he is seen or thought of by himself. When A refers to B as *you*, he is presenting the situation as he (A) sees it; when he refers to him as *yourself* he is asking him to look at it from his own (B's) point of view.

(vii) *My*, *your* and *her* cannot be detached from the rest of the word and made to qualify a noun and a co-ordinated *-self*. 'Kind regards to your mother and self' is vulgar. Say 'Your mother and yourself' or 'Yourself and your mother' (but not 'Yourself and mother'). *Your good self* and *your good selves* are pieces of deplorable business jargon which no self-respecting business house should allow to appear in its correspondence. Even worse, and bordering on an illiteracy, is *your goodself*.

SEMICOLON. (i) The chief point to remember is that, normally, nothing on one side of the semicolon should be grammatically dependent upon anything upon the other side. That is to say, each part could, from a grammatical point of view, be a separate sentence, but since the two have some bearing upon each other notionally, they are put together in one sentence and separated by a semicolon.

> You could not expect it to last very long; it was too cheap.
>
> He is a clever fellow; even his enemies admit that.
>
> And then, of course, there is the question of the missing letter; but we will not go into that now.
>
> She refused to have anything to do with the matter; and I don't blame her, either.

(ii) Occasionally the semicolon may be used instead of a comma to divide a series of subordinate clauses from each other when they are all dependent on the same main clause. The following example is from Macaulay's *History of England*:

> 'It was vehemently argued that this mode of conveyance would be fatal to the breed of horses and to the noble art of horsemanship; that the Thames, which had long been an important nursery of seamen, would cease to be the chief thoroughfare from London up to Windsor and down to Gravesend; that saddlers and spurriers would be ruined by hundreds; that numerous inns at which mounted travellers had been in the habit of stopping would be deserted, and would no longer pay any rent; that the new carriages were too hot in summer and too cold in winter, etc.'

(iii) Sometimes we may hesitate whether to use a comma or a semicolon. We should be guided by the sense of the sentence and by the feeling we want it to convey. Generally, the semicolon, being a heavier stop than the comma, throws more emphasis on to the words that follow it.

He gave his promise, but I didn't suppose he would keep it.
He gave his promise; but I didn't suppose he would keep it.
I prophesied he would fail, and he did.
I prophesied he would fail; and he did.

(There is, of course, no question of the possibility of a comma in the first two examples under (i) above. To use one would be incorrect. A semicolon is the only permissible stop. See under COMMA.)

SENSUAL: SENSUOUS. *Sensual*=appealing to the senses, or to the bodily appetites (usually with a pejorative connotation): *sensual pleasures*. *Sensuous*=appealing to the senses of sight, taste, smell, etc. (generally used approvingly): '*the sensuous imagery of Keats's poetry*.

SEW: SOW. *Sew* (with needle and cotton), *sow* (seeds). The principal parts are *sew, sewed, sewn* and *sow, sowed, sown* (or *sowed*) respectively.

Sow is often used figuratively (*sow dissension, sow the seeds of discontent*), *sew* rarely so.

SEWAGE: SEWERAGE. *Sewage* = waste materials carried away by the sewers. *Sewerage* = system of sewers ('The sewerage of the district has become inadequate').

SHAKESPEARIAN. This spelling is to be preferred to *Shakespearean*.

SHALL: WILL. (See under WILL.)

SHAMBLES. 'After the looting by the enraged mob the interior of the building was a shambles.' This use of the word, as though it meant a scene of ruin, chaos or disorder, is to be deprecated, though it shows every sign of spreading. The correct meaning is *a slaughter-house*. The misuse seems to have arisen from the war of 1939–45, when a heavily bombed district was described as a shambles (i.e. a large number of people were killed). By the ignorant or careless, the word was then applied to the material destruction that was caused, and later was extended to a mere state of disorder, without any suggestion of destruction. Possibly the spread of the incorrect use has been helped by the fact that, in its strictly correct sense, the word is obsolete. Even a slaughter-house is now an *abattoir*

SHAPE. 'Have you anything in the shape of bananas?' — 'Yes, madam: cucumbers.' This should serve as a warning against the totally pointless use of the expression *in the shape of*. The lady meant merely 'Have you any bananas?'

SHEW. Pronounced the same as *show*. At one time it was the accepted spelling for the verb, *show* being reserved for the noun. It is now obsolescent, if not actually obsolete. Use the spelling *show* for both noun and verb. Bernard Shaw always spelt the verb *shew*, and notices of the old Southern Railway read 'All tickets must be *shewn*', but British Railways has altered this to 'Please *show* tickets'.

SHRUNK: SHRUNKEN. *Shrunken* is an adjective, used attributively (*a small, shrunken body*): *shrunk* is the past participle (*The garment has shrunk in the wash*) and the predicative adjective (*It is so shrunk that it will not fit me*).

SHY. *Spelling*: shyer, shyest, shyness, shying: but *shied*.

SIC. A Latin word meaning *thus*. In English its only legitimate use is as an interpolation in a quotation from or a transcription of a document where some obvious error of spelling or fact occurs. E.g. 'On p. 15 of the guide-book we read that "on the outskirts of the village is an old cottage which is supposed to have been the home of Adam Bede, in George Elliot's [*sic*] novel of that name"'. The author of the sentence is, in effect, saying, 'Yes, I know that George Eliot spelt her name with only one *l*, but the mistake is not mine or the printer's. I am quoting it exactly as it is given in the guide-book.'

Sic should not be used to express surprise or disgust, or to convey a veiled sneer, as in the sentence 'This sudden concern of the Socialists for the private trader and the property owner [*sic*] may herald a change of heart, but we doubt it'.

SICK. (See under ILL.)

SIGNAL. As an adjective, means *outstanding, conspicuous* (signal success, a man of signal virtues). The verb meaning 'to pick out from amongst many', or 'to cause to stand clearly out from amongst others' is *single out*, not *signal out*.

SINCE. (Expressing time.) (i) Normally *since* is preceded by a verb in the perfect tense, and followed by a word or expression denoting past time:

We *have lived* here since 1938.

I *have not seen* him since *last Saturday*.

If *since* introduces a clause, then the verb of this clause must normally be in the past tense.

I *have not seen* him since he *left* school.

There are, however, three exceptions to this:

(a) When the sentence is concerned with the total amount of time, counting from the point in the past up to the present, *since* is preceded by a present tense (usually *is*):

It *is* fifteen years since the war ended.

It *must be* almost five years since we last met.

(b) When the sentence is concerned with a present situation or condition which is traced back to an event in the past that gave rise to it, and since when it has persisted, *since* is preceded by a present tense:

She *is* nervous of riding in a car since she was involved in that accident.

(c) *Since* is followed by a perfect tense instead of the past when the reference is to the beginning of something that has persisted ever since, and that still persists:

Since I *have been* at this school we have had three head-masters.

He has never been to see me since I *have been* ill.

Since I was would imply that I am no longer at the school and no longer ill.

It is incorrect, however, to say 'It is three years since I *have seen* him'. This falls under (a) above, and *since* must be followed by the past tense *saw*.

(ii) 'It is ten years ago since my brother left for America.' Incorrect. *Since* reckons from a point of time in the past up to the present; *ago* reckons from the present back to the past. The two, therefore, cannot be combined. (See under Ago.)

(iii) *Ever since* is two words, not one.

SINGULAR OR PLURAL? Usually it is not difficult to know whether we should use a singular or a plural verb, but there are a few words, expressions or constructions over which writers may hesitate. The chief of these are listed below.

(i) On *anybody, anyone, each, either, every, everybody, everyone, none, nobody, no-one, some, somebody, someone*, see under the word in question. On singular or plural verbs with collective nouns like *committee, board, staff*, etc., see Collective Nouns. For nouns ending in *-ics* (as *ethics, physics, economics*) see Mathematics.

(ii) The formal subject *there* usually takes a verb agreeing in number with the 'real' subject that follows (*There is good reason*, *There are many reasons*); but there are exceptions. (See under THERE.)

(iii) The anticipatory subject *it* (in such sentences as 'It is the pace that kills', 'It is the early bird that catches the worm') always takes a singular verb itself, even though the complement that follows it is plural (e.g. 'It is the children that we have to consider'); but when it is qualified by a relative clause with *which*, *that* or *who* as a subject, the verb of this relative clause agrees in number with the preceding complement: 'It is his manner that annoys me', 'It is his manners that annoy me', 'It is John who is to blame', 'It is John and Charles who are to blame'.

(iv) Normally, of course, two singular subjects co-ordinated by *and* take a plural verb ('Bacon and butter have gone up in price'); but if the two co-ordinated terms represent a single idea, a singular verb is used: 'The tumult and the shouting dies', 'All coming and going was forbidden', 'Screaming and shouting was heard coming from the hall'.

(v) When there are alternative subjects co-ordinated by *or* or *nor*, one singular and one plural, the verb agrees with the one which immediately precedes it: 'Neither the child nor her companions have been heard of since'. 'Either the children or their nursemaid has taken the book'. Very occasionally, and in special circumstances, a plural verb is permissible with alternative singular subjects. (See under AGREEMENT OF VERB AND SUBJECT, iii.)

(vi) Though grammatically singular, *a number of*, when it means *several* or *many*, is treated as plural and takes a plural verb: 'A number of people were present. But 'The number of people present was greater than we expected', since here *number* has the more definite meaning of a numerical total.

(vii) Conversely, though *more than one* is notionally plural, it is treated as singular: 'More than one person is involved in this'. 'There is more than one possible explanation'.

(viii) *The greater/greatest part* is singular when it refers to amount or quantity, plural when to number: 'The greater part of the land is uncultivated'. 'The greater part of the apples are bad.'

(ix) Expressions like *two weeks, ten pounds, five miles*, are singular when they are thought of as denoting a single amount or distance: 'Two weeks is a long time when you are ill in bed'. 'Ten pounds is not much for all the trouble we took.'

(x) With the expression *so-many pounds' worth of*, followed by a plural noun, we must have regard to the context and the precise idea to be expressed. If the noun is the significant word, then the verb agrees with that, and is plural; if the value is the significant fact, then the verb is singular, to agree with *worth*: 'Nearly a thousand pounds' worth of cigarettes were stolen' (here we think of the cigarettes, not the worth of them, being stolen): but 'There is nearly a thousand pounds' worth of cigarettes on that shelf' (here it is the value that we have in mind).

(xi) When *one of*, followed by a plural noun, is the subject, the actual subject-word is *one*, and the verb must be in the singular: 'One of the doors is damaged' (not *are damaged*).

(xii) Mistakes are very frequent when *one of* + a plural noun is followed by a relative clause: e.g. 'This is one of the rooms that was damaged in the fire'. 'He is one of those persons who always thinks he is right.' Both sentences are wrong. The antecedent of *that* and *who* is not *one*, but *rooms* and *persons* respectively. It is therefore plural. Amend to . . . 'that were damaged in the fire' and . . . 'who always think they are right'.

But 'One of the documents which is of special interest is a fifteenth-century charter' is correct, for here the relative clause does qualify *one*, not *documents*: it is this one that is of special interest.

(xiii) *What* may also give difficulty. As a relative pronoun it may represent a singular (*that which* or *the thing which*) or a plural (*those which* or *the things which*). When used as a subject it takes a singular or plural verb accordingly ('I can see what appears to be a ship on the horizon'. 'We can see what appear to be camels').

When a whole clause beginning with *what* is the subject of a verb, should the verb be singular or plural? E.g. 'What caused the accident was (or *were?*) two stones which had been placed on the lines'. 'What the children liked most was (or *were?*) his jokes.' Of course, when the complement is singular there is no difficulty ('What I should like most for a birthday present is a camera'); it is with a plural complement that doubt arises.

If the sentence can be remodelled on the *it* . . . *that* pattern, then a singular verb should be used. 'It was two stones that caused the accident': hence 'What caused the accident was (not *were*) two stones'. 'It was his jokes that the children liked most': hence 'What the children liked most was (not *were*) his jokes'. *It* and *that* combine to make *what* (singular).

But 'What appear to be specks on the moon's surface *are* really large craters', since here *what* is plural (= *those things which*).

(xiv) A similar difficulty may arise with *all*. Should we say 'All that remains *is* some broken pillars', or 'All that remains *are* some broken pillars'? Some people, influenced by the plural complement, will write *are*; others will hesitate and find it difficult to make up their mind. But a little thought will show that *is* is required. The fact that the relative clause uses the singular verb *remains*, implies that its subject, *that*, is singular; hence the antecedent of *that* (i.e. *all*), which is also the subject of the disputed verb, must be singular as well, since a relative pronoun is of the same grammatical number as its antecedent.

This line of argument, however, may strike one as begging the question, since it is based upon the assumption that the singular verb *remains* is correct. The choice, it may be pointed out, is between 'All that remains is' and 'All that remain are'. When should we use the one and when the other? If *all* has something of an adjectival force and refers back to a previously mentioned plural (i.e. if it means *all those*), then it is itself plural, and 'All that remain are' is needed: e.g. 'Most of the houses have now been demolished. All that remain are recently built ones.' But if *all* is a pronoun meaning 'the sum total' it is singular, and 'All that remains is' is required: 'All that now remains of the village is a few cottages and a ruined church'. Cf. also 'All that *was* left of them, left of six hundred' (Tennyson, *The Charge of the Light Brigade*).

(xv) Avoid, if possible, constructions of the type 'One of the richest, if not the richest, men in the world'. The objection is not so much that *one of* must be followed by a plural, whereas *the richest* needs a singular, as that *the richest* is followed immediately by the plural *men*, so that a 'clash' results. Either of the following is acceptable: 'One of the richest men in the world, if not the richest'. 'If not the richest man in the world, at least one of the richest.'

(xvi) On singular or plural verbs in inverted constructions like *as was the case*, *as were our intentions*, and on *than was/were*, see under As, Case and Than.

(xvii) A plural noun, when used attributively before another noun, generally becomes singular: *a trouser-press* (not *a trousers-press*), *a scissor manufacturer* (not *a scissors manufacturer*), *a billiard room* (not *a billiards room*, though this seems to have been adopted recently by some newspapers). The rule, however, is not invariable. We speak of a *fives court* and a *works chimney*, though the latter may be accounted for by the fact that, though plural in form, *works* is treated as singular. We speak of *a works*. The plural form is generally preserved also in the names of official bodies: The Mersey Docks and Harbours Board, The Parks and Gardens Committee of the Town Council. Note *the Highway Code*, but *the Highways Committee*.

SKILFUL. One *l* in the middle. Adverb: *skilfully*. Americans prefer *skillful* and *skillfully*.

SLANT. In the sense of *bias, point of view, one-sided view or presentation* ('give a particular slant to a story') a piece of American slang which has been taken up by some British speakers and journals. It is best avoided.

SLATTERNLY. An adjective, not an adverb: e.g. *a slatternly person*. For the adverbial sense we must use a phrase, *in a slatternly manner* (or *fashion*).

SLINK. The past tense is *slunk*, not *slank*.

SLOVENLY. An adjective. Do not say 'She dresses very slovenly, or 'He did his work very slovenly'. 'She is slovenly in her dress' and 'He did very slovenly work' are correct, but for the adverb a phrase must be used (*in a slovenly manner*).

SLOW. *Go slow* is an accepted idiom. The normal adverb is *slowly*, and the comparative *more slowly*, but we say 'The car went slower and slower until it came to a standstill'. Perhaps we feel the word to be semi-adjectival, descriptive of the speed; and in any case *more and more slowly* would sound awkward.

SO. (i) It is incorrect to introduce a clause expressing purpose by the one word *so* (e.g. 'He saved up his money so he might go abroad for his summer holiday'). *So that* is required.

(ii) Equally incorrect is *so as he might go abroad*. *So as* is followed by an infinitive: 'so as to do it', 'so as to get a good seat', 'so as not to be seen', but 'so that he might do it', 'so that they might not be seen', etc.

(iii) *So that* may also introduce a clause of result; in this case it should be preceded by a comma: 'He injured his foot, so that he was unable to play in the match'. No comma is needed before a clause of purpose.

(iv) *To do so* may be used as a 'substitute verb', to avoid repeating a verb used previously, but the verb it replaces must be in the *active* voice; it cannot replace a passive. 'He was asked to move to another seat, but he refused to do so' is correct; here *to do so* replaces the active infinitive *to move*. The following, however, is incorrect: 'The flowers in the park must not be gathered. Anyone found doing so will be prosecuted.' Here the active *doing so* (intended to stand for *gathering them*) refers back to the passive *must not be gathered*.

(v) *So-called*: hyphenated when used attributively, as a compound adjective (*a so-called statesman, the so-called Reformation, the so-called Catholic church*); two words when used predicatively, as participle preceded by adverb: 'He was so called after his father'. 'William Rufus, so called because of his red hair.'

SORT. (i) *These sort* and *those sort* are usually condemned on the ground that a plural demonstrative adjective is combined with a singular noun, but they are frequently heard in speech and sometimes found in print: e.g. 'With those sort of people one must be plain, or one will not be understood' — Anthony Trollope, *The Warden*, chap. v. In conversation we may tolerate them, and Trollope was reproducing conversation, albeit the conversation of Archdeacon Grantly, who was not given to ungrammatical or slovenly speech. But this is the kind of thing that even well-spoken people easily slip into. It is as well to exclude such combinations from writing, however.

(ii) Objection is often raised to *what sort of a . . .?*, the contention being that the indefinite article is intruding where it has no business. But, as is pointed out under KIND, there is room for both the construction with and that without the article. *What sort of . . .?* merely classifies, whereas *What sort of a . . .?* specifies. 'What sort of musician is he?' inquires about the kind of instrument he plays, or whether he is in an orchestra, or a band, etc.; in other words, what is his classification. 'What sort of *a* musician is he?' inquires about his capabilities. It is more personal and individual. This personal element is brought out by the following short passage from R. L. Stevenson's story *Dr Jekyll and Mr Hyde*.

'H'm', said Mr Utterson. 'What sort of a man is he to see?'

'He is not easy to describe. There is something wrong with his appearance; something displeasing, something downright detestable.'

For other points having a bearing on *sort*, see KIND.

SPECIALLY: ESPECIALLY. (See ESPECIALLY.)

SPEED (Verb). 'We sped along', but *speeded* when the meaning is 'went at an excessive speed'. Also *speeded up*.

SPELT. This form of the past tense and past participle is preferable *to spelled*.

SPIRITUAL: SPIRITUOUS. *Spiritual* is opposed to *bodily* or *material*. *Spirituous* corresponds to *spirit* in the sense of a volatile liquid (*spirituous liquors*).

SPIRT: SPURT. A liquid either *spirts* or *spurts*; a runner *spurts*, and *puts on a spurt*.

SPLIT INFINITIVE. There is no rule that an infinitive must *never* be split. Avoid splitting if possible, but if to place the adverb anywhere else than between the stem of the verb and the prefixed *to* would destroy the sense or produce an awkward sentence, then do not hesitate to split. In the following cases the split infinitive seems justifiable: 'to really enjoy oneself', 'to fully understand a thing', 'to better equip oneself for one's task', 'to openly admit something', 'to strongly criticise a person'.

SPOILED: SPOILT. When *spoil* = rob, ravage, lay waste, the past tense and past participle are *spoiled*. When it means *mar* or *ruin*, usage is not fixed, but the general tendency is to use *spoiled* for the former and *spoilt* for the latter. 'A shower of rain spoiled our day's outing.' 'Her essay was spoiled by careless mistakes.' 'The dinner was completely spoilt.' 'The bad egg spoilt the cake.'
   Spoilt is also the usual spelling for the attributive use: *a spoilt child, spoilt ballot papers*.

SPOLIATION. So spelt: not *spoilation*. The word does not mean spoiling in the sense of marring, but of despoiling.

SPURT. (See Spirt.)

STAFF. The older sense of *stick* is now archaic, though it is still preserved in compounds like *flagstaff* (pl. *flagstaffs*) and *staff of office*. The original plural was *staves*, but by back-formation this has given a new singular, *stave*. The collective noun *staff* (those having an established position in an office, school, university, etc.) makes the plural *staffs*.

STANCH: STAUNCH. For the verb either spelling may be used, but the second is the more usual ('to staunch the flow of blood'). The adjective is always *staunch* ('a staunch supporter', 'a staunch friend').

STARVED. 'You look starved: come near the fire and warm yourself.' 'We can't hold the meeting in this room; it's so cold that we shall be starved.' This use of the word (= feel, or be, very cold) is now dialectal. The only meanings of *starve* recognised by Standard English are (i) die of hunger, (ii) be very hungry ('We're starving: we haven't had anything to eat for the last twelve hours'), (iii) provide with insufficient food ('She was so mean that she starved herself and her family'). This, of course, gives rise to the metaphorical use: *starved of affection*; *to starve the mind*.

STATUS QUO. Nowadays often (but wrongly) used to mean the present position. Its correct meaning is 'the previous position' (the complete phrase is *status quo ante bellum* = the state in which things were before the war); hence we can restore the *status quo*, but not preserve the *status quo*.

Note also *in statu quo* (the Latin ablative after the preposition), not *in status quo*.

STAY. 'He did not stay a taxi-driver for very long.' It is quite normal for *stay* to take an adjective as complement ('The cupboard door will not stay closed'. 'The shop stays open till five o'clock'), but when the complement is a noun it is better to use *remain*, unless the noun denotes some condition, status or quality, so that it becomes semi-adjectival: *stay a spinster/a widow/a schoolgirl*. 'She had no intention of staying a spinster for the rest of her life.'

On *stay* and *stop*, see under STOP.

STEADFAST. Now the only accepted spelling, except in the motto of the Boys' Brigade, where it is spelt *stedfast*.

STEM FROM. There seems no need for this German-American expression (from the German *stammen* = spring, arise) when we have so many English words which, until recently, served quite well to express all that *stem from* can express.

STOOD. 'He was stood in the doorway/on the hearth-rug.' In Standard English this can only mean that he had been placed there, though in regional usage it is frequently heard in the speech of even educated persons in an active sense. Correct to *standing*. (See also SAT.)

STOP: STAY. The use of *stop* for the more correct *stay* ('She was stopping with her aunt.' 'If I can't get private hospitality I shall stop at a hotel.') is not of recent growth. Examples can be found in the novels of Jane Austen and throughout the nineteenth century. The difference between the two words is not quite so simple as some text books would have us suppose. The following may be taken as guiding rules.

(a) Use *stop* when the sense is 'cease motion' ('Ask the driver to stop at the "Black Bull"') or 'cease some activity that one is engaged in' ('Stop talking.' 'We couldn't stop laughing').

(b) Use *stay* when the sense is 'remain' ('Stay where you are') or 'reside temporarily' (with a person or at a place): 'stay at a farm', 'stay with friends', 'stay in Paris for a few days'.

(c) It is quite correct, however, to use *stop*, followed by words denoting a period of time, if the meaning is 'break a journey'. 'The coach will stop in Leicester for an hour to allow passengers to get lunch.'

(d) *Stay* is also used transitively with the meaning 'hold back temporarily' or 'partially hold back': *stay one's hand*.

(e) *Stay put* (= stay in position) is a colloquialism; it has no place in formal written English.

STRATA. A Latin plural. The singular is *stratum*. A common error is to speak of *a strata*.

STREAMLINE. Use this word only in its technical sense. There is no need to streamline plans, arrangements, courses, or ladies' dresses.

STREW. Past participle = *strewn* or *strewed*.

STRIDE (Verb). Past tense *strode*. The past participle *stridden* is becoming archaic and is gradually being replaced by *strode* or *strided*.

STRIVE. Past tense *strove* (or *strived*), past participle *striven*.

STUPEFY. Note the spelling, with the medial *e*, not *i*.

STY: STYE. A pig *sty*, but a *stye* on the eye. Plurals, *sties* and *styes* respectively.

SUBCONSCIOUS: UNCONSCIOUS. *Unconscious* means 'unaware of one's surroundings, or of what is taking place'. *Subconscious* is used of impressions made upon our mind, of which we are not aware but which may nevertheless influence our motives or our conduct.

SUBPOENA. An awkward word to convert into a verb, since it is already a Latin phrase (meaning 'under a penalty') converted to an English noun. The difficulty is in attaching endings. Write *subpoena-ed* or *subpoena'd, subpoena-ing.* It means to summon anyone to attend a court of justice *under penalty* for disobedience.

SUBSEQUENT. (See CONSEQUENT.) The preposition that follows *subsequent* is *to.*

SUBSTITUTE. 'All the old typewriters are being substituted by new ones.' Incorrect; they are being *replaced* by new ones, or new ones are being *substituted* for the old. A substitute is something that takes the place of another thing; the verb therefore means 'to put in place of'.

SUCH. (i) An adjective clause following *such,* or a noun qualified by *such,* is introduced by *as*: *such a spectacle* (or *a spectacle such*) *as I had never seen before.*

(ii) For result, *as* is used when an infinitive follows, *that* when a clause follows: 'I am not such a fool as to believe that'. 'There was such a noise that we could not hear ourselves speak.'

(iii) By strict grammatical rule *such as* should be followed by a nominative ('People such as he are not to be trusted'), since it is really an elliptical clause with an understood verb to which the pronoun is the subject (*such as he is*); but when it refers back to an antecedent in the accusative case, the pronoun following *such as* is sometimes put in the accusative also ('I dislike people such as him'), and this is allowable. Perhaps it is felt that the sentence amounts to saying that I dislike him. Cf. also 'It is too expensive for people such as us'.

(iv) Be careful of the placing of the qualifying construction *such as.* The following comes from a G.C.E. essay: 'Some countries have no sea coast, such as Austria'. But Austria is not a sea coast. Obviously, *such as Austria* should have followed *countries. Such as* should be placed immediately after the word it qualifies.

(v) *Such* as a pronoun is confined to literary usage (*such as made verses in writing*), and even there it is almost archaic. Avoid expressions of the type *if such is the case, if such should happen.* Use *this* or *that.*

SUCHLIKE. Do not use this word as a pronoun (*apples, pears and suchlike*). Its only legitimate use is adjectivally. Wyld (*Universal English Dictionary*) gives the example '*Avoid pork and suchlike indigestible foods*'. *Other suchlike* is tautological.

SUFFER. A person suffers *from* (not *with*) indigestion.

SUFFICIENT. (i) In spoken English and informal written style, use *enough* wherever possible (e.g. 'Have you enough money?', 'We have enough food to last us three days').

(ii) Unlike *enough*, *sufficient* cannot be used as a noun. Do not say 'I have said sufficient about that'. 'Have you had enough?' is better than 'Have you had sufficient?', but the latter may be accepted if a noun (e.g. *food*) is understood after it. In the biblical 'Sufficient to the day is the evil thereof', and in 'Sufficient is Thine arm alone, and our defence is sure' (from Isaac Watts's hymn), *sufficient* is, of course, not a noun, but an adjective used predicatively.

(iii) *Amply sufficient* is a vulgarism, and *sufficient enough* an absurd duplication.

SUMMER. *Summer-time* (= the summer season): *summer time* (the system of time, one hour in advance of Greenwich time, in use during the summer months).

SUMMON: SUMMONS. A *summons* is served upon a person he is served with a *summons*, and he receives a *summons* to appear before a court of law, a *summons* to the telephone, a *summons* to the bedside of a sick friend or relative, etc. In other words, in whatever sense it is used, the noun is always *summons*.

As a verb, *summons* can be used only in the judicial sense of 'to serve with a summons'. A person is *summonsed* (served with a summons), and we threaten to *summons* him (to have a summons served upon him), though for the latter *summon* can also be used. *Summon* must always be used when it means 'order or request to appear'. A person is *summoned* to appear before a court of law, *summoned* before his superior, *summoned* to a meeting, *summoned* to the telephone, etc. 'Summoned to the higher life' (not *summonsed*) is a euphemism for *died*. There is an obvious difference of meaning between the two sentences 'He summoned the waiter' and 'He summonsed the waiter'.

SUNK: SUNKEN. *Sunk* is a participle, *sunken* an adjective. A person has *sunken* eyes or cheeks, but a well is *sunk*, and a ship *has sunk*. The past tense of *sink* is properly *sank* ('The ship sank in a very few minutes', 'Her heart sank at the thought', 'The waves soon swamped the small boat and sank it'), but *sunk* is also frequently used, especially when the verb is transitive. Though we need not censure this as 'incorrect' or 'ungrammatical', a writer will always be on the safe side if he avoids it.

Sank can never be used in place of *sunk* for the past participle: we cannot say 'Soon after the ship had sank there was a loud explosion.'

SUPERFLUOUS. Stress on the second syllable.

SUPERIOR. (i) Followed by *to*, not *than*. *Superior* (like its antonym *inferior*) is actually a Latin comparative; it cannot, therefore, have a further comparative. We cannot speak of something being *more superior*.

(ii) One thing is *much* (not *very*) superior to another, but we may speak of *a very superior person*, or say that he thinks himself *very superior*. When used in this way, *superior* has largely lost its comparative sense.

(iii) Just as *superior* cannot have a further comparative, so it cannot have a superlative. We cannot say 'This is the most superior of the three'; but there is no objection to 'He is a most superior person' when *most* is not really a superlative, but an adverb of degree, meaning *very*.

SUPERLATIVE DEGREE. See COMPARATIVES.

SUPPOSE: SUPPOSING. (i) *Suppose*, not *supposing*, should be used to express an imaginary condition, i.e. as an approximate equivalent of *if*: 'Suppose (not *supposing*) you won a hundred pounds, what would you do with it?' *Supposing* is a participle, and is generally used to introduce a reason: 'Supposing the man to be injured, they sent for the ambulance'. It may also be used to state a pre-supposed condition on which a statement holds good, or a similar condition that is to be assumed in giving an answer to a question: 'Supposing everyone who accepted the invitation actually comes, there will be just under two hundred guests', 'Supposing no unforeseen delays occur, how long would the work take?'

(ii) Formally *I suppose* is a statement, but it sometimes has the force of a question, in which case it seems legitimate to use a question mark: e.g. 'I suppose they know how to find the house?' Similarly a suggestion introduced by *suppose* may be given a question mark if it has an interrogative import: 'Suppose we have a round of golf?'

(iii) There is a regional use of *I suppose* which makes it equivalent in meaning to 'I understand, I hear, I have been told': e.g. 'I suppose Freda is getting married in August'. 'We had a visit from the Smiths last Sunday' — 'So I suppose'. 'I suppose there's been a serious accident at the corner of the road.' This is not recognised in Standard usage.

SURPRISE. 'I shouldn't be surprised if it *doesn't* snow.' The negative, to express the idea that the speaker thinks it *may* snow, is illogical, but, despite the condemnation of Fowler, has come to be accepted colloquially. But, of course, the more logical 'I shouldn't be surprised if it snows' is still correct.

When *surprised* means 'taken by surprise', or 'caught unawares', it is followed by the preposition *by* ('The intruder was surprised by the police'); when it means 'filled with surprise' it takes *at* ('I was surprised at his conduct').

SUSCEPTIBLE. *Susceptible to* = easily affected or influenced by: thus we say a person is susceptible to colds, to flattery, to feminine charms, etc.

Susceptible of = admitting of (used predicatively only); susceptible of proof, of verification, of demonstration, of two interpretations.

Susceptible to should not be used in the sense of 'frequently or easily displaying, or subject to', as 'She is susceptible to fits of melancholy'. 'He is susceptible to outbursts of temper.'

SWAP (Slang = exchange). So spelt: not *swop*.

SWAT: SWOT. *Swat* a fly (originally U.S.): *swot* for an examination. The latter, of course, is colloquial, if not actually slang. It is derived from *sweat*. The noun *a swot* has a derogatory suggestion that the verb has not.

SWELL. The past tense is *swelled* and the past participle normally *swollen*, but *swelled* is used as the past participle when the sense is 'increased numerically' or 'increased in amount': e.g. 'Our numbers were swelled by the arrival of a party from Buxton'. 'Several large donations have swelled the fund considerably.' To say that our numbers were *swollen* or that the fund was *swollen* would suggest that they were greater than was good or desirable.

Note also *swollen-headed*, but *suffering from swelled head*.

SWOT. (See under SWAT.)

SYMPATHY: SYMPATHISE. We have sympathy *for* a person who is in trouble (i.e. feel pity), sympathy *with* him or with his views when we are in partial agreement. *Sympathise* always takes *with*: 'I can sympathise with anyone who has migraine, for I suffer from it myself'. 'While we sympathise with you in the views you express, there is little we can do to help.'

The adjectives *sympathetic* and *unsympathetic* both take *to*. The usual meaning of *sympathetic* is 'feeling, expressing or showing sympathy', but Fowler draws attention to another meaning sometimes found in works of literary criticism and copied from the French *sympathique*—that of 'arousing sympathy': e.g. 'I do not find Shylock a very sympathetic character'. It is perhaps pedantic to object to this, provided it does not lead to ambiguity, but it is better avoided.

Sympathetic fallacy: sometimes misused for *pathetic fallacy*, or the attribution of human feelings and sensations to inanimate nature.

T

TALL: HIGH. *Tall* refers to height from base to top, in proportion to breadth: a tall person, a tall tree, a tall spire, a tall lamp standard. *High* refers to distance above — usually, though not always, above the ground or the floor: a high hill, a high window, a high roof. A building may be described as *tall* by a person who looks at it from the ground and sees it towering above him, but anyone who climbs to the top storey climbs to the top of a *high* building, since in this case it is merely the distance that is in question.

A tall order, a tall story are accepted colloquial expressions.

TARGET. 'Our target is £1000.' 'We have set ourselves a target of a hundred new members by the end of the year.' A very much overworked metaphor, which is in danger of becoming hackneyed. Its use, moreover, has many traps for the unwary. In popular jargon targets are set, raised, lowered, reduced, increased, passed, achieved, beaten — in fact anything but hit. To pass the target is supposed to be a more than creditable performance, yet any marksman knows that it is the opposite, as he knows that a small target is more difficult to hit than a large one. How one can beat a target, either in the literal or the metaphorical sense, it is difficult to see; we might as well speak of a horse beating the winning post, or of a runner beating the tape. But the prize for this kind of mixed metaphor, usually the result of carelessness or of hazy thinking, must be divided between the Sunday newspaper which, discussing a house-building programme, remarked that 'we should set ourselves a target and pursue it vigorously' and the Chairman-Designate of the National Coal Board who, if he was correctly reported, declared that he 'would use every weapon in the armoury to carve out and hold a target of two million tons of coal a year'.

TEACH SCHOOL. An Americanism, not idiomatic in British English.

TEENAGER. May now be regarded as accepted English.

TEENS. No apostrophe: 'A girl in her teens'.

TELEVISE. Must be so spelt — not *televize* — since it is a back formation from *television*.

TELEVISION. *Television* is the name of the system of broad-casting pictures, not of the apparatus on which the picture is received. This should be referred to as *a television set*, not *a television*. 'Have you television?' is correct; 'Have you *a* television?' is not. Incorrect also are 'We have just bought a new television', 'I examined several televisions'.

TEMPORAL: TEMPORARY. *Temporal* means 'having to do with time' (e.g. a temporal clause, another name for an adverb clause of time), and hence is often used as the opposite of *spiritual*, as in the expression 'Lords temporal and Lords Spiritual', the Lords temporal being the Peers, and the Lords Spiritual the Bishops. Cf. also 'His [i.e. the king's] sceptre shows the force of temporal power' (Shakespeare, *The Merchant of Venice*). *Temporary* means 'lasting, or intended, for a short time only' (a temporary post, a temporary building, temporary measures).

Be careful of the spelling of the adverb from *temporary*; it is *temporarily*. In British English the stress is on the first syllable in both adjective and adverb. Some American speakers place it on the third.

TEND. 'Her life was spent tending to the sick and the wounded.' Incorrect. *Tend*, in this sense of the word, is a transitive verb. *Attending to the sick*, but *tending the sick*.

TERM (Verb). 'The play may be termed a tragi-comedy' — not 'termed *as* a tragi-comedy'.

TERMINAL: TERMINUS. Usually an air *terminal*, but a railway *terminus*. The plural of *terminus* is *termini*, but *terminuses* is permissible in conversational English.

THAN. (i) Be careful of the case of pronouns after *than*. There is always an ellipsis, and the test is to supply the 'understood' words: 'You can do it better than I (can)'. 'You like him better than I (do).' 'You like him better than (you like) me.' 'That is a task for you rather than (for) me.' 'He is two years older than I (am).' 'You, rather than I, should have the reward' (short for *rather than I should have it*). After verbs of incomplete predication (*be, seem, became* etc.) followed by an adjective, the accusative is, however, often used where prescriptive grammar would require the nominative: e.g. 'His wife was several years younger than him'. This may be accepted.

(ii) '. . . your friend Mr Simpson, *than whom* no-one is more welcome.' By strict grammatical rule, incorrect, but justified by usage. If we adopt the test suggested under (i) above, we get *no-one is more welcome than he*, and *he*, converted to a relative pronoun, becomes *who*, not *whom* (see under WHO); but *than who no-one is more welcome* would sound strange. In such constructions *than* is treated as a preposition, and takes the accusative.

(iii) 'It is warmer today than what it was yesterday.' 'The trip cost us more than what we expected.' Omit *what*. In such sentences the clauses of comparison are short for *than it was warm yesterday* and *than we expected it to cost us*. *What* is, however, correctly used in the following sentence: 'Nothing could give me greater pleasure than what you have just told me'. Here *what*, being a combination of *that which*, serves as both the subject of the understood verb *does* and the object of *have told*.

(iv) On possible mistakes in the number of the verb when *than* introduces an inverted construction like *than was the case*, *than were our intentions*, see under CASE and INVERSION OF VERB AND SUBJECT.

(v) 'There were more people present than *were* expected', if the sentence is short for . . . *than there were people expected*. 'There were more people present than *was* expected' if it stands for *than it was expected there would be*. In all the following only the singular verb is correct: 'There were more casualties than *was* reported' (short for *than it was reported there were*), 'More middle-aged persons suffer from heart trouble than *is* generally realised', 'The really serious cases are fewer than *has* been suggested'.

THAT. (i) As a relative pronoun, *that* may be used to refer to persons as well as to things; we may quite well speak of *the man that built that house*. But whether the reference is a personal or a non-personal one, it can introduce only defining clauses, never non-defining. Normally, therefore, it must not be separated from its antecedent by a comma. In this respect it differs from *which* and *who*. We cannot say 'Sheffield, that is a large industrial city in south Yorkshire, is famous for its cutlery'. In such clauses only *which* is possible. (But for apparent exceptions, see under COMMA (5).)

Fowler suggested that *all* defining clauses should be introduced by *that*, and that *which* should be reserved for non-defining, but the suggestion has never been followed. For defining clauses a speaker or writer is at liberty to use either word, according to which seems the better in a particular context.

Only *that* is idiomatic when the clause qualifies an introductory *it* : 'It is his rudeness *that* I object to'.

(ii) 'Name any book *that* you like.' Correct, if it is meant to exclude books that we don't like; but if the intended meaning is 'any book you like to name', irrespective of whether you like it or not, then *that* should be omitted.

(iii) 'The more *that* I tried to pacify him, the angrier he became.' 'The sooner *that* we start, the sooner we shall arrive.' 'The further *that* we went, the worse the road became.' 'The older *that* we get, the wiser we become.' From all these sentences, and from all others of the same type, *that* should be omitted. It has no antecedent (for the word that precedes it must be either an adjective or an adverb), and hence no place in the syntax of the sentence.

(iv) The use of *that* as an adverb of degree, instead of *so*, in constructions of the type 'It was that dark we could scarcely see an inch before us' is a vulgarism. So are such expressions as *that much, all that far*.

THE. (i) The definite article may legitimately be used with a singular noun as a 'generic singular', i.e. a single one of a species or a group taken to represent the whole, as 'The camel is the ship of the desert', 'The tiger and the cat belong to the same family of animals', 'The child is father of the man'. It must be remembered, however, that all pronouns and possessive adjectives that refer back to a generic singular must themselves be singular. Because a generic singular has a plural idea, it is very easy to slip into such errors as the following : 'The plight of the agricultural labourer was even worse than that of the town worker. *Their* wages were low, and if *they* lost *their* job *they* were turned out of *their* cottages.' Correct to *his* and *he*.

We have an extension of the generic singular in 'to play the fool', 'She was very much the fine lady', 'He looked every inch the judge'.

(ii) When two nouns are co-ordinated by *and*, the article is not repeated before the second one if the two are thought of in conjunction, as 'The King and Queen have visited the exhibition', 'The Plays and Poems of Christopher Marlowe', 'The sons and daughters of the clergy', but if the two are thought of separately, then it is better to use the article before each one : 'God sends his sunshine on the just and the unjust alike'. This, however, should not be regarded as a rigid rule. We clearly must speak of 'the Prime Minister and the Foreign Secretary', as we must of 'the Queen and the Duke of Edinburgh', but it is not incorrect to say, 'The Anglicans and Nonconformists are both opposed to the suggestion', though many might prefer a repetition of the article.

It is always necessary to repeat the article if the combination is preceded by *both*: 'Both the Anglicans and the Nonconformists have decided to oppose the measure'. 'Both the boys and the girls did well in their examinations.' 'The proposals have now been accepted by both the employers and the workers.'

After *or*, the article must be repeated if *or* denotes an alternative ('Do you support the Conservatives or the Socialists?' 'I do not know whether I prefer the blue or the green dress'), but there is no repetition of the article when *or* merely introduces another name for the term that has preceded it: 'The Nonconformists, or Dissenters as they were then called, felt they had a legitimate grievance'.

(iii) Stressed *the* is usually pronounced the same as the pronoun *thee* ('A gentleman — and "quite *the* gentleman", said the landlord of the George Inn — had been looking at Mr Clavering's old house' — Mrs Gaskell, *The Squire's Story*). A pronunciation with the same vowel as the normal unstressed article, however, is sometimes heard.

(iv) Adverbial *the* before a comparative is normal idiom in such expressions as 'The sooner the better', 'The more the merrier', 'The longer I live, the more cynical I become' (though on the incorrect use of *that* in sentences of the last type, see under THAT). It may also be used before a comparative to point backwards or forwards to something which will explain the reason for the excess denoted by the comparative, or which at least has a bearing on it: 'I am the more inclined to believe him because he has nothing to gain by concealing the truth'. 'We were none the wiser for his explanation.' 'If a person was reputed to be rich, she was the more disposed to excuse his faults.' *The* in such sentences means 'in virtue of this' or 'on this account'.

But *the* should not be used:

(a) If it has no such demonstrative function: 'We did not like his presuming on our friendship, but what annoyed us the more was the insolence of his manner'. *The* should be omitted.

(b) When the comparative is followed by an adverb clause of result: 'If he comes early, so much the better' is correct, but 'He is so much the better that he can now go out for a while' is not. *The* has intruded where it is not required.

(c) When the comparative is followed by *than*: 'He explained the matter in great detail, but we were none the wiser than before'. Amend to 'no wiser than before'. The sentence would, however, have been correct if it had ended at *wiser*.

(v) *The* is, of course, normal before any adjective of both the comparative and the superlative degree when a noun is felt, if only vaguely, to be understood after it : 'Of the two courses you suggest, the second would be the more acceptable'. 'Of the three boys, John was the eldest.' 'Which way is the shortest ?' On being shown several different kinds of tea or coffee, we may ask either, 'Which is the cheapest ?' (thinking of the various kinds) or 'Which is cheapest ?' (thinking merely of the price).

Most and *least* are found both with and without *the*, even when a noun is actually expressed after them : 'Of all the people we have been discussing, he has the least cause to complain'. 'The competitor who gets the most points wins the prize.' In both the sentences the article could be omitted, but its use renders the application more specific by singling out the one in question from the others, where the construction without the article takes it in conjunction with the others.

(vi) Superlative adverbs may also be preceded by *the*, though again the sentence would generally be quite idiomatic without it. 'The person who works *the hardest* should receive the greatest reward.' 'Which of these flowers do you like *the best* ?' 'Families without children have to wait *the longest* (for a council house).' We probably tend to use *the* when we feel that a certain adjectival notion is attached to the adverb : 'The person who works the hardest'='The person who does the hardest work'. 'To wait the longest'='to have the longest wait.' 'Which of these flowers do you like the best ?'='Which of these flowers do you consider to be the best ?'

(vii) With expressions like *go to school, go to church, stay in hospital,* as opposed to the same phrases with *the*, the article is used when the reference is to the building, and omitted when the reference is to the purpose or the function of the building, or to the characteristic activity associated with it. We go to school to learn or to teach, go to church or chapel to worship, go to prison as a punishment. We go to *the* school, church, chapel or prison if we merely visit the place on business. The list of phrases in which the omission of the article is idiomatic is, however, limited. We cannot say that a business man 'goes to office'; it must always be 'go to *the* office'; and although a student goes to college, until recently he always went to *the* university. Now 'go to university' is becoming frequent.

The article may also be omitted when the speaker thinks of the building or the institution as in some way closely associated with himself. Just as the lady of the house may refer to 'cook' or 'nurse' when she means her particular cook or nurse, so a headmaster's notice may read 'No boy is allowed in school before 8.30' (though the building and not its purpose, is meant), and a clergyman or minister may apologise for his wife's absence from home when a visitor calls, by saying, 'She's at church, arranging some flowers'. An employee at a branch of a bank or insurance company will speak of 'Head Office' if the reference is to his own company, but 'the head office' of another company.

(viii) With words like *bishop, archbishop, secretary, headmaster, mayor*, the article is used when the person himself is referred to (Dr Proudie, the Bishop of Barchester), and omitted when the reference is to the office or position.

(ix) On *the* in the names of periodicals and in the titles of literary works, see under TITLES, and for 'the Edgware Road' as an alternative to 'Edgware Road', see under ROAD.

THEIRS. No apostrophe.

THERE (Formal Subject). The rule is that normally the verb agrees with the 'real' subject that follows; but a singular verb is used, even if a plural noun or pronoun follows, when:

(i) The plural form denotes a single sum or amount: 'There is five pounds to pay'. 'There is only another two miles to go.'

(ii) When a combination of two or more nouns represents a single idea: 'There was much coming and going'. 'There is duck and green peas for dinner.'

(iii) When the reference is to a situation in its entirety: 'There is my wife and family to consider'. 'There is only two pounds of butter and a few packets of tea left.'

(iv) In enumeration, when the verb is thought of as applying to each one successively and separately: 'There is John, James, Alec . . .' 'When interrogated about "the team for tomorrow", "Let me see," he would reply in a gravely complacent voice, "Let me see; there's Mr Richard Puttridge; and myself; my brother Alfred; Tom Dixon; Mr Jack Barchard; young Bob Ellis — and did I say myself?"' — Siegfried Sassoon, *Memoirs of a Fox-Hunting Man.*

Note that no matter whether the 'real' subject that follows is first, second or third person, *there* always takes a third person verb: 'There is only me to be served now'.

THEREFOR: THEREFORE. *Therefor* is archaic. When it was part of the living language it meant 'for that', *that* referring to something that has been mentioned immediately before: 'The mercies of the Lord endure for ever; give thanks unto him therefor'.

Therefore means 'for that reason', or 'because of that', e.g. 'He has transgressed, therefore he must be punished'. The normal position of *therefore* is at the beginning of a clause, and its function is that of what we may call a conjunctive adverb. In this position it is not followed by a comma; to use one, indeed, would be incompatible with its conjunctive function, since a conjunction joins, whereas a comma separates. If, however, it is placed *within* a clause it becomes parenthetic, and needs a comma both before and after it: 'If, therefore, we wish to put the matter to the test . . .'

THEY. (i) On the common, but incorrect use of *they* with *everybody*, *everyone*, *anybody*, *anyone*, *nobody*, *no-one*, *somebody*, *someone*, and *each*, as well as with the generalising personal pronoun *one*, see under these words.

(ii) 'If anyone is to blame, it's they' is correct from the point of view of strict grammar, but most people would say 'It's them', and this may be regarded as acceptable. (See also ME.)

THINK. (i) 'Did you think to post that letter?', for 'Did you remember?' should be avoided, but 'Did you think to?', 'I didn't think to', etc. in the sense of 'Did it occur to you?', 'It didn't occur to me' is permissible in conversational English. Fowler seems to confuse it with the former use, and condemns the two together — or rather he makes no distinction; but they are clearly on a different footing. We cannot see any objection (in spoken English) to 'Did you think to ask whether there was a dining-car on the train?' 'I didn't think to look in the directory for his address.'

'I didn't think to see you here' is permissible colloquially, but in more formal style *expect* should be used.

Methinks and *methought* are archaisms, which in modern English are used only for humorous effect. They do not mean 'I think' and 'I thought', as most people suppose they do (or did); they are old impersonal constructions, meaning 'It seems to me' and 'It seemed to me'.

(ii) 'What do you think to my new dress?' Regional idiom. Standard English uses *of*.

(iii) 'It is more difficult than you'd think for.' Omit *for*.

The construction is not so much an illiteracy as a rather old-fashioned colloquialism. Several examples occur in the novels of Jane Austen: e.g. 'She is really very sorry to lose poor Miss Taylor, and I am sure she will miss her more than she thinks for.' (*Emma*, chap. i.)

(iv) *Think up* (an expression of fairly recent origin) may be allowable as a short way of expressing the combined notions of *think* and *make up* (as *think up an excuse, think up some story to tell him*), but it should not be used otherwise. It is not permissible in the following: think up some games for the party, think up a scheme, think up a suitable title for the story. Do not let *think up* usurp the place of *think of* and *think out*.

THO'. Not an accepted English spelling. Always write *though*.

THOSE. 'This concession will benefit only those people who pay tax at the full rate.' 'He urged that the new rates should be extended to include those women over fifty.' Fowler objects to the use of *those* in sentences of this type where the adjective clause or phrase is classifying, not merely descriptive. For the first, he contends, we may say either 'those who pay tax at the full rate', or 'people who pay tax at the full rate', but not 'those people who': for the second we should say 'women over fifty', and omit *those*.

Logically, the objection is valid, since *those* specifies particular ones within the general category (e.g. 'those men over sixty-five who have not yet retired', where within the general category 'men over sixty-five' we specify 'those who have not yet retired'); but in the sentences to which exception is taken there is no specification; the whole category is referred to. The construction is, however, so frequent that we may regard it as sanctioned by usage, though if anyone still feels doubtful about it he can avoid it, and quote Fowler as his authority. (There is, of course, no question about the correctness of *those people who* when *those* has its genuine demonstrative function and the adjective clause is descriptive or identifying: 'Who were those people who spoke to us in the café?')

On *those sort of apples, those kind of people*, see under SORT and KIND.

THOUGH: ALTHOUGH. (i) There is no difference of meaning. *Although* is felt to be stronger than *though* and is therefore more frequently used at the beginning of a sentence, and internally when emphasis is desired: 'He insisted on doing it, although I warned him not to'.

(ii) We may say *even though*, but not *even although*.

(iii) To express imaginary circumstances (with the sense 'even if' *though* is more usual than *although*: 'Though all the world were against me, I should still hold to my opinion'. *Though* is also used in preference to *although* when it has a meaning approximating to that of the co-ordinating conjunction *but*:

'There are several theories about how the treasure came here, though we cannot go into them now'. 'I have not yet verified the information, though I think it is correct'. 'No-one is infallible, though there are some people who think they are.' It is just possible that *although* might be used instead of *though* in all of these, but when the word is appended to the end of the sentence *although* is out of the question; only *though* is idiomatic: 'There is an interesting story about how the treasure came to be buried here. We can't go into that now, though'.

(iv) The contracted spellings *tho'* and *altho'* should not be used.

THRASH: THRESH. The two words are the same by origin, though usage has differentiated them. A person is *thrashed*, corn is *threshed*. It is better to speak of *threshing* out a problem than of *thrashing* it out, since it is a metaphorical application of the idea of threshing grain. On the other hand one football team *thrashes* its opponents (gives them a sound beating).

THRIVE. In present-day usage the past tense and the past participle are *thrived*. *Throve* and *thriven* are archaic.

THROUGH. (i) Avoid the spellings *thro'* and *thru*. So far the latter is rarely seen in Britain, though it appears in some American publications.

(ii) 'Congress at Davos, Switzerland, August 8th through August 13th, 1961' (advertisement in an academic journal). This use of *through* to denote a period of time, inclusive of both the dates given, sounds very un-English. It may perhaps become established within the next few years, but in the meantime everything possible should be done to discourage the use of it. It is difficult to see that it serves any purpose that is not served by the normal English idiom with *to*.

THUS. Care is necessary in using this word before a participle: we must make sure that the participle is correctly related, and that the noun or pronoun to which it refers really was the thing (or the person) that did something 'thus' i.e. by this means, in this manner, or on this account. The point is illustrated by the following sentence from a schoolboy's essay: 'All his money was confiscated, thus rendering him penniless'. It is really another form of the error of the mis-related participle, discussed under the heading -ING. According to the syntax of the sentence *rendering* refers to *money*. But did his money render him penniless?' Amend to (a) 'All his money was confiscated, and he was thus rendered penniless', or (b) 'They confiscated all his money, thus rendering him penniless'.

Sometimes, however, the participle is correctly related, but *thus* itself is an intruder: e.g. 'The flood waters swept through the town, thus carrying everything before them'.

TIE. Present participle and gerund, *tying*: past tense and past participle, *tied*.

TIGHT: TIGHTLY. In the desire to be grammatical, and to show that we know the difference between an adverb and an adjective, we may slip into the error of using *tightly* when idiom demands *tight*. 'Hold tight' is idiomatic English: 'Hold tightly' is not. In the following, too, *tight* is correct: 'Don't tie the bandage too tight'. 'See that the lid is screwed down tight.' 'Her dress was drawn in tight at the waist.' 'She clasped the child tight against her body.' In such sentences *tight* is not an adverb, but an adjective used as a complement of result: the sense is 'so that it is/was tight'. Cf. a similar use of *loose* and *firm* in the sentences 'The nut worked loose', 'Allow the mixture to stand till it sets firm.'

Tightly is an adverb of manner: 'He held me tightly by the arm'.

Tight, not *tightly*, is used before a present participle to make a compound adjective, as *a tight-fitting suit*. This is consistent with similar combinations with other words as the first element: paint that dries quickly is *quick-drying paint*, and traffic that moves slowly is *slow-moving traffic*.

TILL: UNTIL. There is no difference of meaning: which of the two is used in a particular context seems to be determined largely by considerations of rhythm or euphony, though there is a tendency to use *till* for a point of time and *until* for duration of time. Thus: 'Don't do anything further till you hear from me'. 'We didn't get home till ten o'clock.' 'The fruit will not ripen till we get more sun.' 'You must stay in bed until your temperature is normal.' 'She lived with an aunt until she married.' 'We shall have to stay here until help arrives.' *Until* is also more usual:

(a) At the beginning of a sentence: 'Until we know the facts, we can do nothing further'. 'Until he was sixteen he had never been away from his native village.'

(b) When result, not merely time, is expressed: 'The frog inflated himself more and more, until finally he burst'. 'They frittered their money away, until they had only a few pence left.'

There is no warrant whatever for the spelling '*til*.

TIME AND AGAIN. Accepted as idiomatic, though *time and time again* is to be preferred.

TIMES. (i) 'In Shakespeare's time', 'In our grandparents' time' (not *times*), but *olden times, past times, these times, such times as these, good times and bad times, modern times.*

(ii) 'The twice-times table', though illogical, is accepted usage.

(iii) On 'three times heavier', 'many times bigger', 'ten times larger', etc., see under COMPARATIVES.

TITILLATE: TITIVATE. The two words are sometimes confused. *To titillate* means 'to tickle' (figuratively), 'to excite a pleasant feeling or sensation': to titillate one's appetite. *To titivate* means 'to smarten up'. It is generally used half humorously, as in the expression 'to titivate oneself'.

TITLES (of literary works, periodicals, etc.). (i) In print the titles of literary works, periodicals, etc. are usually set in italics. In writing or typescript they may be underlined (the equivalent of italics in print) or placed in inverted commas, but both methods must not be used together. We may write either 'Paradise Lost' or *Paradise Lost*, but not '*Paradise Lost*'. The advantage of underlining is that it allows inverted commas to be used for secondary titles, i.e. the titles of chapters, poems, essays, etc. within the main work. Thus 'Browning's "Andrea del Sarto" first appeared in the volume *Men and Women*, published in 1855'. If the title of the individual poem, essay or article is the only one mentioned, then, within that context, it is a main title, and should be underlined.

(ii) If, as with most hymns and some poems, the work is referred to by its first line, it should be given inverted commas, as a quotation, not underlined: e.g. 'The author of "Nearer, my God, to Thee" was Sarah Flower Adams'.

(iii) With periodicals it is usual to exclude an initial *the* from the italics (or inverted commas): e.g. 'He was reading the *Daily Telegraph*'. Exceptions are *The Times* and *The Economist*, who insist on its inclusion. But even with these it must be excluded when it belongs, not to the title of the periodical, but to a noun that follows the title: e.g. 'the *Times* leading article which we have been discussing'.

(iv) For literary works (books, plays, poems, essays, etc.) the article should normally be included (e.g. Hardy's *The Trumpet-Major*, Anthony Trollope's *The Warden*), but it may be necessary, for reasons of euphony, to omit an article, either definite or indefinite, if the title is preceded by a possessive adjective or the genitive of the author's name. We should, for instance, normally speak of 'Gibbon's *Decline and Fall of the Roman Empire*', though the actual title of the work is *The Decline and Fall of the Roman Empire*. Eric Partridge, in both *Usage and Abusage* and *You Have a Point There* (a book dealing with punctuation and related matters), insists on writing 'my *A Dictionary of Slang and Unconventional English*', but not many of us would follow his example; and in any case the argument is not logical. When the first word of a title denotes a *kind* of work (a dictionary, a history, a life of, an essay on, etc.) the article is not on a par with that in a novel or similar work of literature (e.g. *A Pair of Blue Eyes* or *A Room of One's Own*). We could scarcely speak of 'Hardy's *Pair of Blue Eyes*', for (to the ear, at least) this would attribute the blue eyes to Hardy, and it would sound strange to say 'Virginia Woolf's *Room of One's Own*'. But we can say 'Partridge's *Dictionary of Slang*', and Mr Partridge himself need feel no uneasiness about saying 'my *Dictionary of Slang*', for this attributes the dictionary (quite rightly) to its author.

(v) No italics or inverted commas are used for the Bible, for the names of its individual books, or for the sacred writings of the well-known non-Christian religions: the Koran, the Vedas, the Talmud. The article is written with a small letter. (Incidentally, Michael West and P. F. Kimber argue, in their *Deskbook of Correct English*, that since the full title of what everyone refers to as 'the Book of Genesis' is 'The First Book of Moses, called Genesis' it should be shortened to 'the Book Genesis', not 'the Book *of* Genesis'. One sees the reasoning, but is it logical? Surely *of* here expresses an appositional relationship between the two nouns, as when we speak of 'the comedy of *Twelfth Night*'.)

(vi) Inverted commas should not be used for an original title (i.e. one that a writer puts at the head of his own work), or for titles of songs, poems, musical compositions, etc., when they appear as items in a programme or a catalogue, since they are merely transferred, not quoted, titles.

(vii) Titles should always be quoted correctly. A. E. Housman's *A Shropshire Lad* has appeared in print more than once as *The Shropshire Lad*, and Keats's *Ode on a Grecian Urn* as *Ode to a Grecian Urn*. The correct title of J. B. Priestley's play is *Dangerous Corner*, not *The Dangerous Corner*, and Bernard Shaw wrote *Saint Joan*, not *St. Joan*. And while we are speaking of correctness, may we appeal to foreign writers on English literature to refer to authors by the name by which they are

...ally known in England? It is annoying to a British reader
to find, in a critical work by a Frenchman, a German or an
Italian, *The Scholar-Gipsy* (or a quotation from it) attributed to
M. Arnold, *The Grand Babylon Hotel* to A. Bennett and *Brave
New World* to A. Huxley.

(viii) When a work is popularly known, not by its actual
title, but by a personal name with which it is always associated
(e.g. Hansard, Wisden, Bradshaw, Old Moore), so that the
name becomes a 'substitute title', it should not be italicised or
placed in inverted commas. But when initials are used as an
abbreviated form of title for well-known works, these should
be italicised: e.g. *D.N.B.* (*The Dictionary of National Biography*),
T.L.S. (*The Times Literary Supplement*), *C.O.D.* (*The Concise
Oxford Dictionary*).

(ix) A difficulty arises when we have to write the genitive
case of the name of a periodical. Should the '*s* be included in the
italics? The problem can, of course, be solved by avoiding the
genitive, and writing 'in the opinion of the *Daily Telegraph*',
but if we must use the genitive (as sometimes we may have to)
it seems that we shall have to regard the '*s* as a case-ending (as,
indeed, it is) and italicise it with the rest of the word: 'in
the *Daily Telegraph's* opinion'.

But this leads to a further question. Where should we put
the apostrophe in the case of *The Times*, where the title is really
a plural? Normally the genitive case of a plural noun ending
in *s* is pronounced the same as the non-genitive, and, in writing,
the apostrophe is placed after the existing *s*, no further *s* being
added. But we should probably treat *The Times* as a special
case, and say 'in *The Times-iz* opinion', as though *Times* were
a singular, like the proper name *Jones*; so it seems that we shall
have to write 'in *The Times's* opinion'.

TIRE (of a vehicle). (See TYRE.)

TOO. *Only too true, only too pleased,* etc., may be accepted
colloquially, but avoid 'It is too good of you' when the meaning
is 'very good of you'. 'He wasn't too pleased', as an understatement for 'He was rather annoyed', is accepted usage.
Similarly 'He is not too badly off', 'It isn't too warm today'.

TORTIOUS: TORTUOUS: TORTUROUS. *Tortious*=consti-
tuting a tort (i.e. a civil wrong). *Tortuous* = winding ('a tortuous
route', 'a very tortuous chain of argument'). *Torturous* = in-
flicting torture.

TRADE UNION. So spelt. The plural is *trade unions*, not
trades unions; but *The Trades Union Congress*.

TRAFFIC. The present participle and gerund of the verb are spelt *trafficking*; past participle *trafficked*.

TRAIT. Pronounced *tray*, not *trate*. The word is of French origin.

TRANSPIRE. A common mistake is to use *transpire* as though it meant *occur* or *happen* (e.g. 'Many a quarrel has transpired through idle gossip'). It does not mean this. Nor is it synonymous with 'prove to be' or 'turn out' ('To the delight of us all it transpired that the weather was fine, so the fête could be held after all'. 'The driver of the vehicle transpired to be drunk'). It means 'to come to light': 'As a result of the inquiry it transpired that no proper accounts had been kept for the past three years'.

TRANSPORT : TRANSPORTATION. In British English *transportation* is generally reserved for the one-time punishment of criminals by sending them to penal settlements overseas (e.g. *transportation for life*). Americans also speak of the transportation of goods, luggage, passengers, etc., but British English generally uses *transport* for this sense: e.g. 'motorways to facilitate the transport of goods between large towns', 'large tankers for the transport of oil', 'vans specially constructed for the transport of perishable foods'. *Transportation* may, however, be used for a specific project or operation: 'With such large numbers, their transportation across the twenty-one miles of water needed careful planning'.

TRAVEL. In British English the *l* is doubled before a suffix which begins with a vowel symbol: *travelled, travelling, traveller*. The Americans use only one *l*.

TRIUMPHANT : TRIUMPHAL. The first of this pair is often used where the second should be employed: *Triumphant* means *victorious* ('the triumphant army', 'to emerge triumphant from a conflict', 'the Church Triumphant'). *Triumphal* means 'concerned with the celebration of a triumph or a victory', as 'a triumphal march, hymn, arch, procession', etc.

TRY. *Try and do something*, instead of *try to do*, is often condemned as a solecism, but it is well established and can be defended, first on the ground of usage, and secondly on that of meaning; it expresses greater urgency or determination than *try to do*.

ORDS OR ONE? (See ONE WORD OR TWO?)

TYRANNISE. 'Tyrannise *over* people', not 'tyrannise them'. Perhaps the tendency to make the verb transitive has arisen through confusion with *terrorise*.

TYRE. The accepted spelling in British English, though in the U.S. usually *tire*, which was also the spelling used by *The Times* until very recently. Now it has adopted *tyre*.

U

ULT. 'Your letter of 29th ult.' A piece of business jargon, meaning 'last month', as *inst.* means 'this month' and *prox.* 'next month'. Do not use these, either in business letters or elsewhere. Name the month.

'UN (Colloquial or slang for *one*). Usually written with an apostrophe (as *a good 'un*, *a wrong 'un*), though strictly there is no justification for it, since there is no omission. The word is not a contraction of the modern *one*, but a survival of the Old English *an* (=one). An argument for retaining the apostrophe is that the word would look strange and unfamiliar without it.

UN- (Prefix). (i) There is no strict rule about hyphenation. Generally, in established combinations the prefix and the 'base' word are written as one, but a hyphen is used in nonce-combinations. A hyphen *must* be used when the 'base' word begins with a capital, as *un-Christian*, *un-English*, *un-American*, etc. (See under HYPHEN.) When in doubt, consult a dictionary.

(ii) In combinations where there is *non-* as well as *un-*, *un-* generally has a negative import, and means 'the opposite of', while *non-* means 'other than': *an un-Christian act*, *un-Christian conduct*, but *non-Christian religions*.

UNANIMOUS. (i) 'The proposal has my unanimous support.' Incorrect. Amend to *wholehearted*. *Unanimous* can be used only when a number of people are all in agreement.

(ii) A motion is passed unanimously only when everyone present votes in its favour. If no votes are cast against it but a few people abstain from voting, it is not correct to say that it is passed unanimously, or that the vote is unanimous. The correct term in such circumstances is *nem. con.* (short for the Latin *nemine contradicente* (=no-one speaking against).

UNAWARE(S). *Unaware* is the adjective ('They were unaware of what was happening), *unawares* the adverb ('He came upon me unawares'). In a sentence such as the following it is the adjective that is required: 'She arrived home unaware of the surprise that awaited her'. It would be incorrect to use *unawares*, since the word refers back to *she*, not to the verb *arrived*. Only *unaware* (the adjective) can be followed by an *of* adjunct.

UN-COÖPERATIVE. Best spelt in this way, with the diaeresis. Similarly, *un-coördinated.*

UNDER WAY. Now the accepted idiom. *Under weigh* (from the 'weighing' of a ship's anchor) is historically correct, but to go back to this spelling is mere pedantry.

UNDERLINE. 'I should like to underline what the last speaker has said.' Permissible in rather informal style, but *emphasise* is better.

UNDERLINING. (i) The only really legitimate use of underlining in longhand or typescript is to represent italics in print. See under ITALICS, and TITLES.
(ii) In personal letters it may occasionally be used to emphasise, or draw special attention to, certain words or phrases, but it is inadvisable to employ it for this purpose in more formal writing. The very lavish and arbitrary underlining adopted by Victorian ladies in their letters is still occasionally seen in the correspondence of the very elderly, but it should not be copied.

UNDERPRIVILEGED. A word that has come to be very much used in certain circles over the last generation, but a rather stupid expression, especially as it is generally used by those who are opposed to privilege. A privilege is a right enjoyed by a few people only; as soon as it is extended to the many it ceases to be a privilege.

UNDUE: UNDULY. *To show undue concern, to be unduly pessimistic* are correct; they mean 'more concern than is necessary', 'more pessimistic than one need be'. But 'There is no need for undue pessimism' and 'We should not be unduly pessimistic' are mere tautology, since what, in effect, they say is 'There is no need for more pessimism than there is need for', 'We should not be more pessimistic than we should be'.
Do not say 'It is not unduly late' if you mean merely 'It is not very late'.

UNIQUE. *Very unique, rather unique, more unique, most unique* are all incorrect. *Almost unique* is allowable. There cannot be degrees of uniqueness.

UNIVERSITY. *To go to university* (without the article) is rapidly gaining ground, presumably on the analogy of *go to school, go to church, go to college,* etc. It is perhaps too late to object to it now, but 'go to *the* university' is to be preferred.

UNLAWF︐ L: ILLEGAL. (See LAWFUL and ILLEGAL.)

UNLIKE. (See LIKE.)

UNLOOSE. Though, logically, *to unloose* should mean the opposite of *to loose*, it is accepted as a synonym: *unloose the dog, unloose one's shoelaces.*

UNTIL. (See TILL.)

UNTO. Now obsolete, except in verse.

UNWIELDY. So spelt, not *unwieldly*. It means 'difficult to handle, or manage', and comes from the verb *to wield*. An unwieldy sword was one which was difficult to wield, on account of its size or weight. The word is still used literally, of material things, but by an extension of meaning we can speak of an unwieldy organisation.

UP TO DATE. Hyphenated when used, either attributively or predicatively, as a compound adjective: *an up-to-date edition, an edition which is not very up-to-date.* No hyphens when the expression is used as an adverbial or adjectival phrase: 'Up to date, we have collected just over fifty pounds', 'The book has been revised and brought up to date'. 'We have now got the accounts up to date.'

UPSTAIR: UPSTAIRS. Originally *upstair* was the adjective, *upstairs* the adverb, and it is still legitimate to make this distinction (*an upstair room, an upstair window, go upstairs*), but *upstair* is tending to drop out, and *upstairs* to be used for both parts of speech. The same tendency is noticeable with *downstair* and *downstairs*, though it has not progressed so far. As the adjective, *downstair* is probably still commoner than *downstairs*.

USAGE. 'The usage of American spellings in British publications is to be deprecated.' 'The usage of water for washing cars is forbidden.' Incorrect. The word required is *use*. *Usage* means 'that which has become customary', or 'that which has become established by long-standing use'. Thus though 'It is me' violates the grammatical rule that the verb *to be* should be followed by a complement in the nominative case, it has become established by usage, and must therefore be accepted: cf. also the title of Fowler's well-known work, *A Dictionary of*

Modern English Usage, and that of the present book, *Current English Usage*. There cannot be a wrong *usage* of a word, but there may be a wrong *use* of it.

Usage may also be used outside the sphere of language. We may speak of 'the ancient rites and usages' of a livery company or a similar organisation.

USE (Noun). 'This is no use to me', 'Is this any use to you', are accepted as idiomatic, and most people would, in fact, use them in preference to the more formally correct *of no use*, *of any use*, though the purist may be allowed his *of* if it eases his conscience. *Of* must, however, always be used if *use* is not preceded by an adjective (e.g. 'It's no use to me, but it may be *of use* to someone'), while on the other hand it would be out of place in the following: 'It is no use asking him to do it', 'It's no use crying over spilt milk', 'What use is it trying to help people of that sort?' In general, when *use* is felt to have roughly the same meaning as *good*, *of* should, for preference, be omitted; when it refers, even if vaguely, to some use or purpose to which something can be put, *of* should be inserted.

USED TO. (i) Note the spelling — 'I *used* to do it' (past tense), not 'I use to do it'.

(ii) Avoid the solecisms 'I had used to do/be' and 'I was used to do', the latter of which probably arises by confusion with *used to doing*, where *usèd* is an adjective meaning 'accustomed': 'I used to walk to work' means 'I was in the habit of walking to work': 'I was used to walking to work' means 'I was accustomed to walking to work'.

(iii) The usual interrogative form is 'Did you (they) use to?', though 'Used you (they) to?' is not impossible, but it is rather formal.

(iv) In statements the negative is *used not to*, not *didn't use to*, as 'I used not to think so' (*not* applies to the infinitive, not to *used*), but in questions the *didn't use to* form is employed: 'I think I have seen you somewhere before. Didn't you use to live in Birmingham?'

(v) Where habitual or repeated activity or occurrence in the past is concerned, *would* is sometimes used. The following passage from R. L. Stevenson's story *The Body-Snatcher* provides an example:

'After a night of turbulent pleasures . . . he would be called out of bed in the black hours before the winter dawn by the unclean and desperate interlopers who supplied the table. He would open the door to these men, since infamous throughout the land. He would help them with their tragic burden, pay them their sordid price, and remain alone, when they were gone, with the unfriendly relics of humanity. From such a scene he would return to snatch another hour or two of slumber, and refresh himself for the labours of the day.'

Used in this way, *would* differs from *used to* in that it is more specific. It takes one instance as typical of all, implying that this is the kind of thing that happened again and again, whereas *used to* generalises, by merging all together. Where there is no sense of habit, repetition or recurrence, *would* cannot be used. We cannot, for instance, replace *used to* by *would* in such sentences as 'I used to live in Manchester'. 'He used to be much better off than he is now.' 'People used to believe that the earth was flat.'

The use of *would* exemplified above has a counterpart in the present tense in a similar use of *will*: 'She will come home from work, have her tea, and sit reading or sewing until about nine o'clock'.

UTILISE. 'Electricity can be utilised for a number of purposes.' Incorrect. *Utilise* is not a synonym of *use*. It means 'put to a useful purpose, or find a use for, something that would otherwise be wasted'. In certain industries by-products which formerly were regarded as refuse, and treated accordingly, are now utilised.

V

V. (Abbrev.). *Sheffield Wednesday* v. *Notts Forest.* Pronounce *versus* (the full word for which it stands), not *vee*.

VARIOUS. 'We tested various of the samples, but none proved satisfactory.' 'Various of his friends advised him against taking that course.' Both incorrect. *Various* can be used only as an adjective, and cannot be followed by *of*. The alternatives are *his various friends, various friends of his, several of his friends*.

VENAL : VENIAL. *Venal* = 'mercenary : such as may be bought or sold'. It may be applied to a person or to his conduct. *Venial* is applied to a fault, an offence, etc., and means 'pardonable'.

VENTRE À TERRE. To use this French expression in English is an affectation, but if it is used it should be used correctly. It does not mean 'grovelling (with one's stomach on the ground)', but 'at full tilt' or 'at full speed'.

VENUE. A word that has become rather fashionable lately instead of 'meeting-place', perhaps because many of those who use it suppose (mistakenly) that it has something to do with the French verb *venir*, and therefore means a place where people come together. It does not ; it comes from the Latin *vicinia*. It might well be used less frequently.

VERIFY : CORROBORATE. To *verify* means 'to ascertain whether or not something is true' : e.g. to verify a person's story, verify one's facts. But if the truth of one story is borne out by another, the second story does not verify the first ; it *corroborates* it.

VERY : MUCH. *Very* is used before adjectives and adverbs, *much* before participles when they retain their verbal function (*This picture has been much admired, much criticised, much discussed*, etc.). But when a participle is used adjectivally it takes *very* ('I am very concerned about his health', 'He is very interested in stamp collecting', 'We are very pleased to hear of your success').

248

VIA. Use only for the route, not for the method of transport. 'From Liverpool to London via Crewe', but not *via train*, *via the Canadian Pacific Railway*, *via* 'The Golden Arrow', *via B.O.A.C.*

VIABLE. Does not mean 'able to be used as a thoroughfare' or 'workable, practicable', but 'capable of maintaining life' (a medical term). Outside its strict medical sense it may be used figuratively for new-born states or communities, but if there is any doubt about its correctness or suitability it had better be avoided.

VICIOUS : VISCOUS. *Vicious* = characterised by vice. *Viscous* = of a thick, runny consistency, like treacle.

VICIOUS CIRCLE. Not a clique of morally corrupt people, nor merely a course which brings one back to where one started, but a situation in which one evil produces another, which in its turn aggravates the first, which then reproduces the second, and so on : e.g. rising prices lead to demands for higher wages, higher wages cause prices to rise still farther ; this leads to further demands for wage increases, which once again raises prices.

VIEW. The constructions are (i) *in view of* + noun ('In view of the gravity of the situation'), (ii) *with a view to* + noun or gerund ('With a view to easing the difficulties'), (iii) *with the view of* + gerund ('With the view of ascertaining the facts').

In view of expresses reason ; *with a view to* and *with the view of* denote purpose. *With a view to* has the habit of attracting an infinitive instead of a gerund (probably through the influence of the preposition), but it is incorrect : e.g. 'He gave up general practice and went into hospital work, with a view ultimately to become a consultant'. Amend to 'with a view to ultimately becoming a consultant'.

A rather surprising mistake occurs in the following sentence from the report of a well-known company : 'In view of the results, and that the ordinary dividend is covered approximately two and a half times, the Board recommends a final ordinary dividend of ten per cent.' *In view of* is followed by a noun or pronoun ; it cannot be followed by a noun clause. If a noun clause is felt to be necessary, it must be preceded by a noun, such as *the fact*, *the allegation* or *the report*, to which it is in apposition. It is true, we can say 'In view of what has happened', or 'In view of what you tell me', but here the clause introduced by *what* is not a noun clause, but an adjective clause containing its own antecedent. *What* means 'that which'.

VIEWPOINT. At one time an Americanism, but now accepted in British English, though *point of view* is to be preferred. On the confusion between *view* and *viewpoint* or *point of view*, see under POINT OF VIEW.

VISIT : VISITATION. (i) We visit a friend, a town, an exhibition, a cinema, etc.; we in our turn are visited *by* our friends or relations, and the exhibition is visited *by* a large number of people. We are visited (i.e. afflicted) *with* illness, disease or penalties, and a town is visited *with* the plague. A person's sins, misdoings or misdemeanours are visited *upon* him — or sometimes upon someone else : (cf. the biblical 'visiting the sins of the fathers upon the children').

(ii) Americans visit *with* friends; in Britain we merely visit them.

(iii) *Visitation* is not used of ordinary visiting, but only of (a) a formal visit, in an official capacity: 'The Governors' annual visitation of the school', 'the visitation of the sick' (by a clergyman), and (b) visiting in the sense of 'afflicting': (e.g. 'The frequent visitation of Eastern cities by plague'. 'The calmness of the Orientals under such visitation . . . rendered it practicable to dispose of the dead in the usual way' — A. W. Kinglake, *Eōthen*, chap. xviii).

VIZ. The abbreviated form of the Latin *videlicet* (= namely). Do not use *viz.* unless a full explanation follows, as 'The person responsible for the selection of the books, viz. the librarian'. If only examples are given, then *e.g.*, not *viz.*, is required. (See also under E.G., I.E.)

In reading *viz.* aloud, say *namely*. In print it is not italicised.

VOGUE WORDS. Vogue words are words which, at a particular time, become very fashionable, and therefore tend to be overworked. They are not necessarily used wrongly, nor are they objectionable in themselves, but they become rather hackneyed. *Intriguing* (in the sense of 'interesting, arousing curiosity'), *denigrate, intransigent, streamlined, high-ranking, top-level, ambivalent, top secret* have all been vogue words during the past twenty years. Others will arise in the future. A writer should keep a wary eye on vogue words of his own day, and think twice before he uses them.

VOWEL. The letters *a, e, i, o* and *u* should not be referred to as 'the five vowels', for in the first place they are not vowels at all, but merely written symbols, and secondly there are many more than five vowels in English. *Vowel,* like *consonant* and *diphthong,* is a phonetic, not an orthographic term: that is to say, it refers to sound. The same written symbol may represent more than one vowel sound (contrast, for instance, the sound represented by *u* in *cut* with that in *put*), and the same vowel mäy be represented by two different symbols (as in *son* and *sun, park* and *clerk*), while sometimes two symbols are written to represent a single vowel (as in the noun *wound* and the verb *tease*). In many words a single letter or symbol does not represent a vowel at all, but a diphthong, as in *mice, cake, cow.* (See under DIPHTHONG.)

W

WAIT: AWAIT. (i) *Await* must have an object; it cannot be used intransitively, nor can it be followed by a preposition. We cannot say 'I will await here', or 'Await for me at the main entrance'.

(ii) *Await* and *wait for* are not generally interchangeable. We *wait for*, not *await*, a person or a thing: 'I am waiting for my wife'. 'We were waiting for the bus.' 'Wait for me near the ticket barrier.' We *await* some happening, occurrence or development: 'We must await his decision'. 'They were eagerly awaiting the announcement of the results.' 'We await your reply with interest.'

Await may, however, have a personal object when it means 'be in store for', or 'lie in wait for': 'A fortune awaits the person who discovers a cure for the common cold'. 'On arrival at his hotel he found a telegram awaiting him.' 'Little did they realise what a surprise awaited them at home.'

Though grammatically active, there is always a sense of passivity about *await*. 'On coming out of the station he found a taxi waiting for him' presents the situation from the point of view of the taxi; it was standing there ready to pick up the passenger for whom it had been hired. 'He found a taxi awaiting him' presents it from the passenger's point of view.

WANT (Verb). The basic distinction between *want* and *need* is that whereas *need* denotes a necessity, *want* expresses a desire. Many things that we want we do not necessarily need, and sometimes what a person needs he may not want. There is an obvious difference between 'He needs every penny he can get' and 'He wants every penny he can get'. Another meaning of *want* is 'lack', or 'be deficient in': e.g. 'Her father left her a considerable fortune, so she shouldn't want for money'. 'He is wanting in common sense'.

Since a lack of something implies (to some extent, at least) a need of it, and since a desire may be prompted by a genuine need, *need* and *want* often overlap. There are obvious cases, like those given in the paragraph above, where the two are not interchangeable, but there are others where either could be used. We may divide them into two classes, viz. (a) those where *need* can be interchanged with *want* in the sense of 'desire', as 'Do you know of anyone who wants/needs a gardener?', where *want* means more or less the same as *require*, and (b) those where *need* can be interchanged with *want* in the sense of *lack*, or something approaching it, as 'That dress needs/wants washing', 'What you need/want to put you right is a good holiday'. *Want* suggests that the need is an urgent one, which should be satisfied or attended to. When the need is belittled, or represented as trivial, the tendency is to use *need*, not *want*: thus 'My house wants painting from top to bottom', but 'All it needs is a coat of paint'. From this sense of urgency suggested by *want* comes the use of it in conjunction with an infinitive in sentences conveying advice, censure, warning, etc. 'You want to watch that fellow, or he'll cheat you'. 'You think you've got some fine roses, but you want to see mine'.

-WARD: -WARDS. In pairs like *backward, backwards, forward, forwards, westward, westwards*, only the form with *-ward* (without the *s*) can be used adjectivally (*a backward child, a forward movement, a westward direction*). This is sometimes also used for the adverb, especially in the U.S., but in British English *-wards* is more correct: *lean backwards, pitch forwards, journey westwards*. But *forward!* is used as a kind of adverbial imperative ('Forward, the Light Brigade!'), and in the expression *to come forward* in the sense of 'present oneself': 'Several people have come forward with offers of help'. 'No-one has yet come forward with any information.' Cf. the saying 'He is not backward in coming forward', and the phrase 'to put forward a suggestion'. *Forwards*, that is to say, has a spatial sense, *forward* (when used adverbially) a non-spatial.

WASTE: WASTAGE. 'The management complained about the wastage of electricity caused by lights being left on when rooms were not in use.' Incorrect. The word required is *waste*. *Wastage* means 'loss due to evaporation, decay, leakage, etc.' The daily wastage of water from a reservoir is that which is lost through more or less unavoidable causes. The following, from the *Birmingham Post*, also illustrates the correct use. 'Only about thirty-four per cent of boys and seven per cent of girls leaving school, enter apprenticeships or learnerships in skilled occupations. There is a considerable wastage amongst those who do.'

WATCH OUT. Avoid this combination. We *look out* for something, or we *watch for* it, but not *watch out* for it.

-WEAR. *Footwear* and *underwear* have become accepted, but *neckwear* (collars, ties, scarves, etc.), *headwear* (hats) and *eyewear* (spectacles) exist only in commercial jargon. They should not be used in ordinary English.

WED. Except in a few colloquial phrases like *newly-weds, wedded bliss*, etc., the word is now dialectal or journalistic ('Millionaire Weds Shop Girl'). Use *marry*. It is normal English, however, when used metaphorically ('to be wedded to a scheme', 'The Labour Party seem to be wedded to the idea of nationalisation').

WELCH. (See WELSH.)

WELCOME: WELCOMED. *Welcome* is an adjective, *welcomed* a participle: 'a welcome guest', 'a welcome change', 'a most welcome suggestion'. It is mainly in the predicative use that confusion sometimes occurs. 'Anyone who cares to come will be welcome' (not *welcomed*), but 'The guests were welcomed by the chairman'.

In America, anyone begging another person's pardon may receive the reply, 'You're welcome'. In Britain this would be considered a sign of ill breeding.

WELL: GOOD. When prefixed to a participle to make a compound adjective, the word generally used is *well*: e.g. *well-spoken, well-read, well-behaved*. *Well* is also the usual prefix for a pseudo-participle (i.e. a noun with -*ed* or -*ing* added to it, so that it is made to appear a participle). Thus a person with good intentions is *well-intentioned*, and one with good manners is *well-mannered*; but a person with good looks is *good-looking*, possibly because *well-looking* might suggest that he was looking well (i.e. in good health).

WELSH: WELCH. *Welch* is used in the names of certain regiments: e.g. The Royal Welch Fusiliers; for all other purposes the spelling is *Welsh*.

WELSH RAREBIT. A caterers' term, which seems to have originated about sixty years ago. Before that it was *Welsh rabbit*, and this is still really the correct name, though *rarebit* is now so widely used that it is probably useless to object to it. An eighteenth-century cookery book contains recipes for English, Scotch and Welsh rabbit, all of them having toasted cheese as the principal ingredient, though differing in the flavourings and condiments that were added.

WET: WETTED. *Wet* is the usual form of the past tense and past participle when the 'wetting' is not a deliberate act: 'The heavy rain wet us through'. 'That slight shower has scarcely wet the soil.' *Wetted* is more usual for something that is done deliberately: 'He wetted his handkerchief in the stream'. 'She wetted the stamp before trying to remove it from the envelope.'

WHAT. (i) *Difficulties of Number.* When *what* means 'that which' it is singular and takes a singular verb: when it means 'those which' it is plural and takes a plural verb: 'We shall not need any more bread; what we have is quite sufficient'. 'You need not get any more stamps; what we have are quite sufficient.'

When a noun clause beginning with *what* is the subject of a verb which is followed by a plural complement, there is a temptation to make the verb plural; but this is incorrect. It must be singular, since the noun clause represents a single idea: 'What we need *is* more helpers' (not *are*: what we need=our need). Similarly, 'What interested the children most *was* the monkeys' (not *were*), 'What proved his undoing *was* the lies he told'. A useful rule of thumb is, if the clause introduced by *what* could be converted to a question, to which the sentence as a whole is the answer, then use a singular verb. ('What interested the children most?' — 'What interested the children most was the monkeys'.

(ii) *'What'* with *'the same as.'* The same as what is correct when *what* means *that which* and is fully pronominal, e.g. 'What he says now is not the same as what he told me last night'. But when it is semi-adjectival, and refers back to a definite antecedent, it is better omitted, e.g. 'He is wearing the same suit as he wore last Sunday' — not *as what he wore last Sunday*.

When *the same* is adverbial, and means in *the same way* or *just as*, *what* should never be used: e.g. 'Do it the same as what I do', 'He is tall and stout, just the same as what his father was'. In both these sentences omit *what*.

(iii) *What have you?*, in the sense of 'anything else you like to think of' is not accepted English, and should not be used in serious speech or writing ('Pears, apples, bananas and what have you?').

(iv) On *than what* ('He is older than what I am'). See under THAN.

(v) On the difference between interrogative *which* and *what*, see under WHICH.

WHATEVER: WHAT EVER. (See Ever: -ever.)

WHENEVER: WHEN EVER. (See Ever: -ever.)

WHEREABOUTS. When used as a noun, singular: 'His whereabouts is unknown'. Even if the reference is to several persons, each with a different whereabouts, a singular verb is still used: 'She has a brother and two sisters, but their whereabouts is unknown'.

WHEREVER: WHERE EVER. (See Ever: -ever.)

WHEREWITHAL. In its original sense of 'means', the word is archaic. *The wherewithal* (=money) is a vulgarism.

WHETHER. (i) 'Whether any of the tapestries survived the destruction of Berlin during the last war would, I imagine, be improbable.' (From a letter to a historical journal, November 1960.) A confusion of three constructions: (a) 'Whether any survived is doubtful', (b) 'That any survived is improbable', (c) 'That any should survive would be a miracle'. *Whether* always needs a watchful eye kept upon it, particularly in a long and rather involved sentence. It is a word which poses a question, but very often the writer has already made up his mind on the answer, and he is apt to frame the second part of his sentence in the light of this answer, and not of the question with which he started.
(ii) 'Ask her whether she is coming or no.' Allowable, but rather old-fashioned. 'Whether or not' is to be preferred.
(iii) On the substitution of *if* for *whether* in noun clauses after certain verbs ('He asked if he could come with us'). (See under If.)

WHICH. (i) As an interrogative pronoun or adjective, *which* differs from *what* in that it selects from a number of alternatives (though the precise number may not be known to the speaker), whereas *what* is general, and does not take alternatives into account. 'Which train are you going by?' implies that the speaker has in mind several possible trains; 'What train are you going by?' merely asks for the time of the train, and gives no indication that the speaker has any notion of the trains that are available.
(ii) As a relative pronoun, *which* must be preceded by a comma if it is non-defining, but no comma must be used if it is defining, i.e. if it selects a particular one, or particular ones, from amongst

others: 'The house which was burgled is the one at the corner' (defining), 'That house, which was built in 1780, has an interesting history' (non-defining). See COMMA (5).

(iii) Normally *which* should have a specific word as its antecedent, but it is permissible to use it to introduce a continuative clause, when it refers back to the entire notion of the previous clause: 'I said he would withdraw his support at the last moment, which is just what happened'. In such sentences which=*and this*.

(iv) Normally *which* is not used to refer to persons; it is, however, used to refer to a noun which usually denotes a person but which, in a particular context, is de-personalised and represents merely the abstract notion attaching to it: 'If I were a millionaire (which I am not) . . .'

(v) *But which* and *and which* need watching. Since *but* and *and* are co-ordinating conjunctions they must join two words or word-groups of the same kind. When, therefore, they are followed by an adjective (relative) clause introduced by *which*, they must be preceded by another adjective clause of the same type, and the two must have the same antecedent. An example is to be found in the previous paragraph, where the two clauses introduced by *which* both qualify *a noun*.

A frequent mistake is to use *and* or *but* to join an adjective clause introduced by *which* to a totally different kind of construction: e.g. 'The envelope with a foreign stamp on it, and which you promised to give me . . .' (Adjective clause and adjective phrase). 'A house containing six large rooms, and which has a garden at the back . . .' (Adjective clause and participial construction).

This does not mean, however, that if the second of the co-ordinated clauses begins with *which*, the first must also begin with *which*. The following are quite idiomatic:

'Improvements *that* everyone would like to see, but *which* no-one is willing to pay for.'

'The place *where* he lived as a child, and *to which* he always hoped to return.'

The three essential conditions are that both must be adjective clauses, both must be defining or both non-defining (a defining clause cannot be co-ordinated with a non-defining or vice versa), and both must qualify the same antecedent.

An apparent breach of this rule occurs in sentences of the type of the following: 'What everyone would like to see, but which, if it were done, would place the firm in financial difficulties . . .' Here *but* joins a clause beginning with *which* to a preceding one beginning with *what*, and there appears to be no antecedent for either. Actually, however, there is no breach of the rule, for *what* means *that which*, and the idea of *that*, inherent in the *what* of the first clause, is the antecedent of *which*. The sentence is thus perfectly idiomatic.

Nor is there any objection to sentences where the second *which* is understood but not expressed: 'That is a place which many people have seen but few can describe'.

WHILE: WHILST. (i) *Whilst*, though still in use in the spoken language in certain parts of the country, is rapidly becoming an archaism in Standard English. There seems no point in preserving it, since its meaning is no different from that of *while*, which is always to be preferred.

(ii) *While* may legitimately be used in the sense of *although*: e.g. 'While I sympathise with you, I am afraid there is little I can do'). The clause which it introduces must always precede the main clause. It is sometimes found also as a substitute for *and* (e.g. 'His eldest son became a barrister, the second entered the church, while the youngest made the army his career'). Fowler condemned this use, and many others have echoed him, but the arguments against it are not convincing. Fowler's objection apparently is that when used in a temporal sense, *while* is a subordinating conjunction; it must therefore be used only as a subordinating conjunction when employed in any other sense. So it may replace *although*, another subordinating conjunction, but not *and*, which is co-ordinating. But this is mere question-begging. The fact remains that *while* is often used to co-ordinate, and wholesale condemnation of the practice is misguided.

This, however, does not mean that *while* can always be defended. One of the examples quoted by Fowler is the following: 'White outfought Ritchie in nearly every round, and the latter bled profusely, while both his eyes were nearly closed at the end'. Not many people will feel that this is acceptable. Perhaps the writer used *while* to avoid repeating *and*, but still it does not sound right. As a general rule, *while* should be used to co-ordinate only when there is a kind of parallelism between the two clauses, as there is in the example given in the previous paragraph. As *while* contrasts when it is used in place of *although*, so it compares when it replaces *and*. But even so, it is advisable not to use it if it might lead to ambiguity: e.g. 'The vicar conducted the service while the Archdeacon preached the sermon'.

(iii) *While ever* must be written as two words, never as one: 'While ever he remains with that firm he will be discontented

with his position'. 'You cannot hope to get rid of your rheumatism while ever you remain in this climate.'

(iv) In certain parts of the country there is a dialectal use of
while in the sense of *until* ('I did not get home while eight
o'clock'. 'They have invited us to stay while next Sunday'),
but though it was at one time more widely used (there is an
example of it in Shakespeare's *Macbeth*, Act III, Sc. i, line 44) it
is no longer recognised as correct in Standard English.

(v) On *awhile* and *a while*, see under AWHILE. When the
expression is preceded by a preposition, two words must always
be used: 'Let us stay here for a while' (not *for awhile*).

(vi) '*While* away the time', but '*Wile* a person away', i.e.
entice him away by a wile, or a trick.

WHISKY: WHISKEY. Prefer the first spelling, which is always
used by Scottish distillers, though the Irish use the second.

WHITSUN. *Whitsun* and *Whitsuntide* are both used for the
season (the latter is perhaps commoner in the northern parts of
England than in the south), but *Whitsun Sunday* and *Whitsun
Monday* are not correct: they should be *Whit Sunday* and *Whit
Monday*. *Whit week* and *Whitsun week* are, however, both allowable. As an alternative to *Whit Sunday* there is *Whitsun Day* (an
example of metanalysis), which is also permissible.

WHO: WHOM. (i) *Who* and *whom* are normally reserved for
persons, but they may be used of animals when they are thought
of in a semi-personal way ('My dog, who is getting old now')
and of countries when the people rather than the territory are
referred to ('India, who feels very strongly on this matter').

(ii) As relative pronouns, *who* and *whom* are preceded by a
comma when they introduce a non-defining clause, but the
comma must not be used when the clause is a defining one.
(See under COMMA and WHICH.)

(iii) *Who* is used for the subject and the complement of a
verb, *whom* for the object and when governed by a preposition,
but in questions introduced by an interrogative pronoun which
is governed by a preposition which comes at the end of the
sentence, it is more usual to use *who* ('Who is that letter from?',
'Who was this poem written by?').

(iv) A frequent source of trouble is sentences of the type,
'The person who (or *whom?*) we thought was guilty proved
to be innocent', 'The man who (or *whom?*) we feared we had
injured proved to be unharmed'. The temptation is always to
use *whom*, presumably because it is felt that the word is the object

of *thought* and *feared* (or whatever verb takes their place in other sentences); but it is not. In the first sentence it is the subject of *was guilty*, hence *who* is correct, and in the second the object of *had injured*, hence *whom* is required. *We thought* and *we feared* have the force of parentheses, and could be moved to another part of the sentence ('The person who was guilty, we thought', 'The man whom we had injured, we feared . . .'). Even *The Times Literary Supplement* (December 2nd, 1960) had this sentence: 'The German people, *whom* Hitler had determined should not survive defeat, did in fact survive'. Obviously *who* should have been used, since it is the subject of *should not survive*. When it goes with an infinitive, however, *whom* is always required ('The person whom we thought to be guilty'), since we have the accusative + infinitive construction.

If there is any doubt, a useful test is to substitute the personal pronoun *he* or *him*; if *he* would be used, the correct relative is *who*, if *him*, it is *whom*. 'We thought he was guilty' (therefore *who*), 'We feared we had injured him' (therefore *whom*), 'We thought him to be guilty' (hence *whom*).

(v) A similar difficulty may arise with questions. 'Who (not *whom*) do you think she is?', since it is the complement of *is*, not the object of *do think*; but 'Whom do you think we saw?', because it is the object of *saw*. The New Testament 'Whom do men say that I am?' is often quoted, but it proves nothing beyond the fact that it is easy to slip into the accusative in this kind of sentence when the nominative is needed.

(vi) *Whom* is not used as an indirect object. We do not say 'The boy whom I gave the book', or ask 'Whom did you give the book?' It must be *to whom* (or the preposition may be placed at the end).

(vii) *Who* is the same number and person as its antecedent, and takes its verb accordingly: 'It is I who am to blame'.

(viii) 'There was no one but who condemned his action.' Incorrect. Omit *who*. In such sentences *but* is itself equivalent in meaning to *who . . not*; *but condemned* means *who did not condemn*.

The rules regarding the use of the co-ordinating conjunctions *and* and *but* before *who* are the same as those for *which* and *what*, to which the reader is referred.

WHODUNIT. (A crime story, usually one concerned with a murder, in which the interest is in establishing the identity of the criminal.) Now an accepted noun, which has almost gained literary status. At least, it has appeared in serious articles in *The Times Literary Supplement*. No question mark should be used. The word is made up by phonetic imitation of *who done it ?*, a vulgarism for *who did it ?*

WHOEVER: WHO EVER. (i) On the correct use of each, see under EVER, -EVER.

(ii) *Whoever* is used for the accusative as well as the nominative: 'We shall invite whoever we please'. This is also extended to *who ever*: 'Who ever shall we ask ?'

WHOSE. It is legitimate to use *whose* of non-personal and inanimate things: 'a lake whose surface sparkled in the sunlight', 'houses whose trim gardens seemed to indicate the characters of their owners'.

WILE: WHILE (Verb). To *wile* (i.e. trick) a person into doing something, but to *while* away the time.

WILL and SHALL: WOULD and SHOULD. Into all the intricacies of *will* and *shall*, with their past tenses *would* and *should*, there is no need to enter here. It will be sufficient to deal with those points on which difficulty is most likely to occur, though it may clear the ground if we distinguish three separate conjugations, expressing differentiated ideas, in which these two auxiliaries are involved, viz.

(1) *The Future Tense.* This uses *shall* for the first person singular and plural and *will* for the other persons. It merely states what will happen, or a situation that will arise, in the future, without relating the fact to anyone's will, intention, etc.

(2) *Subjective Volition.* This has *will* throughout, and expresses the will, intention, determination, willingness, etc., of the person mentioned in the subject: 'I will' (in the marriage service). 'I will post that letter for you.' 'Boys will be boys.' 'We will see you at the social next Saturday.' This is really a present tense, not a future; it expresses present volition (though what is willed, determined or intended now may not, of course, come to pass until later).

(3) *Objective Volition.* This has *shall* throughout. In statements it expresses, not the will of the subject, but the will, determination, etc., of the speaker *regarding* the subject. The grammatical subject thus stands notionally in something of an objective relationship to it; hence the name we have given to this particular conjugation. 'He shall not enter my house again', 'You shall not insult me in that way', 'All members shall pay a subscription of two guineas per annum'.

In questions it enquires the will of the person addressed,

regarding the subject: 'Shall I open the window?' (i.e. Would you like me to? or Do you wish me to?). 'Shall John carry that parcel for you?' (i.e. Would you like him to?).

The points to notice, then, are as follows.

(i) The first person of the future tense, when no kind of volition is implied, is *I shall* and *we shall*; e.g. 'I shall be forty on my next birthday'. *I will be* expresses intention, will or determination, which would be absurd in such a context. 'We shall be home by ten o'clock' expresses simply futurity; 'We will be home by ten o'clock' is a promise or undertaking. 'We shall never solve this problem' is, again, an expression of mere futurity; 'We will never solve this problem' means that we are determined, or have made up our minds, not to. 'I do not think I shall live to be eighty' simply predicts the improbability of the speaker's living to that age; 'I do not think I will live to be eighty' amounts almost to a contemplation of suicide.

(*N.B.*—What has been said above does not apply to English as spoken in Scotland, or to American English, both of which use *will* for the first person of the future tense, as well as for the other persons. This practice seems to be spreading to England, but it is not yet recognised as idiomatic in Received Standard, and should be firmly resisted, for if the use of *shall* were to drop out of the future we should be deprived of the means of expressing a very material distinction of meaning.)

(ii) First person questions regarding simple futurity have *Shall I?* and *Shall we?*. E.g. 'Shall I have to change at Crewe if I go by this train', 'Shall we see Uncle John at the party?' *Will we?* and *will I?* would be incorrect.

(iii) For second person questions concerning the future, *will you?* is preferable, but *shall you?* may be used if the future situation or occurrence is thought of as being to some extent connected with a person's intention: 'Shall you be at the concert tonight?' (perhaps a little less definite than *will you?*). But where there can be no question of intention, only *will you?* may be used: 'Will you be forty or forty-one on your next birthday?'

(iv) In some parts of the country *shall you?* is used for a request or invitation ('Shall you come this way, please?'). In Standard English this is unidiomatic; *will you?* must be used.

(On the use of the question mark with requests beginning with *will you?*, see under QUESTION MARK.)

(v) The same general differences of usage that exist between *will* and *shall* exist also between their past forms, *would* and *should*, but care is needed when a sentence of direct speech containing *will* or *shall* is put into the indirect form, and a first person is changed to a third. *I/we will* invariably becomes *he/they would*, but with *I/we shall* regard must be had to the precise sense attaching to *shall*.

(a) If it expresses pure futurity, without any suggestion of volition, it becomes *he/they would*. E.g. 'I shall feel better when I have had a rest': 'He said he would feel better, etc.' 'We shall have over fifty pounds when we have collected all the money': 'They said they would have, etc.'

(b) If it is felt virtually to constitute a promise or undertaking or if it expresses strong determination, again it becomes *he/they would*. E.g. 'I shan't be late': 'He said that he wouldn't be late'. 'I shan't do any such thing': 'He said he wouldn't do any such thing.'

(c) If intention is mingled with futurity, *I/we shall* may become *he/they should*. E.g. 'I shall leave the office at 4.30': 'He said he should leave the office at 4.30'. But if there is any doubt about such sentences it is usually safe to use *would*.

(vi) A first-person question with *shall* may be pure futurity (as 'Shall I get there in time if I leave at 10.30?'), in which case *shall* becomes *would* in indirect speech — 'He asked whether he would get there in time'. It may, on the other hand, be an example of objective volition, as 'Shall I close the window?' In this case *shall* becomes *should* — 'She asked whether she should close the window'.

The same rule applies to a question (often in the form of a thought) which a person puts to himself. If 'Shall I catch the 3.30?' means 'Is it possible for me to?', or 'Is it likely that I shall?', then it becomes 'He wondered whether he would catch the 3.30'. But if the speaker is debating in his mind whether or not to catch that particular train, then it becomes 'He wondered whether he should catch the 3.30'.

(vii) *Would* and *should* are sometimes used instead of *will* and *shall* in requests and suggestions. Being more remote, they suggest a certain degree of reluctance, hesitancy or deference. 'Would you lend me thirty pence?' 'Should I ask her to tea?'

(viii) A suggestion requires *I should* (or *I shouldn't*), not *I would* (or *I wouldn't*). 'I shouldn't do that, if I were you.' But the expression of determination or resolution needs *would*: 'Even if I were well off I wouldn't pay that price for a suit'. 'I shouldn't do that, if I were you' means merely 'I should refrain from doing that', but 'I wouldn't do that, if I were you' means 'I should refuse to do that'.

(ix) On *would* and *used to*, see under *used to*. On *should* and *ought to*, see under OUGHT.

(x) The abbreviation *'ll* ('I'll meet you at 7.30') should be used only for *will*. *Shall* should be written and spoken in full. Sentences like 'I'll be twenty-one next August' are often heard in speech, but they are better avoided, and they should not appear in writing.

As an abbreviation of *would*, use *'d*, not *'ld*. 'He said he'd be there', not 'He said he'ld be there'.

(xi) *I won't, they won't*, etc., is to be preferred to *I'll not, they'll not*.

WITHOUT. (i) Do not use *without* in the sense of *unless*: e.g. 'I cannot do it without you help me'. The alternatives are 'without your help' and 'unless you help me'.

(ii) *Without* in the sense of *outside* is in current use as an adverb (*within and without*), but as a preposition it is archaic. 'There is a green hill far away, without a city wall' is often misunderstood. The survival of *without* as a preposition in a few traditional expressions, like 'without the pale of civilisation' and 'lesser breeds, without the law' (Kipling) does not justify its general use.

(iii) On the solecism *without hardly*, see under HARDLY.

WOE BETIDE. Though strictly a subjunctive expressing a wish, (*Woe betide you*=may woe betide you), the subjunctive sense has now been forgotten and the formula has become a fixed expression, used alike for wishes and statements, and of the past as well as the present. 'Woe betide anyone who offends him.' 'Woe betide anyone who offended him.'

WONDER. (i) In such expressions as *It's a wonder, no wonder* (short for 'It is no wonder'); *wonder* is a noun meaning 'a matter for wonder' or 'something to be wondered at'. It is followed by a noun clause in apposition to *it*, specifying the thing or the fact that is regarded as the wonder. In statements the clause is generally not introduced by *that*: 'It's a wonder he wasn't killed'. 'No wonder they were annoyed.' In questions also, *that* may sometimes be omitted, but it is generally used: 'What wonder that we missed the way?' 'Is it any wonder (that) she is always in debt?' *Small wonder*, which has a mild exclamatory force, is usually followed by *that*: 'Small wonder that they refused the offer!'

A wonder may also be followed by a conditional clause ('It will be a wonder if he is punctual') or by an indirect question denoting the thing that arouses the wonder: 'It has always been a wonder to me how he manages to live/where he gets his money from'. In sentences of the last type, *a wonder* means 'something that provokes wonder, or curiosity'.

There is no wonder, *There is small wonder*, and *Is there any wonder ?* are solecisms. One might as well say 'There is no excuse that you did not know the law' (instead of 'It is no excuse') as 'There is no wonder that he never has any money'. In neither is there anything to which the noun clause can stand in apposition.

(ii) As a verb, *wonder* is used with two different meanings:

(a) In the sense of *marvel*. When it has this meaning it is followed by a noun clause having the form of an indirect statement and specifying the fact that excites the wonder. Again, in statement sentences there is no introductory *that*: 'I wonder he wasn't killed'. 'I don't wonder you were anxious about their safety.' But *that* is generally used when the sentence is an interrogative one: 'Do you/can you wonder that no-one trusts him ?'

(b) In the sense of 'ask oneself' or 'be curious about'. When the verb has this meaning it is followed by an indirect question in the form of a noun clause ('I wonder where they have gone.' 'I wonder where that path leads to.' 'I wonder what we had better do.') or an infinitive ('I wonder what to buy my father for Christmas.' 'I wonder what to do.') As with other indirect questions, there is normally no question mark at the end of the sentence, but one is permissible if the *I wonder . . .* formula is felt to be a courteous substitute for an interrogative: 'I wonder whether you could lend me thirty pence?' 'We wondered whether we might beg a lift in your car ?'

(iii) Strictly speaking, a conditional clause which follows *shouldn't wonder* requires the subjunctive ('I shouldn't wonder if they *came* after all' — or 'if they *were to come*'), but very frequently the indicative (*if they come*) is used. This may pass in conversation, but it is hardly allowable in written English, except, of course, when conversation is being reproduced.

(iv) The double negative in sentences of the type 'I shouldn't wonder if she hasn't missed the train' (suggesting that she probably has) is indefensible from a grammatical point of view, but is accepted by usage. Perhaps it is felt (though wrongly) to be akin to the exclamatory 'If she hasn't missed the train !', and therefore to be more forceful or more expressive of feeling.

(v) 'I wonder whether it wouldn't be better to see him personally rather than to write to him.' The negative is correct. It corresponds to the direct question 'Wouldn't it be better ?' suggesting that it would. This, of course, does not exclude the use of the positive indirect form 'whether it would'. The difference is that the positive form leaves the question un-decided, and waits for an answer or for suggestions, whereas the negative form suggests the speaker's own answer. And incidentally it may be noted that just as the negative indirect question implies a positive answer, so, in certain circumstances, a positive indirect question may imply a negative answer: e.g. 'I wonder whether he is speaking the truth' may mean that I believe he is not, and 'I wonder whether it is very wise to do that' may mean that I think it unwise. In this case the indirect *whether it is very wise*, etc., corresponds to the direct question 'Is it very wise to do that?', with the implication that it is not.

(vi) On *I wonder if* in place of *I wonder whether*, see under IF.

WONT (=accustomed). Pronounced the same as the verb *won't*, not like *want*. The word is archaic, and should therefore not be used in writing, but failure to pronounce it correctly when it has to be read aloud from older English may have unfortunate consequences. How often has the present writer heard choirs and congregations sing,

> We turn from seeking thee afar,
> And in *unwanted* ways,
> To build from out our earthly lives
> The temples of thy praise!

WORTH WHILE. (i) Normally written as two words (*The effort was worth while*), but a hyphen is required when the combination is used attributively, as a compound adjective (*a worth-while effort*).

(ii) *To be worth* has the force of a compound transitive verb, and therefore requires an object (e.g. 'It isn't worth the trouble', 'It is well worth the money'). In *worth while* the object is *while*, which originally meant 'the time', but is now used in a general and much vaguer sense. It follows, therefore, that if *worth* already has another object, *while* cannot be used, and that *while* must be used if there is no other object. The following examples will illustrate the point.

That it is not worth keeping. (Here *worth while* would be incorrect, since *worth* already has an object — the gerund *keeping*.)

It is not worth while keeping that. (Here it is necessary to use *while*, since *keeping that* is not the object of *worth*, but is in apposition to *it*, the sense of the sentence being *It* (namely *keeping that*) *is not worth while*. If *while* were omitted *worth* would be left without an object and the sentence would be incomplete.)

Caution, however, is necessary when a sentence starts with *it*, as the following two examples will show.

It is not worth saving. (This is correct if *it* represents some definite thing that the speaker has in mind, such as a small sum of money, a piece of cloth, a cast-off garment, etc.)

It is not worth while saving. (This means, in effect, 'Saving is not worth while'.)

The rule, then, is that when *it* stands for some definite thing, *while* must be omitted. In such cases *it* has a double function to perform: it is the subject of *is*, and at the same time the object of the gerund — or in sentences of the type 'It is not worth arguing about', of a preposition. When *it* is merely an anticipatory subject standing for a gerund or an infinitive that comes later, *while* must be used.

(iii) *Worth while* is usually followed by a gerund, but with *worth one's while* the infinitive is more usual.

> It isn't worth while doing that.
> It isn't worth our while to do that.

WOULD and SHOULD. (See under WILL and SHALL.)

WOULDN'T KNOW. The use of *I wouldn't know* when all that is meant is *I don't know* is absurd and indefensible. 'If you were to ask him he wouldn't know' is, of course, correct: 'If you were to ask me I wouldn't know' is not; idiom demands *I shouldn't know*. 'In which play of Shakespeare does Trinculo appear?' —'*I wouldn't know*' is an absurdity. The question has actually been asked, so there is no question of *would* or *should* about it. The plain fact is that the person concerned *doesn't* know, and he should say so.

WRAPPED: RAPT. *Wrapped*=enclosed by some kind of wrapper, as 'wrapped in tissue paper', 'wrapped in a cloth'. *Rapt*=absorbed in, carried away by: 'rapt in his studies', 'a rapt expression of countenance', 'rapt attention'. The noun *rapture* comes from the same root.

Note the metaphorical use of *wrapped*: a subject is *wrapped* in mystery (not *rapt*, which is hardly ever used figuratively).

X

XMAS. Do not use this spelling. If you come across it in writing or in print, pronounce it *Christmas*, not *Ex-mas*, which is an illiteracy. The initial symbol is not the English letter *X*, but the Greek *chi*, the first letter in the Greek word for *Christ*. It occurs in many Greek words, and is usually rendered into English by the 'hard' *ch*, pronounced as *k*.

Y

YET. 'Is he here yet?', in the sense of *still*, is archaic or dialectal. In Standard usage the sentence would mean that according to the last information we had he was not here. But 'We have yet to learn the full facts' is normal modern idiom.

As yet, which means 'as the position is at present', should not be used if the simple *yet* will suffice, as it would in such sentences as 'We have not as yet received his reply', 'I have not had a chance to read the letter as yet', 'Eight and twenty years I've lived, and never seen a ghost as yet' (H. G. Wells, *The Red Room*). *As yet* implies a certain element of expectancy, or looking forward; it is therefore justified in a sentence like the following: 'We have received only two applications for the post as yet'. The suggestion is that the present position is not expected to be the final one.

YOURS. No apostrophe. *Yours* is a possessive pronoun, not a possessive adjective. It cannot, therefore, be used to qualify a noun. Its adjectival counterpart is *your*. We cannot say 'Yours and my interests'. The alternatives are 'Your interests and mine' or 'My interests and yours'.

APPENDIX

PLURALS OF THE COMMONER FOREIGN WORDS USED IN ENGLISH, TOGETHER WITH THE PLURALS OF CERTAIN ENGLISH WORDS

Note.—(i) An asterisk denotes that the word in question is dealt with in the appropriate alphabetical position in the main part of the book.

(ii) For the general rules regarding plurals of words ending in *-y* and in *-o*, the plurals of compound nouns and the plural forms of proper names, see under PLURAL FORMS in the main part of the book.

abacus – abaci
addendum – addenda
agenda * – agenda
alga – algae
alto – altos
alumnus – alumni
analysis – analyses
antirrhinum – antirrhinums
antithesis – antitheses
apex – apexes (or- *ices*)
aphis – aphides
appendix * – appendices (to
     books, etc.)
  ,,   – appendixes (ana-
     tomical)
aquarium – aquaria (or *-iums*)
archipelago – archipelagos
armadillo – armadillos
autobahn – autobahns
automaton – automata
axis – axes
ay – ayes ('The Ayes have it')

bacillus – bacilli
bacterium * – bacteria
bamboo – bamboos
banjo – banjos (or *-oes*)
basis – bases
beau – beaux

bonus – bonuses
buffalo – buffalo (or *-oes*)
bus – buses

cactus – cacti
calix – calices
cannon * – cannon (or *-ons*)
canto – cantos
cargo – cargoes
cherub * – cherubs, cherubim
chipolata – chipolatas
commando – commandos
concerto – concertos
contralto – contraltos
conversazione – conversazioni
corps – corps
corrigendum – corrigenda
coup d'état – coups d'état
crematorium – crematoria
crisis – crises
criterion – criteria
crocus – crocuses
crux – cruces
cupful – cupfuls (see under
 -ful *)
curio – curios

dado – dadoes
datum.* – datal

desideratum – desiderata
desperado – desperadoes
dictum – dicta
dodo – dodos
domino – dominos (cloaks)
   ,,   – dominoes (the game)
dragoman – dragomans
dwarf – dwarfs
dynamo – dynamos

echo – echoes
effluvium – effluvia
elf – elves
embargo – embargoes
emporium – emporia
encomium – encomiums
enigma – enigmas
equinox – equinoxes
erratum – errata
Eskimo * – Eskimoes
euphonium – euphoniums

facsimile – facsimiles
factotum – factotums
fait accompli – faits accomplis
falsetto – falsettos
fish * – fishes *or* fish
flamingo – flamingoes
fly – flies (the insects)
   ,, – flys (the vehicles)
focus – focuses (*foci* in scientific contexts)
folio – folios
formula – formulae (occasionally *formulas*)
forum – forums
fresco – frescoes
fulcrum – fulcrums
fungus – fungi

gas – gases
genius * – geniuses
genus – genera
geranium – geraniums
gladiolus * – gladioli

grotto – grottoes
gymnasium – gymnasiums (but *gymnasia* for the German High Schools)

halo – haloes
handful – handfuls
handkerchief – handkerchiefs
harmonica – harmonicas
harmonium – harmoniums
hero – heroes
hippopotamus – hippopotamuses (or -*mi*)
hoof – hoofs (occasionally *hooves*)
hors-d'œuvre – hors-d'œuvre
hydrangea – hydrangeas
hypothesis – hypotheses

igloo – igloos
ignoramus * – ignoramuses
impetus – impetuses
impresario – impresarios
index * – indices (mathematical)
   ,,   – indexes (to books, etc.)
innuendo – innuendoes
isthmus – isthmuses

kilo – kilos

laburnum – laburnums
lacuna – lacunae (or -*as*)
larva – larvae
lasso – lassos
lay-by – lay-bys
libretto – libretti or librettos
linoleum – linoleums
loofa – loofas (sometimes spelt -*fah*(*s*))
Lord Justice – Lords Justices
Lord Lieutenant – Lord Lieutenants
Lord Mayor – Lord Mayors (similarly *Lady Mayoresses*)

maestro – maestros (or -ri)
magneto – magnetos
mango – mangoes
manifesto – manifestoes
Maori – Maoris
matrix – matrices
mausoleum – mausoleums
maximum – maxima
medium – media
      ,, – mediums(spiritualist)
memento – mementoes
memorandum – memoranda
menu – menus
Mikado – Mikados
minimum – minima
minus – minuses (for the sign)
momentum – momenta
mongoose – mongooses
mosquito – mosquitoes
mother-in-law – mothers-in-law (see IN-LAW in the main part of the book)
motto – mottoes
mulatto – mulattos (-oes)
mummy – mummies

naiad – naiads
narcissus – narcissi (or -uses)
nasturtium – nasturtiums
nebula – nebulae
negro – negroes
no – noes (The Noes have it)
nostrum – nostrums
nucleus – nuclei
nuncio – nuncios

oaf – oafs
oasis – oases
octavo – octavos
octopus – octopuses
omnibus – omnibuses
oratorio – oratorios

pagoda – pagodas
parenthesis – parentheses

parvenu(e) – parvenu(e)s (the e for the feminine)
peccadillo – peccadillos
pendulum – pendulums
pergola – pergolas
phenomenon – phenomena
phobia – phobias
photo – photos
piano – pianos
piccolo – piccolos
pick-me-up – pick-me-ups
plateau – plateaux
plus – pluses (the sign)
Poet Laureate – Poets Laureate
polyanthus – polyanthuses
portfolio – portfolios
portico – porticoes
portmanteau – portmanteaus (or -x)
potato – potatoes
premium – premiums
prima donna – prima donnas
prospectus – prospectuses
proviso – provisos
purlieu – purlieus

quarto – quartos
quiz – quizzes
quorum – quorums
quota – quotas

rabbi – rabbis
radio – radios
radius – radii
ranunculus – ranunculuses
referendum – referendums
rhino – rhinos
rhinoceros – rhinoceroses
rhododendron – rhododendrons
rhombus – rhombuses
roebuck – roebuck
roof – roofs
rostrum – rostrums
rota – rotas
rotunda – rotundas

saga – sagas
salmon – salmon
salvo – salvoes
sanatorium – sanatoria (occasionally -*iums*)
sari – saris
scarf – scarfs *or* scarves
scenario – scenarios
schema – schemata
scherzo – scherzos (or -*zi*)
seraglio – seraglios
seraph * – seraphs (in Scriptural contexts *seraphim*)
serf – serfs
series – series
serum – sera
shako – shakos
shampoo – shampoos
sheaf – sheaves
sheriff – sheriffs
siesta – siestas
silo – silos
simile – similes
sinus – sinuses
ski – skis
solarium – solariums (less frequently -*ia*)
solo – solos
soprano – sopranos
spatula – spatulas
species – species
spectrum – spectra
spermatozoon – spermatozoa
sphinx – sphinxes
spoonful -spoonfuls
staccato – staccatos
stadium – stadiums
staff – staffs
stamen – stamens
stand-by – stand-bys
stanza – stanzas
stiletto – stilettos
stimulus – stimuli
stratum * – strata
studio – studios

stylo – stylos
stylus – styluses
subpoena – subpoenas
substratum – substrata
surplus – surpluses
syllabus – syllabuses (*syllabi* is pédantic)
symposium – symposia
synopsis – synopses

tableau – tableaux (sometimes -*s*)
taboo – taboos
talisman – talismans
tango – tangos
tattoo – tattoos
taxi – taxis
terra-cotta – terra-cottas
terminus * – termini (though -*uses* is becoming accepted)
thesis – theses
tiara – tiaras
timpano – timpani
tiro – tiros (see also *tyro*.)
tobacco – tobaccos
toga – togas
tomato – tomatoes
tornado – tornadoes
torpedo – torpedoes
torso – torsos
trade union – trade unions
trapezium – trapeziums
trauma – traumata
tremolo – tremolos
trio – trios
triumvir – triumvirs (or -*viri*)
trousseau – trousseaus
tuba – tubas
tumulus – tumuli
turf – turfs
two – twos
tympanum – tympana
tyro–tyros
ultimatum – ultimatums
Utopia – Utopias

vacuum – vacuums (but *vacua* in
   scientific contexts)
veranda(h) – veranda(h)s
vertebra – vertebrae
veto – vetoes
virago – viragos
virtuoso – virtuosi
virus – viruses
vista – vistas
volcano – volcanoes
volte-face – volte-faces

vortex – vortices

wharf – wharfs (sometimes
   wharves)
will-o'-the-wisp – will-o'-the-
   wisps

yogi – yogis

zero – zeros
zoo – zoos